# WILLIAM GRANT STILL

# A VOICE HIGH-SOUNDING

Judith Anne Still

A series of published and previously unpublished essays about the "Dean of Afro-American Composers," his racial attitudes and his artistic, spiritual and cultural beliefs, written by the composer's daughter.

THE MASTER-PLAYER LIBRARY
Flagstaff, Arizona

Copyright © 1990 2003 by The Master-Player Library

All rights reserved by William Grant Still Music. No part of this publication may be reproduced, stored in a retrieval system, or transmitted, in any form or by any means, electronic, mechanical, photocopying, recording, or otherwise, without the prior written permission of the publisher.

All inquiries should be addressed to:
The Master-Player Library
P. O. Box 3044
Flagstaff, AZ 86003-3044

Library of Congress Catalog Card No. 2003-101701

**First Edition**
Published in May 2003

ISBN 1-877873-14-4 (hdbk)
ISBN 1-877873-15-2 (ppbk)

PRINTED IN THE UNITED STATES OF AMERICA

## DEDICATION

This book is dedicated to the parents of the author, William Grant Still and Verna Arvey, in tribute to their courage, self-sacrifice, and unceasing love for God and humankind.

"We all rise together,
Or not at all."

*William Grant Still*

A photograph autographed by William Grant Still for his daughter, Judith Anne Still, in the 1940's.

*"To the sweetest little girl in the world."* Daddy

# TABLE OF CONTENTS

Foreword ..... v

## I. Essays about the Composer

Carrie Still Shepperson: The Hollows of Her Footsteps ..... 3
In My Father's House ..... 13
My Life as a Composer's Daughter ..... 25
From Composer to Composition: The Visionary Path ..... 65
"In the Beginning... :" The Genesis of *Ennanga* ..... 75
William Grant Still: A Voice High-Sounding ..... 83
The "Little Life" of William Grant Still ..... 97
The Last Shall be First: The Crucifixion of the World's Famous Composers ..... 105
William Grant Still: Solving the Mystic Puzzle ..... 119
Turning Pages ..... 155
The Gleaming of a Random Light ..... 159

## II. Essays about the Composer's Color and Culture

Prejudice: An Acquired Deficiency ..... 163
Why Black Isn't Beautiful ..... 191
An Educational Approach to Negro Individualism ..... 221
For the Man Who Fails ..... 233
Restoring Paths to Dwell In ..... 255

Index ..... 293

# PHOTOGRAPHS

**Preceding Foreword**
Photograph of William Grant Still, autographed for the composer's daughter, Judith Anne, in the 1940's.

**PHOTO INSERT**
**For "My Life as a Composer's Daughter"**

Myself, Judith Anne.

William Grant Still, Judith Anne's father.

Verna Arvey, Judith Anne's mother.

Duncan Allan Still, Judith Anne's brother just after his graduation from junior high school.

Bessie Lawson Blackman, (a registered nurse, friend of the Still family and a direct descendent of Martha Custis Washington, wife of President George Washington) with Judith Anne.

Dr. Bessie Arvey (Judith Anne's maternal grandmother) and her family: Verna (Judith Anne's mother, standing) with her sister and brother, Edna and Dale.

The Still's house in Los Angeles with the old 1936 Ford in the left foreground.

Marjorie and Arthur Lange, life-long friends of the Still family.

**PHOTO INSERT**
**Following Section I: Essays about the Composer**

A page from William Grant Still's personal scrapbook: The composer, his forebears, and his wife and children. His forebears include: Anne Fambro (grandmother), William

Grant Still, Sr. (father), Carrie Still Shepperson (mother), and Charles B. Shepperson (stepfather).

William Grant Still with his wife, Verna Arvey, and their children, Duncan and Judith Anne, at the piano in the year 1944.

William Grant Still making toys for Judith Anne and Duncan in 1944.

William Grant Still and Verna Arvey with their children and their dog, Shep, in Los Angeles, 1944.

William Grant Still and Verna Arvey at work.

William Grant Still and his family listening to a broadcast of Still's music in 1944.

William Grant Still proofreading one of his compositions.

William Grant Still with Judith Anne in 1972.

# FOREWORD

To hold one mirror up to another and to look into both, is to see an image reboundingly reflected, reflected and miniaturized, until that image is unintelligible and diminished. In many instances modern scholarship consists of images minimized by reflective minds: academicians study the works of the Masters by reading critical interpretations, they collect, summarize and comment upon the interpretations, and their students internalize and react to that commentary. The students then become commentators themselves, and pass their reactions to critical viewpoints on to those who follow them.

Somewhere in the recessive corridors of learning the pulsing flesh of human achievement--the intent and motivation of creative effort--is lost. In graduate school, when I was a student of English literature, a professor of mine made an excellent case for Marxism in Shakespeare's dramas, while a colleague of his "proved" that Robert Frost was absolutely a Freudian. Today I watch in dismay while musicologists applaud the whimpering, degenerate Mozart of the play, *Amadeus*, and a certain composer who pirated most of his melodies and treatments is lauded as the originator of the "truly American idiom" in music. The more educated I have become, the less I have been taught to trust my own knowledge about the ingredients and significance of artistic genius. It seems that only in Socrates' time were thinkers encouraged to make judgments according to immediate logic, experience and human concourse. At this point in history, men judge others, not by what they have done, but by what is said about what they have done.

Certainly much has been said about the work of my late father, William Grant Still, both before and after his death. It is, in fact, ironic that his music was frequently more talked about than performed up until the current decade. Not until 1983 did the Still concerts and recitals increase astonishingly, and it was not until the last three years that there were over 24,000 reported performances of Still works, as well as over five-million pages of the composer's music and writings distributed to the public.

More Still works are being played, and, more and more, the life of William Grant Still is a subject of study and written observation. It is only a matter of time before the man and his work will be partially obscured by the self-perpetuating myths of "critical commentary"--his declarative intentions, his arterial convictions--will be reflected, rephrased and altered into an "Accepted View" of the composer. This "Accepted View" will then be hung proudly in historical, sociological and musicological galleries, where it will always be consulted before the music is assessed by future generations.

All but two of the essays in this volume were written between 1974 and 1989 in order to shatter the brilliant but uninformed judgments that enter so often into the making of an "accepted view" of someone or something. They attempt to lead anyone who does not know the composer into his private mind, and to unveil the recesses where erroneous conclusions may seek to gain a foothold. Unfortunately, this book was yet unpublished when the University of California Press brought out its study of Still that was, in my opinion, filled with damaging and erroneous conclusions. Therefore this volume also includes my year 2000 review of their unauthorized effort as written by Catherine Parsons Smith.

Admittedly, my own eyes have not always been open where my father was concerned. For most of my younger years he was simply "Daddy"--the busy, attentive man who played "this little piggy" on my baby toes, who built furniture for my dolls, who sang funny songs like "Frog Went a Courtin'" and "Twenty-four Robbers at My Door," and who read the Oz books to me at bedtime. He was the one who taught me to fashion music-makers out of combs and tissue paper, and spinning toys out of large buttons and loops of string. He was the protective father who caused a commotion when he demanded that a concessionaire at Ocean Park stop a loop-the-loop ride because he thought that I was frightened and wanted to get off. He was the sadly victimized parent who was cozened into believing that I was "the sweetest little girl in the world"--a belief that was one of his few displays of unreasonable prejudice.

As I grew older, he was firm and kind, and he sometimes talked to me about spiritual and philosophical precepts, as well as about artistic and racial matters. He told me that one day I would have to take good care of the music, because it was to become an instrument for brotherhood. Unfortunately, my respect for the things that he was saying was shaded from the light of day by our personal relationship; love has a way of intruding itself between humanity and philosophy, a way of suggesting that it is all-important, and that, next to itself, words, philosophical and otherwise, are lacking in longevity.

It was only after my father died, (after I had long since discovered that I was not the sweetest little girl in the world) that the things my father told me assumed intrinsic value. I read his diaries, his letters and his various writings, and I realized that the concepts he had struggled to explain to me were thoughts that he had hoped to pass on to any who would listen. The immense sorrow of his eighty-three years was that so few would listen, and many who did listen did not do so without incredulousness or bias.

It is for the subversion of bias that the essays in this book were written, and for the clarification of a drifting image. Although some may see the composer hereafter through a glass and darkly, I will make an attempt at the outset to wipe that glass as clean as I can.

-- *Judith Anne Still*
August 31, 2002

# ESSAYS ABOUT THE COMPOSER

# CARRIE STILL SHEPPERSON: THE HOLLOWS OF HER FOOTSTEPS[1]

"Hath not a Jew ahs," drawled a slender, walnut-skinned Negro boy, holding a large volume of Shakespeare out in front of him.

"Not ahs, ... *eyes*," interrupted the teacher firmly. "And do stand straighter, young man."

"Yes'm, Mrs. Shepperson," answered the boy, then squared his shoulders purposefully.

Neither the teenage Shylock nor any of his classmates sitting on the sidelines cared to defy the directions of their teacher, Mrs. Shepperson. Her word was law.

The time? The first decade of the twentieth century in Little Rock, Arkansas. The milieu? Brick and frame schools near small businesses, theaters, blacksmith shops, and cane fields. Sun-bonneted ladies, watermelons selling for five cents each, and the bodies of the Negro and White bandits displayed, bullet ridden, in the funeral parlor window.

Of the two colored English teachers who were teaching at the all-Negro M.W. Gibbs High School, Mrs. Shepperson was the more strict and more beloved. It was not only that she helped the students to put on Shakespearean plays so that they could earn money for a library; it was not only that she taught them to sing and to do fine needlework and to use perfect grammar; it was also that she believed in the abilities of her students to handle all of these difficult tasks. She always looked at them circumspectly, as if she knew how much more they could do if they only worked long enough and hard enough.

Her name, before she married Charles Shepperson, was Carrie Lena Fambro Still. Though she was an Afro-American, her features were not essentially Negroid. She had mulatto skin and

---

[1] Reprinted here by permission of *Forum* magazine at the University of Houston (XV, Spring 1977, 60-65), of the *Phi Delta Gamma Journal* (XLIII, May 1981, 40-45), and of *The Arkansas Historical Quarterly* (XLII, Spring 1983, 37-46).

penetrating dark eyes beneath low-slung eyebrows. She had coal black, Spanish hair, worn parted in the middle, long in back, and fluffed around an aristocratic forehead. Her lower lip was set, as if it were riveted to the middle of her jaw.

Those who remember her, oddly enough, have difficulty describing her. They say that she was attractive, that she was of medium height, straight of stature, and that her voice was cultured. Beyond that, they will say only that, when she walked into a room, everyone snapped to attention. Like Melville's Ahab, she was magnetic and predominant.

She exercised discipline fully and without favoritism. Her only son was in her class at school, and in order not to appear that she indulged him above the other students, she was often more severe with him than with the others. Once when he was reading Chaucer aloud to the class, he laughed coarsely at the word "dung." Without warning, his mother's ruler came down on his wrists. Then, when he pouted, she snapped, "Pull in that lip, young man."

The boy had met his match in his mother, in spite of his precocious and stubborn nature. He seldom got away with dipping pigtails in inkwells, or throwing crayons at poor Professor Gillam--and only once did he play hookey to watch the trains pass through town. In fact, sometimes he was even punished for the pranks of his friend, Leander McDowell. Leander was fond of putting tacks and water on chairs of both teachers and students.

Speaking of Mrs. Shepperson in later years, her son has said, laughing, "She had an educated whipping strap. If I crawled under the bed to escape, the strap curled under ahead of me."

But the discipline kept the mischievous child in tow, and he became valedictorian of his class and, afterwards, one of the most important composers in America. In fact, much has been written about Carrie Fambro's son, William Grant Still, the dean of Negro composers--the man whose opera was promoted by Eleanor Roosevelt and Mayor Fiorello LaGuardia, and the first man of color to conduct a major symphony orchestra in the Deep South. Little, however, is really known of his mother.

Recently an educational filmstrip was made about Still for the elementary schools, picturing Carrie Still as a simple homebody, clad in an apron, cooking wonderful meals in the kitchen while young Still and Mr. Shepperson listened to the latest pre-1910 classical recordings. But the image was false. Carrie was no Hattie McDaniel. Her attempts to cook had always resulted in disaster--like the time that she seasoned a roast with bluing. She was fortunate that she had her mother, Anne Fambro, to prepare meals for the family.[2]

Of course, her lack of culinary talent did not concern her overmuch. She had too many things to interest her outside of the kitchen. Most significantly, she did not give over any of the cares of child upbringing to the grandmother. When little William was impish, and the grandmother tried to tell the daughter that it was his "Injun blood" showing, Carrie just frowned at her and dealt with him in her own stalwart fashion.

She was firm with her son because she saw that he was a handsome, sensitive lad with great genius. She knew that he was vulnerable to those who would prey upon his sensitivity and his genius, and that, without habituation to difficulties, he would soon lose heart. As William Still himself put it later on,

> In shaping my attitudes, my mother had a most important role to play. She was constantly "molding my character," trying to keep me from "following the path of least resistance," impressing on me the fact that I **must** amount to something in the world.... . She gave me chores to do: cutting the kindling and the wood, bringing it and the coal indoors; starting the fires every morning; sweeping the house. When in high school I wanted long trousers like the other boys, I had to go to work to pay for them. My mother could easily have given them to me, but it was part of her discipline to let me earn them.[3]

In addition to the stress on physical output, Carrie worked on vocabulary building, pronunciation, and grammar. She said that good English could help her son to reach people who were worth reaching and who would not listen otherwise. She made sure that

---

[2] Anne Fambro took her last name from the slaveowners in whose house she worked in Atlanta, Georgia.

[3] Robert B. Haas, ed., *William Grant Still and the Fusion of Cultures in American Music* (Los Angeles, 1972), 76.

## William Grant Still: A Voice High-Sounding

he, and his fellow students, always said "get," not "git," and "she and I," not "her and me." For the rest of his life Still could tell why, grammatically, one cannot say, "It is me," instead of "It is I." And he could tell how such knowledge opened doors for him in the field of serious music.

Knowledge and talent had opened doors for Carrie too. She was born on June 15, 1872, in Milner, Georgia, the daughter of a light-skinned plantation owner from Florida, and Anne Fambro, a light coffee-colored Negro-Choctaw house servant. Her Spanish father was fond of his charming, sagacious daughter, and saw that she was well-dressed and educated in the arts of embroidery, painting, music and language.

From the first she showed signs of fierce pride. If some hapless child in her Georgia neighborhood made derogatory remarks about her "half-breed" origins, she was more than likely to beat him soundly. Then, after the conflict, she would tell her mother without shame, "I won't take anything from anybody."

And she never did.

Deciding that she wanted to teach, she went to Atlanta University. Then, with degree in hand, a trim and handsome teacher of English, she took a position in Alabama. It was not too long afterwards that she decided to solidify a relationship with a math teacher whom she had met in Atlanta, William Grant Still, Sr.

Racially, Still was a Negro-Scotch-Irish-Indian, with a fine Harry Belafonte face and a smartly-trimmed moustache, "good hair," and a broad-leafed mouth. Most important, he was a man of spirit. In his early twenties he had protested the fact that Negro teachers were paid less than Whites, and was burned out of a one-room schoolhouse in Woodville, Mississippi. On the same occasion, a friend of his was shot. The incident did not deter him, however, from his interest in teaching.

When he and Carrie had met in Atlanta, they were immediately drawn to each other by the similarity in their natures--their mutual sense of the justice of things and of their personal abilities to combat hostility. Still, however, had to dissolve a friendship with another woman in order to woo and wed Carrie. The other woman, who was of a servant mentality, was jealous, bitter and vengeful. It was in spite of her anger, then, that Carrie became Mrs. Still on June 26, 1894, and the mother to the son, William, on May 11, 1895. But the marriage was not destined to survive. The couple settled in Woodville, and, mysteriously, the elder Still died suddenly when his son was only a few months old. Rumor had it that the rejected lover had taken her revenge with poison, having been set on to the deed by the murderous Whites who had burned Still out of his schoolhouse.

So Carrie was a bride, a mother and a widow almost within a year. Deeply within herself she grieved. But outwardly, she set her lip and promised her baby that he would never suffer materially for the loss of a parent. She considered going to live near her father--he had sent word from his Florida plantation that he wanted her to come. He promised her a home and an orange grove.

Carrie wanted to go, but she had her son to consider. Little William was not as fair as his mother and father. He was readily identifiable as a colored person. If he and his mother lived in Florida, they would have to put up with the Florida "Jim Crow" laws, which were possibly more stringent than racial restrictions in other areas of the South.

Carrie would not give up her dignity in order to have an easy life; once again her pride and high temper won out. She said of her son, "He's not a stereotyped Negro, or Indian, or Scotch-Irishman. He's an American, in the finest sense of the word. He must never let anyone take away his humanity with a label."

Ultimately, she went to Little Rock, Arkansas, to try to earn a living. She and her son moved in with their Aunt Laura at 912 West 14th Street, two miles from the main part of town.[4] Little Rock was a rural city then; it had a "downtown" area, but it also had many open lots dotted with grazing cattle, as well as cane fields on the outskirts of the houses.

Carrie, through her teaching, was able to purchase the house in which they were living--a fine, two-story gray frame house, with shingles and a broad front porch, standing in a middle-class interracial neighborhood. Oddly enough, interracial neighborhoods

---

[4] This was Laura Oliver Hyatt.

were not unusual in the South in the early part of the century. Only in recent years has the idea become current that Blacks in the South have always lived to themselves in poverty and ignorance and bitterness.

The truth was that Carrie and her son, and her mother who came to live with them, were not ignorant, poor, or hated. They co-existed peacefully with their neighbors, and among their neighbors were people of all races. In fact, down the street lived a German boy named Billheimer who was later to become president of Silverwoods. Also nearby was the house of a White boy named Allan, who, like Leander McDowell, was always to be a devoted friend of William Still.

And yet there was more to it than co-existence. The good life that they came to enjoy was also the result of Carrie's many community services and exemplary talents. In the hot summers she went into the backwoods of Arkansas to thatched one-room school houses of places like Olmstead, a small community northwest of Jacksonville, to teach. There, where barefoot boys and scorpions both tried to make places for themselves in a world of naïveté and raw courage, she taught the people to say "fire" instead of "far," and "sit" instead of "set."

When the summers were over, Carrie returned to bring culture to Little Rock. She spearheaded the formation of a Lotus Club, or literary group, whose members read the classics and the latest "best sellers," and discussed the books at meetings. Carrie's fondness for her Lotus Club work even led her to write a book herself, which has since been lost. The manuscript, done in her beautiful scroll-like penmanship, concerned the prejudices against Negroes and women in her day. It was entitled, *Orange and Lemon*.

Besides being an author, she was also a musician. An accomplished pianist, she formed and directed a group of spiritual singers. Sometimes she filled the neighborhood with music when she led her family in song out on the front porch on warm evenings. Sometimes she wrote little songs for the children to sing at school and in church.

At other times she taught fine embroidery to young girls, and won prizes for her beautiful needlework at the Fair. Her own wardrobe was enriched with the high fashion garments that she created, some in silk and taffeta, and most with the leg-o-mutton sleeves and high collars of the day. She did not care too much for bustles, and her favorite dress was a blue-lavender with delicate flowers on it.

In her spare time, she painted china. Today, only one piece of her hand-painted china remains--a beautiful double-handled sugar bowl. Its shades of misty green and blue-gray materialize mystically out of a white, gold-trimmed background, and evolve into a string of orchids around the middle of the bowl.

Because Carrie was talented, thorough, and well-proportioned, she soon had many suitors. And yet she was a lady to be treated with respect. Once when a saucy streetcar conductor took the liberty of calling her by her first name, she confronted him angrily and would not let the car continue until she had received his apology.

Eventually, of course, she found a good man. She married a well-fixed postal employee named Charles B. Shepperson on November 27, 1904. Charles Shepperson was a man who loved the arts and appreciated classical music. He was destined to introduce his stepson to the best in serious classical recordings and in Arkansas theatrical productions.

Once married, Carrie Shepperson's financial status was enough enhanced that she was able to pursue the goal dearest to her heart: the financing of a library for the Colored people in Little Rock.

Carrie felt that the most important thing for people to have in a growing culture--besides freedom--was education. But in those days, though Negro and White usually lived together amicably, the slave era was still near enough in memory that no White person thought it necessary to make books available to the non-White population. Negroes could buy books, but not borrow them.

So Carrie ordered and paid for theater costumes, through a mail order catalogue, and in a Fall semester started her students rehearsing plays to enact before the citizens of Little Rock. Her son William played Little Hiawatha in one of the first dramatic productions. He remembered his disappointment when his Indian dance did not draw the penny-tossing applause that another boy received when he sang "Back to Baltimore."

Later his mother helped the high school students to produce *The Merchant of Venice* and *A Midsummer Night's Dream*, leading them staunchly through the intricacies of Shakespeare's vocabulary. Tickets sold well for all of these productions, and soon the anxiously-awaited library was set up within the confines of Capitol Hill School.

The students and the other townspeople were satisfied with the library, with the Shakespeare, and with the unflagging cultural pride of Carrie Shepperson. Further, they were fond of the English teacher for her other qualities. She could laugh on occasion. She laughed when little Will sneaked some homemade sherbet in the kitchen and tried, bug-eyed, to conceal a mouthful of the icy stuff when she came in. She laughed with Charles Shepperson too. Once when she was playing a very tedious piece called the "Burning of Rome," Shepperson hauled in a large pail of water and set it by the piano.

"What's that for?" she asked, surprised.

"To put the fire out," was the answer.

She smiled about that the rest of the day.

She might have smiled also had she heard some of the comments that are made today about the people of her time. "Negroes seventy-five years ago were ignorant, and were not allowed to develop their talents." "White men built America." She would probably tell anyone who made such statements that the nation-builders were not all White, and that they were not all men. And then she would demand that the misguided apologize for their ignorance.

Indeed, it was Carrie who had tried to teach her son about nation-building. Although she insisted that he be a top scholar, and nurtured his love for music by sending him to violin lessons regularly, she hoped that he would use his intellect to become a doctor of medicine rather than a musician. Negro musicians in her time were commonly thought to be an immoral lot, and she hoped for better things for him.

Young Still, wanting above all to please her, went to Wilberforce University to study pre-medicine for four years. And yet the lure of the musical world was too strong. He made it clear to her that he had to realize his desires, and she eventually understood. She told him always to follow the inner sense of dignity that great men keep within themselves, and, when in need of real help, to turn to the Ninety-first Psalm for strength.

> For He will deliver thee from the snare of the fowler, And under his wings shalt thou take refuge: His truth is a shield and a buckler...

So he tucked the Psalm and his mother's faith in among the keepsakes of his soul, and went off to Boston and to New York to begin a musical career with W. C. Handy, Paul Whiteman, Artie Shaw, and Edgard Várèse.

While Still was in the East, he received word that his mother had cancer and was not expected to live. He returned to Little Rock just in time to be with her at the last. He found her hair whitened and her eyes weakened by the illness. Although she was in a great deal of pain, she expressed maternal anxiety over her son's vulnerability to greedy, deceptive people. She cautioned him to take care of his material and spiritual inheritance. Then she died.

She left him a solid square block of twelve houses in the center of Little Rock,[5] some emerald jewelry, a pinkish-ivory cameo brooch, a watch pin, her painted china, and the book she had written. As it turned out, her worries about her son's credulous nature were prophetic. He subsequently lost all of these things that she had willed to him to a dishonest aunt, a capricious first wife, and an avaricious property manager. He was much too busy with his music to care for his possessions properly. Only one thing remained that had been hers: the uncompromising moral

---

[5] This block of houses was said to be on Ninth street between Cross and Ringo streets in Little Rock. Melba McDowell, who lived in Little Rock, told Verna Arvey (Mrs. William Grant Still, the author's mother) that Carrie Shepperson owned all twelve houses at her death. However, when questioned recently, Josie Gilkey, a classmate of William Grant Still who now lives in Los Angeles, California, insisted that some of the property was disposed of prior to Carrie's death, leaving the son just a row of houses.

strength and integrity to overcome the prejudices and jealousies that would confront him in his lifetime.

Carrie Lena Fambro died on May 18, 1927,[6] at the same time that Lindbergh made his historic flight across the Atlantic. And, like Lindbergh's, the force of her influence has extended over the years. William Grant Still, returning to Mississippi in 1974 for the successful presentation of his opera, *Bayou Legend*, thought of his mother once again in "the quiet gentleness of respect and grateful love."

We too can know fine people by the mystic aura that their incredible spirits spread over the decades. We can know Carrie Shepperson--we can look at her orchid-wreathed, sea-green china and feel her sense of purpose and dedication--and yet we may fall like sand into the hollows of her footsteps. For there was something in the quiet majesty of her mind, and in the splendid rigidity of her soul that somehow went into the making of the nation.

---

[6] Carrie Shepperson was buried in a perpetual care grave in the Fraternal Cemetery in Little Rock. She was laid to rest next to her husband, Charles B. Shepperson, who had died years earlier of drowning.

# IN MY FATHER'S HOUSE[1]

His was a life of challenges. In fact, when he and I first became acquainted with one another, he was doing a job he had never done before--helping a registered nurse bring me into the world.

Monday, August 31, 1942. The war raged. Newspaper headlines told of German attacks on Stalingrad and vicious battles with the Japanese forces in New Guinea. But in our small, one-story, stucco house on Cimarron Street in Los Angeles, the war was, for the time being, secondary. Mother had been in labor all night. With her were my father, and a nurse, Bessie L. Blackman, who was also a beloved friend of the family. At high noon I was ready to be born, but the doctor had not arrived. So my two-year-old brother, Duncan, was put in the music room to amuse himself at the piano, while Mrs. Blackman took charge of the delivery.

My brother had been a reddish color at birth, but I was a remarkable shade of bluish-purple. I refused to breathe. Mrs. Blackman told my father to bring in pans of hot and cold water. Then she dipped me in each pan in turn, spanked and dipped, spanked and dipped, until I cried. Father said, teasingly, when I had grown up, that I had not stopped crying since. The observation represented one of his few errors in judgment. My father was William Grant Still.

During the thirty years of my association with him, prior to his last illness, my father never changed appreciably in his ability to meet challenges, even though the world picture changed greatly. Men turned from global conflicts to more personal battlefields, chanting, "We shall overcome." The words of the song were compelling, persuasive. But the words often spoke of things as they were not, not of things as they were. Too many

---

[1] Reprinted with minor changes in verb tense and wording, courtesy of Dr. Eileen Southern and *The Black Perspective in Music* (III, Special Issue #2, May 1975, 199-206). The author also offers belated thanks to Dr. Willis McNelly, of California State University, Fullerton, for his help and encouragement with the original.

who sang them thought only of what they had not accomplished owing to racial hatred . They had forgotten the men who had "overcome" already, repeatedly, in times less fortunate than those.

Among such men was William Grant Still. He was a man who never said, "I cannot achieve because I am a Negro." His milestones were reached in spite of racial discrimination. In 1931, his *Afro-American* Symphony was the first symphony written by a Negro to be played for an American audience. Five years later, he was the first of his race to conduct a major symphony orchestra in this country, and, before the decade closed, his *Rising Tide* became the theme music for the 1939 World's Fair. During the forties, the Still opera, *Troubled Island*, was the first opera by a Negro to be produced by a major American company. Then, in 1955, he was the first Negro to conduct a major orchestra in the Deep South. Among those who helped him were Eleanor Roosevelt and Mayor Fiorello LaGuardia of New York; among those who admired him were Jean Sibelius and Leopold Stokowski. Indeed, the citation attached to his Bates College Honorary Degree reads:

> Some men have improved race relations through court instruments; others have written flaming books, or moving plays. William Grant Still's contribution has been as a dedicated man who strongly believes that if a Negro's creativeness is of the first quality, he will be ranked among the leaders in interracial influence. In this endeavor he used the method he knew best--music.

In other words, racial battles are often won, not by riotous dissidents, but by men of integrity who give their peculiar gifts, unselfishly, to the world. And, so prismatic was William Grant Still's work, so magnetic was his personal integrity, that those who met him or heard his music did not care whether he was White or Black or Yellow or Red.

In fact, when racial cares cease in the distant future, William Grant Still's skin color will be totally irrelevant. He will then be a legend--a legend, because people who have deep hopes and harmony of spirit make legends. His music speaks to the complex melodies of the soul, striking chords of a universal nature, urging humanity toward eternal transcendence and peace in self-realization. Above all, it is music that does not exact day-labor to be understood. It is freely given, as was the bread that nourished the multitudes, and will be freely accepted by succeeding generations.

And yet the legendary quality of his music was not alone responsible for his ability to "overcome." Racial barriers are crossed by men who give of their talents and, beyond talent and intellect, by men who engage in the struggle to uphold the four great loves of humanity: love of God, love of men, love of self, and devotion to work. These four loves distinguished the career of William Grant Still. Further, they are the aspects of his life of which I, as his daughter, can speak with special intimacy.

Let me speak of his devotion to work first. For my father had a great many abilities other than musical ones, and he knew what power, satisfaction, and dignity accrue to those who develop all of their potentialities. Thus, being a father and householder led him to tackle many creative tasks outside of composing.

Carpentry was one such task. He made doll furniture for me and wooden trains for my brother. With a tiny coping-saw blade, he cut out complex jigsaw puzzles for us to assemble, or at least, for us to try to assemble. Learning to glue various kinds of woods together, he shaped the glued pieces into bookends and decorative boxes. He also made adult-sized furniture for the house--bookcases, cabinets for curios, tables, a desk, a lazy susan and a tea wagon. All of the hand-crafted items are things that we have used for many years and still use today. Now my children, the four Still grandchildren, play with the toys and puzzles.

Just as my father loved his carpentry, so also he loved gardening. A "green thumb" is the sign of a man who has a viable communion with the consciousness of nature. And my father's consciousness of nature was revealed both at his piano with blank staffs in front of him, and in his garden. He truly did have a green thumb. In his Victory Garden, planted in our diminutive backyard during the war, he produced gigantic tomatoes, yams, onions and carrots. The vegetables were lush and abundant, and it pleased him always to pick more than we could eat so that we could share some with the neighbors.

The munificence of his domestic labors carried over to his recreational interests. Always fond of reading, his literary world encompassed poetry, historical novels, and occult philosophy. His favorite volume among the hundreds on the family bookshelves was *The Life and Works of Paul Laurence Dunbar*. My father's adulation of poets of Dunbar's caliber was closely allied to his fascination with words in general. He gloried in opportunities to look up the meanings and pronunciations of words, and he worked difficult crossword puzzles for relaxation.

Beyond words, variety in scenery was also important to him. We visited all the educational sites in California when I was young: the Southwest Indian Museum, the Museum of Natural History, the harbor and the beaches, the Rosicrucian Museum, and the Griffith Park Planetarium and Bird Sanctuary. My father also indulged my brother's interest in trains. We spent time together at model-train clubs, hobby shops, and at railway stations. The wistful call of the steam engines reminded the Mississippi-born composer of a time when a lone night-whistle was a summons to duty as well as a promise of adventure. It was this promise that the composer built into the train set that he constructed for my brother's electric train--a model set compacted of scale buildings, trees and accessories, and fashioned with the same care that he used in making miniature sets for his operas.

Whether involved with leisure-time pursuits or manual labor, my father learned to discipline himself to accomplishment. Arising at nine on most mornings, he would compose until lunchtime. The sounds of slowly evolving chords and harmonies coming from the workroom piano were as familiar to us as the smells of the evening honeysuckle or of the sheets fresh from the clothesline. After lunch, he would record in ink what he had written in the morning. Then Mother, the concert pianist in the family, would play the new measures for him, for the piano was one of the few instruments he did not play well. In the evenings, he orchestrated and extracted parts from the completed score. If necessary, he worked late into the night. If not, he would spend the evening hours reading, working crossword puzzles, and discussing future plans with my mother. Together with the puzzles and the plans, there were bedtime stories for my brother and me--the miracles of

*Oz* by L. Frank Baum and the never-never lands of Hans Christian Andersen. Following this schedule, he brought his total number of finished symphonies, operas, songs and ballets up to 136 compositions.

Such disciplined production was not only the result of his love for work, but also it was the outgrowth of a deep and positive love of self. Self-love does not necessarily mean egotism; in its best sense it means pride of accomplishment and self-reliance. It means realizing that no other belief is possible without belief in one's own integrity and potential. From the moment that William Grant Still, valedictorian of his high school class, gave up medical school for music, he accepted the responsibility for the course of his own career. He believed in his choice. He taught himself to play many instruments and to orchestrate. While developing his serious talents, he played in pop bands with so little recompense that he was often cold and hungry. And then he began orchestrating for Artie Shaw and Paul Whiteman.

Even after coming into his own as a composer, however, he was never well off financially. All too often he was cheated of jobs, commissions and performances, sometimes because of racial prejudice, but more often because of political and professional jealousy. He was cheated because it has rarely been fashionable for a Negro to be intellectual, artistic, hard-working or patriotic. Among political left-leaners it was especially frowned upon. Subversive groups, already speculating in the thirties about the overthrow of the American government through militant violence, tried and failed to woo my father's support. They found, to their disgust, that there was nothing downtrodden about the "Dean of Negro Composers" or his music. A glad servant of his country in World War I, he expressed his feelings of patriotic heroism in the pieces, *In Memoriam: The Colored Soldiers Who Died for Democrary*, and *To You, America*. Furthermore, he put his thoughts into words, when he said:

> I know that I shall always be grateful to the many White friends who helped me. I could not have made it in a community solely of Negroes for the simple reason that Negroes did not have the facilities of the large orchestras, publishing houses and so on, which I needed in order to advance. White people made these facilities available in

every instance... .
    Make no mistake about it: the future of our music is tied immutably to that of the individual musician, and the future of the race as a whole is bound up in the future of America. What is good for our nation is good for the race. We must never allow ourselves to think otherwise, nor allow ourselves to be duped into a separatist philosophy, no matter how frustrated we may feel. We and our fellow Americans are in this together... . We have an investment in this nation... .

Such a commitment to national brotherhood, as a real and achievable goal, was rarely seen in his day. The bigots tried to put my father "back in his place," while the militant liberals dismissed him as an "Uncle Tom." Both viewpoints betrayed their own peculiar kinds of bias.

Yet, whatever the bias, it was necessary to meet it with an Aristotelian mingling of honor and common sense. Vivid in my father's memory was the incident that took place in a large Hollywood studio, just after his short-lived career in film music began. While walking past the open door of an office in the Music Department, he heard a White film composer exclaim in astonishment, "What? A nigger in this line of work?"

The only way to meet such antagonism with honor was to discount it completely, which, of course, Father did. But the most difficult opposition for him was that which could not be dealt with on any terms, because it took the form of insidious conspiracy. This kind of conspiracy was unearthed when the Still opera, *Troubled Island*, was produced in New York in March 1949. At the opera's opening performance, the audience was so favorably impressed by the work that the applause brought the composer to the stage for twenty curtain calls, alone and with the rest of the cast. The reception was unprecedented, almost ecstatic. It was a mystical height for my father, whose greatest love was opera. Yet, a shadow hung over the triumph. The night before the opening, one of the New York music critics had warned, behind the scenes, that his colleagues were planning to "pan" the opera, regardless of its success or failure. And so they did. The reviews were so noncommittal that the production withered on the vine. Even the Voice of America recordings of the production, first issued and played abroad, were later recalled. To have achieved the success he had long dreamed of and then to have had it snatched away was the crowning irony of his life.

My father returned from the New York production wrenched by disappointment. I remember how he looked in his long, charcoal gray overcoat and brown, wide-brimmed hat, wearily taking his suitcases out of our 1936 Ford after we had brought him home from the airport. So might Galileo have looked after the Inquisition. Characteristically, however, he had not forgotten to bring presents in his suitcases for my brother and me, as he usually did when he came home from his trips. Then, my mother asked him how things went. He took out the little notebook in which he always jotted down notes when he did not have my mother there to remember things for him, and he glanced through it. "Well, Verna, he said, "I just don't know. I just don't know what to say." He did, of course, go on to tell the story in low, hesitant tones. He turned to my mother for support, and found in her infinite resources of strength and stability.

Because of his personal stamina and with my mother's help, he survived this and other defeats as the years went by. He survived without losing his moral principles. Always a gentleman, he was never given to indulgence in obscenities or hard liquor. He even stopped smoking in the forties, when his fondness for cigars and pipes showed signs of affecting his health. True, opposition took its toll. Sometimes he was stubborn and temperamental. And other times he was strict and intractable. Even so, his pride in his music remained. Now and then he was forced to wear frayed collars or to see his children in hand-me-down clothes. Yet he knew that his music transcended all of that.

My mother echoed his faith--talking always about the "big break" that was coming someday. Meanwhile, she struggled patiently, making a little money go as far as it would. She sometimes manufactured her own lye soap, sewed some of our play clothes by hand, crocheted rugs, and made monk's cloth slipcovers for our deteriorating couches. In addition, she was the one who handled all of Father's letter-writing, publicity, libretti, and lyrics.

Both of my parents consistently demonstrated an ability to

endure, a deep devotion to honest work and a pride of self. Significantly, however, my father's pride never made him completely satisfied with his music. For him, knowing that a piece was good did not mean knowing that it was beyond improvement. He always went back to his pieces, reassessing and revising them. Creation was not being for him, it was "becoming." Like Aristotle, he believed that reality was a continuing process of generation, and that at the end of the process was God.

Truly, the faith in God--the personal knowledge and love of the immutable Creator--was one of the most impressive loves of William Grant Still's career. He believed that writers and composers who worked without awareness of ultimate harmonies produced melodrama, dissonance, or discordant "mood" music. On the other hand, he felt that artists who sensed a power greater than themselves could write lasting music. Such pieces as his "A Psalm for the Living" emanated from the sense of a higher power, as did the inscription on all of the Still scores, which reads, "With humble thanks to God, the Source of inspiration."

When my father spoke of inspiration, he spoke also of the vital forces in prayer and meditation. By opening his consciousness to spiritual influences, he always found the creative impulse. This is not to suggest that we were a church-going family, adhering to the doctrines of a particular religion. My parents never found a denomination which they considered able to answer to all of the miseries, aspirations and doubts of people in any corner of the cosmos. But there is more to religion than churches.

The "more" often lies in the realm of occult awareness, in the best sense of the word "occult"--that is, hidden. There, heaven is an educational spiral continually moving the soul upward towards pure light. In a lesser sense, the "more" to religion comes in being able to see a prayer as an avenue to solving problems, and in finding passages in Scripture which seem to have been written only for the individual seeker. My father habitually advised, as much for himself as for me, that I pray over anything that troubled me. And he often read his favorite passages from the Bible out loud, particularly the Ninety-first Psalm, which his own mother had loved:

For he will deliver thee from the snare of the fowler,
And from the deadly pestilence.
He will cover thee with his pinions,
And under his wings shalt thou take refuge:
His truth is a shield and a buckler.

Another of his favorites was:

> In my Father's house there are many mansions; if it were not so, I would have told you; I go to prepare a place for you. And if I go and prepare a place for you, I come again.... . And whither I go, ye know the way (John 14:2-4).

He accepted this last passage in its deepest occult sense--that a soul must travel through many stages, and many lives, of trial and error, failure and achievement--just as a servant might pass from room to room in a large house in search of his master. And, in God's house there are no rooms reserved for "Colored" or "White Only." Advancement is solely determined by the individual's willingness and ability to advance through love and good works.

The belief in the power of individual commitment and dignity, inherent in the natures of both of my parents, attracted many people of many races to them. Friends of all colors and talents found a welcome at our house. W. C. Handy, "Father of the Blues," Miriam Matthews and Wendell Coon, librarians; Arthur Lange, composer, and his wife, Marjorie, runner-up to Miss America in 1926; Joseph Portanova, the sculptor of the Kennedy Medallion for the Los Angeles Coliseum, and his wife, Mary Portanova, and Louis and Annette Kaufman, virtuosi; Mr. and Mrs. Theodore Phillips, educators; Leopold Stokowski, conductor; Mildred Hines, mother of the Metropolitan Opera star, Jerome Hines; L. Wolfe Gilbert, song-writer. Very few of these people who came to the house have failed to become fast friends.

Significantly, the fact that my parents were intermarried (my mother being Jewish), never put a blight on their friendships. Strangers might have turned them away, but others who knew them personally found that racial distinctions were inoperable. It is therefore surprising that so many people fear interracial marriages and believe that such marriages are the most likely to cause "trouble" for both the marital partners and for the offspring.

Strangely enough, the fear-mongers arrive at their conclusions in spite of the U.S. Census Bureau statistics, which suggest that the greatest causes of marital troubles are economic deficiencies and problems of immaturity related to the ages of the brides and grooms. And the greatest cause of emotional and social trouble among youngsters is not racial: it is lack of love in the home. In actuality, when couples must overcome social obstacles in order to affirm their love, their concern and affection for themselves and for their children is likely to increase, not decrease. Love that is fire-tempered is the purest kind of love and the most lasting.

When I tell people that my childhood was secure and full of love and hope, and that whatever conflicts arose were no more serious than those which arise in any family, many of these people are dubious. A common reaction is, "Well, you are the exception to the rule." Yet, these same people have had no other contacts with mixed marriages in sufficient number to justify their conclusions. Their reactions arise from the secret hope that the exception is not the rule, and that racial and religious distinctions will continue to make a difference. They are afraid of a world where black can be white and white can be black.

The simple truth is that racial and religious distinctions do not matter to the child who knows that his parents love each other and that they love him. Only the "little things" matter to a child. What then, are the little things which make a difference? The things my mother had to give up in order to buy me a fifteen-dollar dress for graduation; the hot-buttered toast that my father made for us some mornings, which he called "honest-to-goodness toast;" my mother's sympathy when I was learning to sew and inadvertently sewed my doll dress to the bedspread; the way my father struggled up a steep bank at Santa Monica beach to retrieve me when I had climbed up and was too frightened to come down again; the candle my mother burned for me when I was very ill; the way my father rubbed my neck and back to make me feel better, assuring me that he did not like for his "little girl" to be sick.

Nothing else matters when a family has these special moments. The moments create their own reality of strength and truth; the moments, and the people who share them, become capable of overcoming any barriers. "We shall overcome" is suddenly history, rather than a relevant rallying standard for the present. And among the people who have made it history, there was one who was also blessed with the four great loves of humanity--love of self, love of God, love of men, and love of work--and he will be the one who will be, therefore, of legendary greatness. His name was William Grant Still.

# MY LIFE AS A COMPOSER'S DAUGHTER[1]

> Written during the summer of 1956, at the age of 13 years, this work represents the childhood memories of Judith Anne Still, the daughter of composer-conductor, William Grant Still, and of pianist-journalist, Verna Arvey. While unrefined in its compositional skill, this work provides an otherwise unsupervised look at the Still's family life, at least through the eyes of a young girl. The reader will be charmed by the author's youthful confidence yet overall innocence as evidenced in the work.
>
> Judith Anne Still later developed her skills to become an accomplished writer and has received numerous commendations for her literary endeavors.

---

[1] The following text is presented in its original 1956 form, except for a very few changes of syntax and the addition of footnotes to clarify where needed.

The dedication of this work reads "To my family without whom I would not have had a subject for this book."

## CONTENTS

| | | |
|---|---|---|
| Chapter I | And I Was Born | 27 |
| Chapter II | The Story Of My Parents | 29 |
| Chapter III | I Now Pronounce You Man And Wife | 34 |
| Chapter IV | School Days | 36 |
| Chapter V | A Normal Day At Home | 43 |
| Chapter VI | Trains, Trains, Trains | 49 |
| Chapter VII | All About Me | 52 |
| Chapter VIII | Our Travels | 56 |
| Chapter IX | Religion And The Stills | 60 |
| Chapter X | May We Rest In Peace | 63 |

## PHOTOGRAPHS

Myself, Judith Anne.

William Grant Still, Judith Anne's father.

Verna Arvey, Judith Anne's mother.

Duncan Allan Still, Judith Anne's brother just after his graduation from junior high school.

Bessie Lawson Blackman, (a registered nurse, friend of the Still family and a direct descendent of Martha Custis Washington, wife of President George Washington) with Judith Anne.

Dr. Bessie Arvey (Judith Anne's maternal grandmother) and her family: Verna (Judith Anne's mother, standing) with her sister and brother, Edna and Dale.

The Still's house in Los Angeles with the old 1936 Ford in the left foreground.

Marjorie and Arthur Lange, life-long friends of the Still family.

# CHAPTER I
# And I Was Born

It happened in August, in August of 1942. The place was the very house I have lived in for 13 years. The event was my birth.

They tell me there was quite a lot of confusion and hysteria over me because the doctor didn't make it to the house on time to deliver me.

Fortunately we had with us (I say "we" because in the actual physical concepts I was there too) a very dear friend who was a registered nurse who took care of my mother when my one and only brother (I had no sisters) was born. Her name was Mrs. Blackman and she patiently stayed up with my mother all night to wait for me.

When day came everyone was anxious, and before long the minutes became hours and still no sign.

Soon the time was coming closer and my father felt it necessary to notify the Doctor. He telephoned him immediately as it came closer and closer to twelve noon.

When my father looked around he saw my little two-year-old brother standing there waiting with them, the picture of complete innocence. My father instructed him to go into the room in the back of the house, which served as my father's composing room, and stay there until it was all over. Very obediently, he trudged down the hall and into the room to amuse himself in his own way for a little while.

Now the seconds seemed like hours until all of a sudden at exactly twelve o'clock noon, Standard Time (it was Daylight Savings time then and the clocks really said one o'clock at that time), I was there before anyone even realized what had been happening. I was told many times over about the fact that just as I arrived my tiny brother, only two years old, was trying to play the piano in the back with his little chubby fist to welcome me and introduce me to music just as soon as I was born, although I'm sure he didn't have any idea what significance it would have. He banged happily away while much more important things, unknown to him were going on probably a great deal nearer to him than he realized.

There was probably more anxiety after I was born than before, because instead of being red when arriving like most normal babies I was very purple indeed. The problem was that they were not able to make me breathe at all very quickly.

Like any really good nurse, Mrs. Blackman took charge and saved the day. She made herself a self-appointed doctor and immediately initiated my very nervous father as a temporary nurse to help her.

First, she asked for some hot water and my father brought that to her. Then she asked for some cold water and that was also brought. Then she took me by my feet and held me upside down and dipped me in the hot water, after which she similarly dipped me in the cold water. Then she spanked me, and I know that after all that went on for about a minute, I should have started to cry. Believe me, that is exactly what I did. My father always said after that that I hadn't stopped crying since. Of course, you know how adults are.

After all the excitement was over I am very sure that if I had been aware of things right away I would have been very embarrassed indeed. Now I realize, though, that it was necessary to save my life before it began.

My father threw off his role as nurse as fast as he could right then and gained a new one as a father of two children.

My mother was happy too, and promptly declared that she wasn't worried at all. She knew I was going to cry at one time or another.

It was only a few minutes after I had entered the world when the doctor came. Breathlessly he explained that contrary to his first decision he failed to ask for a police escort across town so he could get there on time, so that was probably the reason he was late. We didn't blame him for anything because everything turned out fine, so there was nothing to blame him for. He was glad to see mother and baby doing fine and so was I.

Sometimes it takes a long time for mothers and fathers to think up a name for a brand new baby, but my mother and father had it all figured out for me. You see, my mother named my brother when he came after his great-grandfather on my father's side, so when I came it was my father's turn to name me, so my name became Judith Anne Still along with my brother's name of Duncan Allan Still.

Ever since my birth I have been proud of the fact that I was born at home instead of in a hospital as my brother was. It seems to me that being born in a hospital is not quite as exciting as being born at home, especially with such circumstances as the ones that occurred when I came into the world. In these modern times, almost every child in the civilized world meets the world in a hospital, so you can imagine how proud I am.

Of course, I give due credit to Mrs. Blackman because she is a real friend of the Still family. Ever since those early days there has never been a truer friend. Ready to come at any time if really needed, even if there was nothing in it for her. We always have such a wonderful time talking over that incident in 1942 with her.

I understand I was a regular every day baby after that and cried just as much as any other, especially at night.

Sometimes I wish I was still somewhat of a baby because then I had a lovely head of blond hair. Now my hair has turned brown and may even become almost black like other girls and the saying now is that gentlemen prefer blondes. I would have never known that I had blonde hair then had it not been that I came across an old envelope labeled, "Judith's hair, August 9, 1945," and another labeled "Judith's hair, November 1944," and they both had blond hair in them.

Really though, I shouldn't complain, I ought to be glad I was born in the first place!

## CHAPTER II - THE STORY OF MY PARENTS
## Part I: The Story of William Grant Still

My father's story began in the deep South, way down in Mississippi. It was in Woodville that Carrie Lena Fambro Still gave birth to a baby boy on May 11, 1895. He was a Colored American as was his mother.

His father was teacher of music at the Alabama Agricultural and Mechanical College. Both his parents loved their little child very much indeed.

# William Grant Still: A Voice High-Sounding

He was named William. William Grant Still, frequently called, "baby Will," after his father.

Unfortunately one of the greatest tragedies of this innocent child's life was to occur when he was only six months old, before his life had even begun. It was at this time that his father died.

Grief-stricken, his mother packed up, and when he was nine months old, she left for Little Rock, Arkansas, so that she could live with her sister and mother and try to make a living to support herself and her only child. There they made their home and, until my father grew up, it was his home town.

He grew into a fine boy...a lover of music and of the finer things of life.

As soon as he was ready for school, he began at Capitol Hill Elementary School right there in Little Rock, where his mother had become a public school teacher. Because his mother was teacher and a very strict and honorable woman, he had to be exceptionally good in school and wasn't able to get away with all the mischievous things his playmates got away with. He had to get good grades and if he did anything bad, it was "spare the rod and spoil the child" for him.

His friends actually felt sorry for him at times because he had to be so good all the time.

When he was nine years old, his mother remarried, to a Mr. Shepperson who held a job as a postal clerk and had an incessant love for classical music, especially opera.

This probably was another factor which kindled a closeness to music in his little stepson.

The family went to concerts together and enjoyed music immensely.

My father stayed in Capitol Hill school until the eighth grade when the officials of another elementary school, the Union School, insisted he was living in their district all that time, so he had to finish off his elementary school there.

He didn't like it there because he had left all his friends behind and didn't have time to make new ones.

When he went into high school at M. W. Gibbs High, his mother went there to teach while he was there and for many years afterward.

## My Life as a Composer's Daughter

In 1911, he graduated from high school as valedictorian of his class and went on to Wilberforce University.

His mother didn't want him to be a musician because, in her opinion, there was no future in it, so he took science classes to make her happy. In the end, he didn't enjoy doing science and other such things and ended up in music.

During his college years, he played in the band and from playing many, many different instruments he learned how to orchestrate and arrange and started to write pieces for band. One time at Wilberforce, a whole program of his works was played.

My father quit Wilberforce and school for a few years to take jobs in music in Columbus, Ohio.

After those few years, he went back to school at Oberlin College to study composition, and when World War I came around he joined the Navy in 1917.

After getting an honorable discharge from the Navy, he worked in music more until he went into the New England Conservatory of Music in Boston, Massachusetts.

In 1923, his stepfather, Mr. Shepperson, died by drowning. This was quite a coincidence because for some strange reason all through his life, Mr. Shepperson knew he would die that way. He had always been afraid of dying that way and it was strange that he really did in the end.

When my father had just started to build up his profession, he orchestrated for such people as W. C. Handy, Don Voorhees, Paul Whiteman, Sophie Tucker, Artie Shaw, and Willard Robison. He was also connected with the stations CBS and WOR when he arranged and conducted for the Deep River Hour.

In 1925 and '26, he finally began to be known as a serious composer and people recognized him as such.

Another tragedy entered his life in 1927 when his mother died. While in New York in that year, he received a telegram saying that his mother was very sick and was not expected to live. He hurried back to Little Rock as soon as he could to be by her side and that is where he was when she passed.

After this, he returned to New York, heart-broken, to continue his work in radio, to build up his serious works and his career as a serious composer, which he did.

In 1934, he received a Guggenheim Fellowship and with it it was possible for him to come to California to continue his work. This he did and after coming out to California, he made a permanent home in Los Angeles.

This action proved to be the turning point in his life as he added more and more wonderful experiences to his already full and distinguished life.

## CHAPTER II - THE STORY OF MY PARENTS
## Part II: The Story of Verna Arvey Still

Just about the time my father turned fifteen, something was going on in the Old Crocker Street Hospital in Los Angeles on February 16, 1910. This something was the birth of a little baby girl who turned out to be one of the most important persons in his life later on.

The baby's mother was Doctor Bessie Arvey, wife of David Arvey, a well-liked paper salesman. They were both Jewish. She made her career as an accomplished chiropractor and she raised her family in a practical sensible way, with a useful knowledge of the powers of God.

She named this first child of hers, Verna, after a good friend of the family.

Although my mother happened to be the first of the children, she was not the only child. She later gained a sister and even later a brother.

She was brought up well in the family.

They changed addresses many times in the city, but that didn't hamper the education of the children any. They all went to different schools because of the many moves, but all got the complete amount of education they were to have.

My mother first went to Western Avenue Elementary School for her kindergarten and the first grade and then transferred to Ninety-fifth Street Elementary School to finish her elementary schooling there.

At the age of nine years, she began her piano lessons with a lady by the name of Merle Gaskill.

## My Life as a Composer's Daughter

Then she went into John Muir Junior High School and was in the very first graduating class that came from there.

When she started in high school she began studying with a piano teacher named Marguerite d' Aleria. She went into Manual Arts High and made her name there. She belonged to the Scholarship Society, and won two prizes in Spanish competing with students all over the city. She was a reporter on the school paper which gave her a running start in her journalistic career, and she also belonged to the debating club.

On the side, she learned to be an accomplished concert pianist during her school years, and when commencement exercises took place at graduation she played a piano solo on a new piano which her class had bought for the school.

She graduated in the summer of 1926 class from Manual and after doing this she took a post graduate course at Los Angeles High and then took up a career as a pianist playing for dancers and singers and giving recitals for various women's clubs.

She concertized in the United States and in Latin America, and made her name in that field along with her writing career.

In 1927, the same year my father's mother died, her parents separated and her mother went on a trip around the world while she kept the house in order. She did this because of her love for travel and to see different places and things. Before this trip, she had taken a trip to Hawaii and that had only whetted her appetite for traveling, and she finally decided to really see the world in its entirety.

After 1927, my mother became a soloist in Raymond Paige's Orchestra over CBS.

During the time after she left high school she studied with such instructors as Rose Cooper Vinetz, Alexander Kosloff, and Ann Eachus.

She wrote articles for the *Etude* principally, along with other magazines of importance. She tried her hand at writing some novels which she later discarded but which had served to give her more experience in that field.

She continued in this way, always trying and never relenting if she failed at one time or another, not knowing that soon she would meet someone who would change her entire life.

## CHAPTER III
## I Now Pronounce You Man and Wife

Soon after my father moved to Los Angeles to stay he got together with a young man from Manual Arts High School whom he knew. This man was going to write the libretto for one of his operas.

This young man knew of a promising pianist and writer who went to school with him, so he introduced her to my father.

Of course, this person was Verna Arvey. As soon as the two met, they knew they were suited for one another, and before long they began to work together as they knew each other better.

My mother helped my father with his correspondence and played some of his new pieces for him on the piano as he wrote them so he could see how they would sound when played after being written. They put on concerts together in leading California cities at different times and in this way, by working together all the more, they became very dear friends.

My father dedicated one of his pieces, *Kaintuck'* to my mother and, when she played with the Philharmonic Orchestra under Otto Klemperer, she played this piece.

She played many of his works and soon each of their lives became as much of the other's concern as his own. After seeing a lot of each other, they found they just couldn't get along without each other.

Intermarriages were very rare in those days, and still are, but you don't have to be in love to know that when you really love someone you don't think about race or color.

Finally, there was no question about it. My mother and father were meant to be married.

And so it came to pass that one day in February, the eighth to be exact, in 1939, my father got in his car, a brand new 1936 Ford, and took his dog over to pick up my mother and they all drove down to Tijuana to get married. They had to go to Tijuana because it was illegal to intermarry in California at that time.

When they arrived in Tijuana they sought out the Mexican Justice of the Peace and after doing all the necessary things they had to do before getting married, they were married peacefully in the tiny quarters of the Judge. The entire ceremony was in Spanish, but I'm sure it couldn't have been more romantic if it had been in English.

On the way back from Mexico, something happened that added a sour note to their complete and unbreakable happiness. As they sped down the highway they were far too happy to even notice the speedometer and soon someone in a familiar uniform pulled up beside them and compelled them to pull to the side of the road. Obediently, they followed orders and sadly watched the officer as he wrote out a ticket for speeding, as calmly as calm could be. Now this ticket wouldn't have been quite so harassing, but they just happened to be in a little unknown town called National City when they received it, many miles from Los Angeles. They couldn't have stayed there to wait for their case to come up in the court there, so they had to go back to Los Angeles and when they received the summons, mailed the fine back with the extra money charged because they weren't there in the court. The entire fine amounted to exactly twenty dollars complete and this gave them their first wedding present.

Later my father gave my mother her wedding ring which was a present from his father to his mother, which my mother has always worn faithfully for seventeen years.

Before the marriage took place, my mother prepared for it by buying a small, three-bedroom house in the center of the city. We are still living in that house now although it has been our desire to make a change which we are working on now.

For many long years now my mother and father have belonged to the American Society of Composers, Authors and Publishers (ASCAP) which has helped them immensely through giving them a suitable outlet and income and, in turn, they have always tried to help it too.

Much of their time was spent after their marriage settling in their new home and, before anything, preparing for a family. They made ready for one as soon as it was possible.

God wasted no time in seeing that they had their wish. On January 21, 1940, their first blessed event came to keep them company. It was a boy, and as you already know, it was my mother who named him Duncan Allan.

It was only two and a half years later that I came along to be his little sister and make up the last addition to the family circle. I was glad to be the second child because almost everyone seems to think that it is better to have the boy first and the girl later on.

Even though my mother and father spent most of those early years with my brother and myself, they kept working as much as they could, trying to accomplish what they could and give to the world what knowledge they had, and, in that way help its progress in some way.

My mother continued her writing for the magazines *Etude*, *Ritmo*, *New York Times*, *Musical America*, *American Mercury*, and other well-known magazines.

She also reached a greater goal by writing a large book in 1941 called *Choreographic Music* which was published by the Dutton Publishing Company and showed what experience gained through the years can do.

My father did far too many things in those years to add to his list of accomplishments to put here in their entire form. He acquired four honorary Doctor's degrees, and in 1949, he went to New York to see his inspiring opera, *Troubled Island*, done. It was indeed a huge success. The audience applauded so that my father and the cast together took way over twenty curtain calls. Another time, he went to New Orleans to make another "first" as the first Colored man to conduct a major symphony orchestra in the deep South when he conducted the New Orleans Philharmonic Orchestra in 1955.

So, you must see now that the marriage of my parents was indeed a harmonious one and has served to show the world what love really is; beside the fact that when God puts a pair together it means that they are really meant for each other, and may the brotherhood of man be put up the stairs one step because of it.

## **CHAPTER IV**
## **School Days**

The first thing that you go through now in school in these modern times is kindergarten, but that doesn't include me or my brother for that matter.

When it came time for my brother to enter kindergarten, my mother and father discovered a law which stated that all parents could keep their children out of school until they were eight years old as long as they gave them the same education at home as in the schools.

So, it was decided to keep my brother out of school until he was eight so they could have him home a little longer because they didn't want to lose him so quickly.

Then my mother went out and bought a set of books belonging to the same grades my brother would miss and each night he had a lesson until he learned everything he was to know, and perhaps even more.

Because I was exactly two and a half years younger than my brother, it just happened that I was supposed to enter kindergarten just at the same time he started back to school at eight. Because this was so, my mother and father decided against keeping me out until I became eight so we could both enter school together.

So on the day of enrollment, we all drove over to the school, Sixth Avenue School by name, to get enrolled. It was unfortunate that just at that time there was no room in the kindergarten classes for them to take me. This made me very unhappy and I remember crying all the way home after we had left my brother there at school.

They didn't want to see me unhappy and they wanted to get me in school with my privileged brother so we waited a year so I could be entered into first grade.

This time nothing stood in our way and I was successfully gotten into the first grade, with no trouble whatsoever.

Hardly had I gotten into the swing of things at my first alma mater when a minor disaster came about. I developed a case of chicken pox.

Well, that was all. From then on, I was kept out of school until the age of eight and learned my ABC's at home.

This didn't bother me so much later because I found that when I got back into the B3, I knew a lot more than I was supposed to, which gave me an easier start just as it did for my brother.

After all that, there wasn't much more to my elementary

school days except that I got out of them as much as I could. I have gained many pleasant memories, beside the three cases of measles developed during that time.

The experiences I can recall the best are so deeply embedded in my mind that I don't think I'll ever forget them as easily as I have many of the other things that happened during the earliest years of my life.

Always at our school we had a carnival at Halloween every year. Everyone dressed in bright and fancy costumes on that day and paraded around the school and through the auditorium so all the parents could come and look at them and say, "That's my child!" I was in that crowd of merrymakers too, and I enjoyed it just as much of the rest of them. After the parade was over, there was always a big circus after school right on the grounds. They had a different kind of animal each year for the animal act part of it, and there were acts and concessions where you could risk your money to win a prize.

But then there was always Christmas after that, and every year we had a pageant of some sort. One year they had a part for a little girl in the first act to be a child anxiously awaiting Christmas and holding a short, but significant, conversation. Because I was small and yet in a high enough grade to play the part, that part was given to me. I didn't mind and everything started off fine and ended fine for everyone, even me.

Then, there were school trips, fun assemblies, and PTA drives.

There was always entertainment at the PTA meetings and, at one of these meetings, my mother and father were asked to give a short program of some of my father's piano pieces with my mother at the piano. That was one of the only nights that we ever went to a PTA meeting although we belonged.

I belonged to the chorus at Seventh Avenue under the leadership of a dear little lady named Mrs. Merriweather who flitted into our classes every day to give the class a much needed music lesson.

Needless to say, I liked the last grades at elementary school (until the seventh grade) the very best because it was then that I started to learn things.

## My Life as a Composer's Daughter

At Sixth Avenue, we were unfortunate to have student teachers from college practicing teaching on us for their teaching degrees at college, so we never learned as much as those in schools without student teachers.

In the last grades of school, a few of the children from our school were chosen to go to a special school in Los Feliz to help children who wanted to go farther and learn more to go ahead. I was among those children. For a few weeks on every Wednesday we went out to the school before noon to learn things and take tests. That, in itself, was a wonderful experience.

Also in elementary school, I got on the Safety Council and worked my way up to secretary of the Student Council so that I was in on all the big school decisions.

The real experiences that I honestly associate with Sixth Avenue School in a big way were my early television careers.

I was first introduced into television when the very wonderful principal of the school, Mrs. Holt, who was very understanding and nice and always willing to give me a chance, recommended me for the Art Linkletter program when some of the heads of the show asked her for suggestions of people that would be good to be on his show.

So I was on his "House Party" program in the school children's section, as calm as I could ever be. I thought I wouldn't be scared for my first time on television and I wasn't. I was, as I say, calm, cool and collected until after the program when I got home. I was really sick! The sickness was disheartening enough, but as a prize for being on the show, I was given quarts of ice cream, a large case of soft drinks, and other things which happen to be my favorite sort of treats which ended up in the stomachs of my brother and the rest of the family, and not me!

Later, they made a film of the same program with the children for another show which was never shown to my knowledge.

My last chance at television came when I was in sixth grade. They were putting on a show about how the public schools took measures to help those who couldn't read as well as they should when they got to higher grades on a Board of Education program on television called "Learning '54."

I didn't know a thing about the program, even the fact that the children to play in this particular show were to come directly from our school.

The day I first learned of the plans, Mrs. Holt asked me to tell my mother to come to school and talk to her when she brought me back to school from lunch. Well, I didn't have any idea what she wanted to talk to her about so without inquiring, I did as she asked.

My mother did go to see her, and while I was in class one of the boys whom I later learned was to be in the show told us the news that they were putting on this show and they wanted me to play the part of a little girl who couldn't read and then they would base the story around that. At first I didn't believe it, but after prodding everyone I got hold of, I found it was true.

After school my mother told me that was what Mrs. Holt talked to her about and she had said "yes." So the play went forward and we practiced our parts almost every day.

The day the show went on was very detailed so I won't tell about it here, but it was all very exciting. I suppose I did all right, but what was better was I didn't get sick afterward. I got myself a real television background then, along with all my other friends on the show. They all did a fine job.

Those are just a few of a great number of happy experiences that I gained in elementary school. I liked the oneness of the school. The many nations and peoples represented in the school were all one and the same. They weren't judged by their races or colors but by just what they could accomplish. We were all friends because we understood that we were all part of the human race no matter how we looked on the outside. The Mexican, the Japanese, the Negro, and the Jewish, and no one ever thought of race, creed, or color because it was absolutely silly to them. The world could well learn a few things from children.

When it was time for me to graduate, I was a chairman of the graduation committee along with another girl who was the only other chairman. Unfortunately for me, at the last minute she hurt her arm and was out of school for the whole last part of school.

I wonder how I ever even handled things even with the inadequate job that I did. I was running all over the school during graduation, before and after. Although I didn't know what was

## My Life as a Composer's Daughter

going on myself, we graduated in spite of it all and I went streaming off to a new phase of my school life in junior high school.

My brother, Duncan, had already passed that stage and gone on, but he probably had his memories too.

During elementary school, he got better grades than he had gotten in high school, because as he got older he did just as all other typical boys do and became more and more mischievous and interested in other things. He dropped from excellent to good and average which is bad when you have a good enough brain to do better. As you know, boys seem to take things more lightly than girls, so I'm glad that he is normal. Boys get as good grades as they can to stay on top and save their time for the things they really want to do, which has been the way with Duncan.

I have, of course, been speaking of the average every day boy that I've really had experience with.

Duncan went through junior high school at Foshay Junior High School and I followed him right through. While I was at Foshay, he went to Manual Arts which, as you remember, was my mother's old alma mater. There he reached very high grades. When he took the Iowa tests which were given to students all over the country he made 99% which meant that he was better in brain power than ninety-nine other students out of one-hundred. He remembers things well and gets the highest grades in the classes in which his interest takes root.

Of course, Duncan had his moments in high school. I well remember the time he had in his Latin class. His regular teacher in that class happened to get sick and a substitute came to take her place and teach the class temporarily. Well, unfortunately for him, he turned out to be a very short man with white hair and, according to my playful brother, he looked very funny indeed.

Duncan and his friends began by making fun of him behind his back. They always told the joke that, when you saw him behind his desk, he looked as though he were sitting, but when he walked out from behind it, they discovered he was standing all the time. They said he was once run over by a roller-skate too. None of Duncan's friends seemed to like him, but I know they did underneath. They never did anything to him or played any tricks on him, but the stories they told were really something. Duncan himself is taller than any of us in the family and still growing. He is stocky too, with hard muscles and a gentle nature as are all of his friends, so this caused more joking because said Latin teacher was allegedly just the opposite.

One day, just as Duncan had gotten on the streetcar to come home after school and the streetcar was just about to go away, his Latin teacher came running up, puffing and panting, tugging a large briefcase along with him. He yelled at the conductor to let him in and the unsuspecting conductor, not knowing what it was all about and apparently not noticing the teacher's white hair said, "All right, you'll have to wait for the next car, sonny."

When I got in junior high, I really began digging into my school work and had many more experiences there that have all been added to my list. One of the most wonderful experiences of that period before high school happened right there in junior high school.

Each year at each school, the American Legion holds an essay contest on a different subject of patriotic significance. Every year, I entered the contests with no hope of winning anything. Then one year when I was near the middle of my three years at James A. Foshay, I entered as always with still no hope. The essay that year was on the Liberty Bell and as usual I patiently copied and recopied and redid the essay meticulously until it was just right, and handed it in. Then I forgot all about it and went on about my regular business.

It wasn't long before it was time for the American Legion Awards to be handed out. Then there was an American Legion Awards Assembly at school, and we all went. I sat in my seat next to one of my friends who wanted to win very badly. I calmly sat there paying almost no attention to what was going on as I drew pictures on my hands with an indelible pencil. When they began the announcements, I stopped to listen. The honorable mention went to the anxious friend of mine next to me. I was very happy for her and before I could tell her how happy I was, they began to announce the first prize winner. To my surprise, they were saying my name! It was my name and I was sure of it. It was with very wobbly legs that I went up on the stage to receive the award, which turned out to be a gold cup with my name on it. I couldn't get over it, especially because I had never won anything before and never expected to. To add to the state of shock I was in, I was also told that I had won for the district too, which was a check. I suppose I shall never get over that experience because it was my first.

Like my brother, I got on the school club of Foshayettes and Foshaymen which was the school police force, shall we say. I also got in the Scholarship Society.

We got movies and dances and class trips to entertain us at school, besides the hilarious faculty talent shows and "Hi Jinx" shows every once in a while.

I know that high school, with its wealth of activities and opportunities, will be even more wonderful to me. But I'll always remember the first of my school days, too.

All in all, I think we find that the good old school days were grand old times while they were here.

## **CHAPTER V**
## **A Normal Day At Home**

Most people's normal day begins when hubby rushes off for work and the children run off to school while the lady of the house stays home to work around the house.

That most certainly is not the case in our house. It is true that my brother and I go to school in the mornings and my mother stays home, but my father does not rush off to work because his place of business is right at home. Because he, as you know, is a composer. After taking my brother and me to school, he comes back home and begins work in his work room, only taking time out for dinner or to keep an appointment. This is hard on him just as it is hard for a man to work in a factory all day doing hard labor. But, he and my mother (who also works very hard during the day) are both in a remarkable state of health and our family is all the better because of it.

When someone asks me what sort of work my mother does, I find it almost necessary to say that she leads four lives. These include housekeeper, secretary for my father, pianist (she only takes this occupation up every once in a while now), and a writer in the journalistic field. She keeps up on her work and still finds time for recreation which seems almost impossible.

My father leads only one life...a musical one, which is much harder to follow than you think. You need to know about the theater, how to play many different instruments, about the art of singing and voice, you need to have a knowledge of how far you can stretch the capabilities of the performer and how to do all the things required to write a piece. Besides this, you must have a personality, be able to speak, to know what the public wants, and present a good appearance; aside from the fact that you have to know how to write a pleasing melody, and to be able to be sort of a part of what you are writing.

Even if you are familiar with all these things, it still takes a lot of effort and patience to write a good piece. My father knows about all of these things and yet he has a lot to do before he can present the final composition to the expectant public. First, he must get the inspiration. This usually comes to him at night and he gets up at off hours to write down whatever came to him. This constant working at night doesn't bother him because he is glad to have the inspiration in the first place, and because he is older, he doesn't need as much sleep as children would, or as all females seem to need. He does some of his work when he wakes up in the morning, too.

The first steps of composing a piece are long drawn out processes and they almost always require hard struggles between the composer and his ideas, so it really does end up to be "ten percent inspiration and ninety percent perspiration."

After my father gets the idea, he lives with it and works with it for weeks at a time and watches it grow. He plays with it on the piano, looking at the different forms of the theme until it begins to tell him things about itself and begins to take a definite shape.

Sometimes he leaves spaces between notes until he gets the right thing to go there. While he is doing the developing of the music, he decides what kind of a piece it will be, and after he has done this he begins to fill in the outline of the piece. Then he makes a pencil sketch of it to be gone over many, many times at

## My Life as a Composer's Daughter

the piano with my mother. Every day they spend careful minutes inspecting each section of the music and debating its possibilities. After the music is pretty well in order my mother puts words to it if it requires words.

Of course, if the piece is to be for orchestra my father begins to orchestrate it at this point. He makes parts for each instrument, making it so it can be played by an orchestra, and this process is called orchestrating.

Even after this, his job has not just yet been finished. He finishes the job by extracting parts, which means copying them from the score, after which he has the piece printed.

So, you see, that is a lot to do for one piece, especially when you turn out hundreds of them in your lifetime. Even at this, my father does other things in spite of it. He builds things when we need them for the house and works on his flowers which he plants around the house. When my brother and I were just little children he made almost all of our toys. He made lovely furniture for my dolls (which I still have) and skillful wooden engines for my brother with cars and scenery to match them.

During World War II, he planted a "victory" garden which was such a success that we have never eaten or have seen such delicious or beautiful fruit and vegetables again.

My father also took to making jig-saw puzzles and later, when I got bigger, he made me a good supply of puzzles to work.

In his spare time, after his working day has ended, he works crossword puzzles out of magazines that he gets each month and I would say that they are his favorite pastime.

He used to smoke cigars and pipes, but it hampered his health so much that he stopped and feels very much better because of it.

In my mother's spare time, she reads, rests, and watches television. Her writing is usually done in her spare time, although she does a lot of it in her working time because that is work in itself. She supplies the words for many of my father's works which need them besides her journalistic and secretarial work.

Life is always easier for the children of the family though. When I and my brother are not going to school, we're doing what helping we can around the house, participating in the family business, doing the things we like to do and watching television.

At this point, I would like to add that I am not the only television star in the house. My father has been on television three times as a serious composer, and I hope it won't be long before the rest of the family will become television stars, too.

Besides these other things that we in our family enjoy doing, we like to go places and do interesting things on the holidays we have. My mother and father have holidays from work and, when we do so, we can all do things together.

It used to be that we always had a family dog to be our companion, but after our last dog, Ozma, we have not gotten another one. Our first dog was named Shep. He was my father's dog before he and my mother were even married and there was a family. I was so small when we had Shep, I hardly remember him anymore. I remember the day he passed away, though. He was very sick at that time because he was so old. We tried to keep him well and frisky, but finally it was no use anymore. So one day I was told that for Shep's own good, we would have to have him put to sleep. That day my father, brother, and I took Shep in the car to the vet and had him put to death. We were happy that he did not have to suffer any longer, but we were sorry that we had to lose him.

After Shep, we got two more dogs who ungratefully proceeded to run away. Then we got Ozma. She was a very wonderful dog. You could talk about her almost as you could talk about a human being. (Of course, all dogs feel that they are human beings.) I liked Ozma because I had a chance to know her from the start, and I was older so I could appreciate her companionship better.

We got Ozma on a day when I wasn't feeling too well. I had been sick for the past few days, but when I seemed to be getting better, we all decided to go to the S.P.C.A. (Society for the Prevention of Cruelty to Animals) to get a dog. We went down the long rows of cages with dogs in them and talked each one over. When we came to one of the cages, the little toy shepherd inside, who was only just a puppy, greeted us happily and literally chose us to take her home. We decided right away that this little dog was the one for us and she had already shown us that she felt the same way, so we got her. We were planning to name her Jo-Jo,

## My Life as a Composer's Daughter

but that was a boy's name and we found out that she was a girl so we ended in naming her Ozma. We took the names from the celebrated *Oz* stories by L. Frank Baum. I went right back to bed when we got home again because I was sick again, but they brought Ozma to see me in bed while she was still wet and limp from the animal shelter. After that, she was our constant friend and companion. Unfortunately she died when only seven years old because she developed a bad case of mange and she suffered so we simply had to put her to sleep. It was the loss of the best friend we could have had.

We didn't always have just dogs as pets, there were other animals too. Once a cat came to the house of its own free will and made its home at our house for awhile. We took care of it until Ozma came and chased it away, at which time we knew we would never see it again, in our house. It did come once or twice and sit in the tree by the side of the house and peer at us until Ozma saw it there. The cat had been at the house before we lost Shep, but Shep was such a gentle-hearted dog, he didn't mind him a bit.

Besides the cat, we acquired some ducks at one time. A friend gave us a large duck called Daisy. Soon we decided she needed a companion, so we bought two baby ducks named Dora and Donald. It wasn't long before they grew up and ate up all our grass in the back yard of the house. This wasn't a very good thing for the yard, but we had an even greater problem. The male duck, Donald, was very mean and especially greedy. He stole food from Dora and Daisy and tried to bite us several times. Finally, we decided to put a stop to it, so my father sharpened the ax and the next morning he got a good hold on Donald and did a little chopping. I didn't watch the execution because it was far too horrible for me, but I didn't mind the delicious roast duck dinner we had that afternoon which we all enjoyed very much indeed.

We have another kind of pet now. She is much smaller than all the rest and she belongs to me. She is a turtle. The way I got her was a rather round-about way of getting a turtle. I suddenly got the urge to get one one day and decided I wanted one very badly. I couldn't get one too easily because they didn't sell them at places where it was simple to just drop by any day and come back with one.

One day (although I hadn't exactly planned it) I got sick. It was in 1952 that this happened and I remember it all perfectly. I had come down with a very bad case of influenza which proved to stick with me for a total of four weeks. As each day passed, I got less hungry and consequently I wouldn't eat which made me get thinner and thinner as the meals went by. After I was able to keep things on my stomach, which was one of the reasons I wasn't hungry before, I still wouldn't eat because the thought of food was even repulsive to me. My mother was extremely distressed. She promised me that if I would eat before I starved to death, she would get me a turtle for sure. That seemed like too good a proposition to turn down, so I began to eat again. My grandmother wanted to help the situation out a little, so she found that turtles could be bought in quantity in the five-and-ten cent store across the street from her house. In a very few days, she brought it over in a cardboard box and I've had her ever since.

I named her Anne because I had decided beforehand that she was indeed a girl turtle (especially since I wanted her to be a girl) and I am sure she is a girl. My father calls her Andrew instead of Anne because he insists she is a male turtle, just because he thinks she hasn't laid any eggs yet. I contend that none of us in the family know what turtle eggs look like in the first place, so what do we care!

She and I are very fond of each other and the whole family seems to like her too. A very hungry turtle she is, too. She eats like a horse and is especially fond of moths, sowbugs, dried flies, and all other such things. I even took the liberty of asking the neighbors if they had any available bugs on their side of the fence for her breakfast, lunch, or dinner.

Anne is very opinionated, also. When I put her in the water ditch on one side of the driveway, and she feels that she wants to be in the flower beds on the other side, she wastes no time in going where she wants to go no matter how many times I put her on the side I want her to be on. She is very fast for such a small creature, contrary to common belief that turtles are slow. She never moves fast unless she wants to, and takes a lot of time to make decisions, which I think is a good trait for any person to have.

Another constant companion that we've had since a few years ago, is our television set. At the end of a usually tiring day, we all settle down to a wonderfully full and entertaining evening of good old-fashioned television as most average American families do. There is really nothing better if you don't ever go to moving picture shows which our family never does. We think it is loads of fun to go to movies once in awhile for a change, but if we went all the time it would become somewhat of a bother to us. We, in this country and other lucky countries, should feel quite priviledged to have such a wonderful thing as television, also radio and the movies. I'm sure at times we all tend to take them for granted.

Our day begins and ends like the day of every other average American citizen, but it is different just as everyone else has differences in their lives. I find that it takes many, many different kinds of people to make a world, and to make a good world with enough setbacks to make people appreciate the good things when they come, and enough good things to keep people reaching out for them and opening the doors to new and better things. Because of this thought, I find myself thanking God that we are what we are and we'll always be that way.

## CHAPTER VI
## Trains, Trains, Trains

"Railroaditis"
This is just a warning
In case you haven't yet
Been taken by an 'itis
You really shouldn't get.
Now, if you've ever ridden trains
Or have seen them charging through,
Don't get too drawn
By their charming sound,
Although you're human too.
Don't listen to the whistle
Of a graceful 440
Or measure up their drivers

From the top down to the toe.
These are just the very things
You really mustn't do,
Or that sneaky railroaditis
Will be sure to get you too!

Due to unavoidable circumstances, the Still family has always been connected with railroading and everything connected with trains.

When my brother, Duncan, was just a little baby boy, he became a confirmed train man.

When he went on trips as a child, he saw the trains whizzing by and the railroad yards with rows of cars both dingy and sparkling clean, and track and other such scenery, it always made him excited and he loved every minute of it. From that time on, he never could get enough of railroads, and it was that early experience that was the root of his love that exists today for everything connected with trains.

Because of this undying passion of his we find ourselves in the most undesirable places, standing on the siding of an out-of-the-way junction, surrounded by all the things you find at such places: hobos, grease, trainmen, switches, semaphores, and everything else. We make frequent trips to a small, hot town around fifty-seven miles from Los Angeles, parking the car at a station there where all sorts of engines and cars come roaring in while Duncan photographs them and takes down their numbers.

He keeps piles of railroad books, magazines, pictures, timetables, and data. He is really interested in that sort of thing and because of him we have a soft spot in our hearts for it too.

It makes me chuckle to think of the fact that Duncan can turn so many people his way when it comes to thinking of trains. When he meets someone who likes airplanes, trucks, and busses instead of the railroads, he is sure to set them straight with the true facts.

In the tiny house we are living in at this time, it is almost impossible for Duncan to have a "real" model railroad but he has the makings of one. Piles of boxes with buildings, scenery, cars, engines and track for a model railroad line the walls. This being the condition, it is hard to plan for a model railroad, but Duncan keeps working on it anyway.

Besides himself being a model railroader, Duncan has many friends who are also model railroad fans. When the boys get together there is no room for me, so off I go to listen to the railroad language at a distance.

After Duncan's first model train, which was a little rubber train from babyhood, he got a transfer to the large wooden trains that my father built for him. When he wanted to turn to bigger things, he went to the O gauge Lionel electric trains. When he tired of this, he traded the entire outfit of handsome buildings, expensive engines and cars and scenery to a cowboy who gave him a few paltry engines and cars for all of it. Then he went into smaller size of model trains which was HO scale. He hasn't yet traded this set but he'll probably change many more times before he goes into full sized railroading.

Someday Duncan says he is going to be a railroad superintendent and try to improve his railroad. He wants to make the country stronger by the use of rails. He has ideas for the betterment of railroads and industry in general, but wants to keep them as secret as possible. He has sound, sensible and fascinating ideas and someday he might have them carried out.

He isn't the athletic type, but doesn't care that much about athletics, although he goes in for sports once in a while. He has brains for mechanical things, though. He could write volumes and volumes on trains and model railroading and there would be many millions of people to read it because the number of train fans is increasing by the day.

Besides Duncan's other talents, he has a remarkable sense of direction which suits him because he loves to travel. He likes to study maps and travel folders, and likes nothing better than to drive around town in the car, even if he only goes to the market.

He loves the northern section of California and says that someday he will live there.

He also likes to know what is going on in the world and never misses a chance to read the newspaper from cover to cover. He listens to the opinions of others and putting the facts together he forms his own opinions, so that he is not the really gullible type. He weighs each side of the story carefully before deciding what he thinks is right which I think is a good quality. Sometimes I wish I had some of the qualities he has because they are good ones to have around at times.

Duncan is more of the businessman type and he has put over some good deals in his lifetime. Our family doesn't have to be good enough in business to weigh both sides of the story to know that we all hope he will someday make the railroad. Since Duncan hopes the same thing, I won't debate the subject but just pray that it will happen.

## **CHAPTER VII**
## **All About Me**

I find that it is one of the hardest things in the world for me to write about myself. I think it is good for people to express their opinions and ideas and to listen to the opinions of others, but when I want to express my opinions they seem to end up sounding very silly, indeed.

Aside from my opinions, I don't know as much in the way of music as I should. I want someday to become a singer but although I know certain cut-and-dried things about music, I don't know how to play an instrument as yet. I think that this is necessary for the development of a really tops singer. Of course, I want to take up singing in the operatic field and nothing else. I am very glad that I know what I do about music, but as a composer's daughter I ought to know almost everything there is to know about it.

I would also like to advance more in the field of writing, composition, and journalism. This sort of thing is what my father favors to a musical life because he feels that the public would understand something of beauty better if you wrote it down in black and white for them than if you expressed it in music. I agree with him from that standpoint but I also feel that if the public has it to understand in music and in writing, they will understand it twice as well with both of the forms of expression explaining it to them.

I think I should be more like Duncan and be more interested

in world affairs than I am, but I can not help my poetic nature so I never push myself. When it comes to a poetic nature, you might say that my poetry isn't as good as it should be, but I have tried my hand at it anyway. I write a lot of poetry. You can get everything from humorous poems to sentimental type poems to just plain poems from me. When I write poetry (or am in the mood, shall we say), I think what I write is pretty good, but a few days later when I read it over it seems pretty bad. I have only three poems that are better than the others but even they aren't fit to be read. Just the same, I want you to read them so you can get an example of my poetic genius:

### "Ants"

Ants are little insects
Of importance they rank none,
And they hardly even weigh
One ten-trillionth of a ton.

I'm sure they haven't got a brain
'Cause all they do is eat
And really when you look at it
They aren't very neat.

I really never think of them
Until a picnic comes along,
Then they start a-comin' at me
In a force ten thousand strong.

They eat all that's around me,
Over me and under;
That they leave the dishes
Is quite the greatest wonder

And so of ants I'll finally say,
They're really very small,
But when you lay your picnic out
They'll gladly take it all!

**"A Storm"**
A storm is just a symphony
Across the rain-drenched lands,
Along the sandy beaches,
Across the coral strands,
Its thunder is a kettle drum
Rumbling with all its might;
The lightening is a cymbal
Flashing through the night.
The mighty winds
Are the violins
Whistling through the trees
And the pattering rains
Are the harps sweet strings,
And the strong wind blows
As the water sings.


**"A Tranquil Sea"**
I felt the salt spray on my face,
I faced the sea with living grace--
The tranquil sea.

I saw the waves grasp the shore,
And the sands silently waited for--
A tranquil sea.

The waters called me to their home,
By their shores I'll always roam--
By a tranquil sea.

So you see, those are my masterpieces, and I am sure if I keep trying I might become something of a poet some day soon.

I have, as I have said, many ideas to credit what little experience in life I've had. I second the ideas of the family on the subjects of prejudices, religion, spiritual and political beliefs. I believe in gaining all the experience and knowledge that a person can gain in his lifetime.

## My Life as a Composer's Daughter

I think that a person should always try to be doing something and keeping busy. In that way they can better themselves and find more ways to better themselves. They should of course always be trying to do good things that will help others while they are doing things, even if it wouldn't profit them in any way.

I try to keep getting ideas and carry them through as best I can, and if they aren't good ideas, I learn from experience.

I like to work with my hands very much. When I have nothing better to do I get out the old handicraft books and make something. I know that not everyone likes to do things like that so I don't urge people to do it, but for my type of person it is one of the best things to do in your spare time.

I also like to have a quiet chance to think and come upon new possibilities and angles on different subjects. It is good to have a chance to think things out and straighten everything out in your mind a little once in a while.

Another thing that is good to do once in a while is to clean up your things. I know I like to clean my things up and change them around every month or so to keep my mind refreshed with a feeling of having something new. It does something to my room to change it around because it not only gives you a chance to get the dust out of the way but to keep your things neat and orderly. I think that if you keep things neat and orderly, your mind is also kept neat and orderly at the same time.

Another one of my crackpot ideas is that the world can't get along without evil along with the good influences. No one would know the value of good if there wasn't evil so there would be no use. If it were not hot we wouldn't be able to appreciate a nice, warm, wonderful day.

These are the things I believe in now, but as I grow I hope I will hear more opinions and views and then my own beliefs will broaden and I will be able to express them much better. All young people should at least have some ideas and thoughts and learn as they grow older.

Someday I may be able to express my thoughts to the world, but now I'll just use my energy to form opinions in the first place!

## CHAPTER VIII
## Our Travels

Whenever anyone talks of traveling, everyone sits up and takes notice because it is such a fascinating subject to talk about.

Actually, our family has never gone across the ocean to foreign lands together, although my father and mother have done a lot of traveling out of the country in their youth.

Whenever our family goes somewhere we always go together. Even when we were small my brother and I were never left home with a baby sitter because we are all so close to one another we want to be with each other. Before I was born my brother went to the San Francisco World's Fair with my parents. In these modern times the average parent thinks far too little of his children and will gladly leave them home while they go out and have a lot of fun. If they don't want to bother with the child, why did they bother to have a child anyway? The child needs affection and love and maybe because so many children don't get this love is the reason there is so much juvenile delinquency. In our family we are always glad we go places together and share our fun.

Most of the many places we have gone have been in some way connected with my father's or my mother's work. The other part of our travels has been for pure fun and recreation, and for interesting experiences that we could have.

The first big trip that we made in my time was when I was four years old in 1947 when we went to Seattle, Washington. We went there because my father was going to conduct the University of Washington Orchestra. That was also my first big train trip that I have taken. I thought it was very exciting. I remember how the whole family ran back and forth from one side of the train to the other to see Mount Shasta from the windows. It was one of the most beautiful sights I have ever seen. It is always wonderful for everyone to see a tall, majestic, snow-capped mountain before you. I almost wish I had been older when I saw it so I could have enjoyed it more.

In that very same year of 1947, we took a trip in our old 1936 Ford, which we aptly named Neo, to Oberlin in Ohio. We made the trip because the College of Oberlin presented my father with his third honorary degree. I enjoyed this trip very much because of the beautiful scenery at Oberlin. Majestic, towering trees lined the lanes at the college and ivy climbed its walls. We especially loved the delicious ice cream they sold there. The days were delightfully warm and nice, and the air was crisp and clear. Later they sent us pictures of the winters there and I wished we could have stayed until winter came to see it clothed in its white gown.

After this trip, we did not make another such long trip together as a family.

In 1949 my father, as I have mentioned before, went to New York to see his opera done and much later to New Orleans to conduct the orchestra there. In all, he went to New York several times besides his two trips to West Point and Bates College in Maine. He went to West Point in 1952 to conduct his band piece there with the band of the West Point Military Academy. There he met the outstanding director of the band, Colonel Resta. Later when Colonel Resta came out to California the rest of the family met him too.

In 1954, my father went to Bates College where he received his fourth honorary degree. Also getting an honorary degree with him was the very famous and outstanding assistant to President Eisenhower, Sherman Adams. The two of them immediately became good friends and I only hope I will have a chance to meet him personally some day. Every year he sends us lots of pure Vermont maple syrup which makes us want to have pancakes and waffles much more than we usually do.

The entire family made a shorter trip in 1953 to San Jose, California at which time the very distinguished director of the San Jose Municipal Chorus, Leroy Brant, collaborated with the city to make May 22, 1953 "William Grant Still Day" there. At that time, my father made a speech at a Chamber of Commerce luncheon for the local dignitaries and at a concert that evening he was given the keys to the city. The trip was a very enjoyable for me. We were taken on a tour of the city and spent most of this tour at the beautiful and noteworthy Rosicrucian's Egyptian Museum. This museum contained both authentic things from Egypt of thousands of years ago and replicas of other more rare and valuable articles, along with data and historic exhibits. I loved the life-size replicas of tombs of ancient rulers of Egypt which made it just as though you were in Egypt at that time so long ago. Besides the excitement, these sights contributed to my enjoyment of the trip.

We got up early to see the real glory of the morning and ate huge, luscious breakfasts at the Brant's. My brother and my father didn't fail to make a trip to the local railroad station there, and my mother and I simply loved the wonderful fresh bread we got piping hot at the bakery across the street from our lodgings. Of course there were pictures for the newspapers, and for one whole evening, Mr. Brant thrilled us with his striking slides of the Mayan country in Mexico. To top it off, while we slept in our beds at night, the police kept a constant watch on us which made us more like big officials. It was a wonderful experience and all the people there were so nice and sincere we hated to leave.

We came back to San Jose once again on our way to San Francisco in 1955 on a vacation trip which we had planned for years. On that trip we really had fun. We saw some of the important visitors' points there and in other places in California. We saw a lot of the Ferry Building and Fisherman's Wharf and didn't miss a chance to ride on the cable cars. We went through Oakland and then up to Roseville, one of the chief all-railroad towns for Duncan's benefit. Then we came through Sacramento and saw the State Capitol as well as the famous landmark of Sutter's Fort. I enjoyed that experience very much because it is always so thrilling for me to see old landmarks and the things that people had done many years ago.

One of the nicest things about the trip was that my brother and I both had hamburgers and Coca Cola for breakfast every morning of the trip. We had nice varieties of dinners, too. Mexican food in Monterey (where we spent considerable time too), a fish dinner in San Francisco and a wonderful barbecued dinner in San Jose on the way home. The entire trip only took around four days, but we certainly saw a lot in those few days.

Aside from those trips, my brother, my mother, and I went to Catalina on my birthday in 1948. That was a nice trip also, but from that trip I can only bring back the memory of a crocodile and alligator farm and bird farm.

## My Life as a Composer's Daughter

When our family digs up a little recreation time aside from visiting people and taking care of business we decide on some nearby, nice place to go in or near the city and just pack a lunch and go there. We love the beach on hot afternoons and the Griffith Observatory and at times we go to an extensive Indian museum called the Southwest Indian Museum. We enjoy looking at things concerning Indians and like the individual craftsmanship of their work. We take to the mountains and passes and only once have we been to Palomar Observatory, which we enjoyed tremendously.

We have also frequented the Hollywood Bowl, and many times we have gone there to hear my father's works played.

Being the child of a famous composer, I had chances to meet famous people, like Louis and Annette Kaufman, and to circulate in a society of musical people at receptions and concerts. We go to concerts almost all the time and find that they take up most of our traveling time. All our lives, my brother and I have gone to concerts and talked to famous adults, and have enjoyed every minute of it. It turns out that it is much more fun to talk to grown-ups than to converse with other children because they know so much more than we do and have had so much more experience in life. It is a routine part of our lives to entertain people who have already made their marks on the world.

At a ripe old age of a few weeks, I met Leopold Stokowski at the house one day. Now by meeting Metropolitan Opera Stars, I have become more and more enticed by the wonders of a life as an opera singer for myself. I have learned from Mattiwilda Dobbs to be charming and gracious and always keep promises. I hope that I can someday be as great as they are.

When my father was just getting ready for the New York World's Fair, he met the well-known designer, Henry Dreyfuss. I had a chance to meet him too when we went to his home and office one day. He showed us some of the many articles which he designed and some of the revolutionary changes in design that are just coming out now.

It is a lot of fun to talk to people like this and to have these contacts. But, believe me, if everyone had the opportunity, they would think nothing of it because it is such a routine thing. These people are just like all other people and I would rather idolize a person than be able to meet him every day.

There is nothing to our meeting these people personally, and there is nothing to our travels. But let me say that it is the memories of these things that make it all so wonderful and it is the memories that inspire us to want to travel more. I hope that if you have not traveled much as we have, you will be inspired now to see more of our great land and of other lands around us. So Bon Voyage!

## CHAPTER IX
## Religion and the Stills

Everyone in the world is entitled to his own opinions and to tell others about them, and everyone has different opinions.

When it comes to our religion, our family has no really set religion. We do not go to church, but do whatever praying we want at home. We believe that being alone while praying is much better. We know that all churches believe in the right thing and so we don't accept only one to be ours, but all of them. In our eyes, all churches work for brotherhood, and yet a few of them blindly tear down brotherhood by telling people to come to their church because only those who belong to that church shall be saved. Others hurt brotherhood even more when they think it is wrong to belong to any other church but their own and refuse to associate with those of the other church. These people are becoming lesser and lesser each year so we are sure that the problem will soon be solved.

It would be much better, though, if there was only one church instead of different ones because all of them believe virtually in the same thing, it is only the customs of the churches that seem to differ so greatly. This change would have to come gradually because people like so much to stick to tradition.

It is good that many of the churches now are telling the people to leave their prejudices behind and take up the cry of the brotherhood of the entire world, not only nations and races.

Many people talk in the United States of the caste systems of other countries, but do not realize that we in our country have that same sort of prejudice, only against races and not castes. Our family has always and will always fight against these prejudices that grow so strangely in mankind.

We also will fight against the more evident evil which is Communism. We have always been against this new form of communism in the Communist Party and its principles and are glad to see level-minded citizens striking out at this menace. We feel that Communism today represents everything ungodly and adverse to right, so we think that citizens who just sit by and watch an evil monster sticking its nose in their doorways and plundering the righteousness built up by their forefathers are saying in effect, "take our country and our freedom and conquer the world, we don't care." People say that they cannot do anything about it, but that is certainly a feeble, lazy excuse which shows that they don't want to do anything, else they would at least try.

As long as we are able we will fight these things and at the same time try to give the world something of beauty from our hearts.

Our family has been a spiritual family from the roots. We are tremendously interested in occult things and have been blessed with many interesting experiences in that line, which we have reason to believe in.

Our beliefs may be different from the beliefs of others, but we believe in good and the strength of brotherhood and right, and whoever chooses to believe in those things is certainly on the right track.

When I speak of spiritual experiences I want to tell you about one in particular. For many years, my father and mother have known well the distinguished conductor-composer, Arthur Lange. Mr. Lange now conducts the Santa Monica Symphony Orchestra and has written many pieces to add to his musical accomplishments. He married a lovely lady who had a wonderful career as one-time winner of the title, "Miss Washington of 1926," and runner-up to "Miss America" in that same year. She was an actress who held top jobs during her life. Soon she became more and more interested in occult things and before long she was up to her neck in it. One night while talking to her, we found that she possessed very wonderful talents in that field. She had developed the talents of automatic writing which enabled certain beings to talk to people through her mind. These beings called themselves the WW's and expressed the wish for it to be known that they were not fortune tellers, but teachers of love and good in the hope that someday their teachings will lead the world out of its darkness into light. They hope that they can in some way make the world strive for peace, and through doing that, come upon the right answers to their problems and spiritual questions. They don't want to make people listen, but if they want to it is fine. Mrs. Lange has a club of women who come regularly to listen to the WW's teachings. We believe that whoever these beings are, that they aren't false, and we will only disbelieve them when they are disapproved, and even then we'll continue to believe in their teachings.

Everyone has to have something to believe in and cling to because life wouldn't be worth living if there wasn't anything to have faith in. If most everyone had beliefs in right maybe someday we might all stumble on the really right answers to some of our most puzzling questions. Our family feels privileged to have been able to listen to such vast and beautiful teachings, and at the same time feel privileged to be able to understand their meanings. They call themselves forces of light and love.

We have had many lesser experiences but this has given you an example. We do not try to disagree with the opinions of other people, but we listen to them in the hope that we can learn something to benefit us from them. We try to give people some of our views too, and "compare notes." We believe that things could be so until such things are proved false, to a certain extent.

When it comes to flying saucers, this same idea holds true. We see that all the factors point to the existence of such things, and so we not only do not disbelieve but are reasonably sure they are such. We know that there are unidentified flying objects and we have studied all the matter that we could get a hold of and have found all of it in favor of the idea that they are from other planets. We have heard that many, many people have not only seen them, but have met and talked to humans from the saucers. We know that some of these "crack pots" are big fakers, but can all of them be faking? This question is another one to be debated, but I am sure the truth about the subject will come out soon.

No matter what a person's beliefs happen to be, whether they are political, religious or whatever, I know we all want the world to join in working onward for peace, love, and brotherhood.

## CHAPTER X
## May We Rest In Peace

In these past nine chapters, I have tried to give you the complete history of the Still family; our thoughts, actions, opinions, and feelings. I have also tried to show you the outline of another story, which is the story of the activities of the family of a composer with music in their hearts and imprinted in the paths of their lives.

Besides this, it has been the story of just another family with perhaps tiny differences in opinions, likes, and dislikes from the others. We certainly aren't the same as the family of a baker or of a political official, but maybe by reading this book you will be given the urge to learn about their lives too.

We are a happy family. We work and hope and pray because we have something to work, hope, and pray for. We need something that we can keep hoping for, because it gives us all the courage we need to go on doing and trying to do. We work because there is work to be done, problems to be solved. Only the striving of little people like ourselves can accomplish the tasks which so dearly need to be done. We pray because we have faith in divine powers.

Someday I hope to become a fine woman full of the virtues which make the woman. When I do I will always try to work for things that our world really needs. I will try to bring beauty, peace, and happiness to the world. There is always room for people who are glad for what they have and are willing to bend a little for it and whatever more they want. After all, the world owes you a living only if you pay for it. In this complicated world of ours, we do not need people who keep complaining and complaining and destroying the good deeds of others by it. It is the doings of those, and only those, who have a cheerful outlook on life that repairs the awful damage that people without hope or faith can do. The world may be in a turmoil, but it will be the calm, open-minded, peace-loving people who will at one time or another set it straight. The world is summarized as a place to live and learn, and not a place to rule or make material wealth from.

Perhaps in a child you can find the answer to the innocent virtues of life and at the day's end, a glorious sunset can give you the answers to questions about beauty, love, and the vastness of nature.

When we die perhaps we will be remembered and perhaps not, but our spirits will live on in the hearts of able-minded people and we will find that with death there is birth in a new world of eternity. With this last thought in mind, may I hope that you and everyone else rest in eternal, restful peace!

Myself, Judith Anne.

William Grant Still, Judith Anne's father.

Verna Arvey, Judith Anne's mother.

Duncan Allan Still, Judith Anne's brother, just after his graduation from junior high school.

Bessie Lawson Blackman (a registered nurse, friend of the Still family and a direct descendent of Martha Custis Washington, wife of President George Washington) with Judith Anne.

Dr. Bessie Arvey (Judith Anne's maternal grandmother)
and her family: Verna (Judith Anne's mother, standing)
with her sister and brother, Edna and Dale.

The Still's house in Los Angeles with
the old 1936 Ford in the left foreground.

Marjorie and Arthur Lange,
life-long friends of the Still family.

# FROM COMPOSER TO COMPOSITION: THE VISIONARY PATH[1]

O chestnut tree, great rooted blossomer,
Are you the leaf, the blossom or the bole?
O Body swayed to music, O brightening glance,
How can we know the dancer from the dance?

(W. B. Yeats, "Among School Children," 1928).

The problem in the understanding of music, dance, literature or art is that, too often, no one wants to separate the "dancer from the dance." We find it easier to approach an artistic work by thinking of the creator and his creation as inseparable.

In other words, we enjoy searching the biographies of great men for clues to the meaning of their work. When it is found, for example, that Puccini's father died when Giacomo was six-years-old, and that a close relationship developed thereafter between the boy and his mother, we begin to look upon the composer's full and sympathetic portrayals of his operatic heroines as the result of his affection for his mother. Or, because poet Robert Frost suffered tragedies like the loss of a child to suicide, we may be led to accept the frightening winter landscapes in his work as proof that he became a nihilist out of personal despair and loneliness.

The dark mood of Mozart's *G Minor Symphony* (K550) is sometimes thought to mirror the composer's poverty and illness. On occasion, Wagner's absolute tones and unrelenting progressions are taken as evidence of his aggressive personality, his egotism and his sense of ethnic superiority. Chopin has been said to have lost power and versatility through the tyranny of his relationship with George Sand. The originality and longevity of George Gershwin and Irving Berlin is tainted, for some, when it is noted that these composers took material from unknown Negro song writers or from the cabarets of Harlem.

---

[1] Reprinted here with permission. First published by *Piano Guild Notes* (34, September/October 1984, 8, 40-41), after which portions of it were reprinted by *Keyboard Classics* (5, July/August 1985, 6, 8-9).

# William Grant Still: A Voice High-Sounding

It is both natural and interesting for us to probe the private lives of the artistic greats for insights into their work. Achievements are subjected to the Medusa-touch of close scrutiny, and our discoveries about the achievers are transformed into the stone monuments of historical praise or blame.

Unfortunately, the meanings of these achievements can sometimes be sullied by this sort of scrutiny. Chopin might have written the same works had he never met George Sand that he wrote under her influence. Robert Frost's own comments on his poetry have indicated that his winter landscapes and storms are not images of nihilist despair. Mozart's *Jupiter Symphony* (K551), written in the same year as the G Minor, reveals no dark thoughts of impending destruction. All too often it appears that compositions were better left free from the frailties of their creators, and from the manipulations of history.

Indeed, I have seen the tendency toward the manipulation of the truth on a personal level. My father, William Grant Still, long known as the "Dean of Negro Composers," died in 1978. Since his death, the fictions regarding his life and work have begun to accrue to his accomplishments.

The small fictions, based on obvious error, are easily dealt with. When Calvin Simmons, Music Director of the Oakland Symphony, drowned in Lake Placid, a northern California newspaper memorialized him as the first Negro to conduct a major symphony orchestra. Had the reporter who wrote the story made a cursory check of encyclopedias and music textbooks, he would have discovered that the first Negro to conduct such an orchestra was William Grant Still, when he directed the Los Angeles Philharmonic at the Hollywood Bowl in 1936. Still was also the first Negro in the United States to write a symphony which was performed by a major orchestra, the first to have one of his operas produced by a major company, and the first to conduct a major orchestra of White musicians in the Deep South. All of these events in the composer's career are readily verifiable.

But then, there are larger fictions which are beginning to develop, based on what is not publicly known about Still's life. Rumors have drifted back to the family recently that William Grant Still's college education was paid for by his stepfather, the

## From Composer to Composition: The Visionary Path

inference being that his natural father and mother were poor and uneducated, and unable to afford tuition. The tale is also told that Still abandoned his first wife and children and ignored his daughter Gail at her death. Further, it is said that Leonard Bernstein has not played the works of the composer because Still's opera, *Troubled Island*, was poorly received by audiences in New York.

Perhaps these notions will never loom large enough to damage a fair concept of the composer's output. After all, the rumor that Shakespeare treated Anne Hathaway callously was never dangerous enough to spoil our appreciation for *Hamlet* or *Twelfth Night*. Even so, the record should be cleared, in order to open the path between the composer and our understanding of his compositions.

Some of the misconceptions will eventually be dispelled by my mother's book, *In One Lifetime*, the biography of my father's career published by the University of Arkansas Press. Some will remain clouded, at least for a time, for it is not possible now to reveal the whole truth about the composer's first marriage. Others must be approached part by part, as falsehoods materialize, by those who seek the truth.

And the truth is that William Grant Still's education at Oberlin was paid for by a legacy from his deceased father, received in 1923, and that, had there been no legacy, his mother, who was highly-educated and well-fixed, could certainly have afforded the tuition. Moreover, Still did not leave his first wife--it was she who left him, taking the four children to Canada. In spite of having been abandoned, however, he continued to support his four children until they came of age, and did what he could for Gail prior to her death. As for *Troubled Island*, the opera was so vigorously applauded on opening night in New York that the composer and cast took over twenty curtain calls. The failure of the work, if there was a failure, should be laid at the feet of the New York critics, who let my father know before the performance that they were planning to damn the work with faint praise.

Beyond the discovery of facts surrounding personal and public events, there is also work to be done in unveiling the composer's philosophical and musical intent in his compositions. As scholars begin to study the over 150 operas, ballets, orchestral works, choral compositions, instrumental pieces, and songs by Still, they frequently attempt to categorize or stereotype his efforts. They make a case for the influence of Edgard Várèse and the atonalists upon the success of his efforts. Or, they look at the composer's use of Negro idioms, claiming that he was either a writer of "Black music," championing an ethnic cause, or a seeker after classicism who could not avoid his origins.

Hopefully, the problem of composer vs. composition, "dancer vs. dance," will someday be solved by careful study of Still's private papers (papers which are now being shipped to their final resting place in the University of Arkansas). When these papers are assessed, the scholars will be forced to conclude that the composer's accomplishments cannot be easily categorized. He learned the techniques of the atonalists, but was not molded by them. As he put it himself, "I discovered that, if I wanted to write music that was recognizable as Negro music...I could not use that [ultra-modern] idiom, because the identity was lost" (From an interview with R. Donald Brown, California State University, Fullerton, 1967).

While repudiating the atonalists, however, Still did not take up, unconditionally, the Negroid idiom. Again he explained, "I did not want to confine myself to that particular idiom because I think [that] here in America we have so many idioms. The Indian music, the Creole music, and so on," (CSUF interview). In other words, he made use of all forms of musical expression, from atonal devices in *Darker America*, to classical consonance and harmony in the *Fourth Symphony*, to the blues themes of *The Afro-American Symphony* and *Lenox Avenue*, to the multiple idioms of *The American Scene* and the *Folk Suites from the Western Hemisphere*.

As for being a "Black composer," Still was the first to disavow the epithet. "I don't know what people mean by 'Black music,'" he would confess privately. "Are they saying that Negroes can only write music in a certain way? Are they trying to make it appear that White people and Colored people are so unlike each other that their work can't share in scope or competence? For me there is no White music or Black music--there is only music by individual men that is important only if it attempts to dignify all men, not just a particular race."

This is not to say, of course, that Still did not express his racial heritage in his music. He did most assuredly. Yet, his primary goal was to say something melodic to which people in all walks of life would respond. In a letter to Homer Hathaway on August 9, 1968, he noted that good music was not necessarily classical music, as there were some jazz compositions that were good and some classical pieces that were bad. Good music, he affirmed, "awakens a response in a person's emotional self." It is the enjoyment of the listener which makes a piece "a part of our lives and gives it significance and vitality."

There is evidence that Still succeeded in his efforts to touch his audiences. Music critic Frank Gagnard wrote in 1968, "Symphony audiences today are used to working for their rewards in the concert hall," but "William Grant Still's music is so accessible... [it] almost effortlessly establishes the roots of blues in religious and musical expression, and raises this expression to the heights of personal nobility (New Orleans *Times-Picayune*, April 17, 1968).

The question remains, now, how did Still, or how does any artist, open doors to the inward nature of the human audience? Where lies the path from composer to composition? What is the secret of creativity? Here, again, it is helpful to go to the artist himself for revelation. In a letter to Miss Rose Heylbut on August 29, 1948, Still cited the importance of spiritual inspiration over and above craftsmanship:

> Inspiration is the prime requisite in composing. Many of the compositions we hear today are, in my estimation, uninspired. An uninspired composition is like an inanimate body: it lacks the breath of life, which only God can give it. No amount of craftsmanship can atone for the lack of a God-given life-force. Thus it would follow that a composer, to be worthy of the name, *must* have in his nature a spiritual quality which would enable him to contact the divine source. I always place at the end of each composition this inscription: 'With humble thanks to God, the Source of Inspiration,' for I believe that anyone who manages to accomplish anything at all worthwhile has been in contact with this Source, and should

recognize it and express gratitude.

As this passage readily intimates, the composer was a devout religious spiritualist, harboring a faith that surpassed the casual study of numerology and psychic phenomena. In his diary on December 17, 1930 he wrote, "For years I labored in vain to master scoring for the orchestra. Then, one day, God showed me that I must turn to Him and rely solely on the Hand that knows no failure. Immediately, upon so doing, that I could not do before became easy. My Lord showered blessings of inspiration upon me."

Bolstered by his belief that a composer is merely a channel for the voice of Godhead to be transmitted to humanity, Still would begin work on a piece of music by opening his "psychic" senses to the "vibrations" of the Source. Seated in the captain's chair in his workroom, he began with a prayer, then sat quietly in a state of suspension and sensitivity until the messages came through to the physical. According to one of Still's good friends, Nola McGarry, the composer once told a theosophical group that he could hear the music before he wrote it down, and that sometimes it came to him so rapidly that he hardly had time to get it on paper. Mrs. McGarry also observed, from her own reading, that other important composers, such as Rachmaninoff, have attested to having heard their music before writing it down.

Suffice it to say that Still believed in the spiritual power of music, a power that seemed to be bound up somehow with the life-force. He may or may not have studied scientific reports which show that music causes factory workers and beasts of burden to increase their productivity by 11% (*Coronet*, XIII, November 1942, 131-134). He certainly was aware that music enhances the growth of plants, because the vegetables that he grew in the garden behind his music room were twice the size of normal produce. But regardless of the extent of his experiments with this Power-source, his most widely-acclaimed compositions were the result of his beliefs.

Moreover, the unexpressed meaning of many of Still's works often lay in his spiritualist views. It was frequently true that the composer's mind and the intent of his compositions were inseparable. Perhaps the best place to look for evidence of Still's mystical ideas is in his piano pieces.

The compositions for piano by William Grant Still have always been popular. The good recording by Natalie Hinderas of the *Three Visions* (Desto Records, DC 7102/3) is doing well; as is one by Felipe Hall (Da Camera Schallplatten Records, SM 93144). An excellent rendering of the *Three Visions* by Richard Fields has just been released by Orion Records (ORS 82442), and very soon John Kniest will put out a magnificent album of the complete piano works, with pianist Albert Dominguez, on the Grand Prix or the Legend label.

In the notes which are included in her album, Natalie Hinderas suggests that the *Three Visions* by Still are like tone paintings which have consistent rhythms and an "aura of gentleness." In one of the selections in the *Visions* called "Summerland," Miss Hinderas finds a nostalgic meaning, or, the "relaxed timelessness one feels on a hot summer day." While she is a fine pianist, Hinderas speaks out of her own feeling for the work, and not out of a sure knowledge of the composition.

The composer's own papers must be studied for a proper concept of his intent. In a letter to Miss Mildred Ellis on December 20, 1950, Still explained that each *Vision* described, abstractly, "a different dream, the individual titles indicating the character of the dreams." This allusion to dreams was significant for Still, as his diaries and journals recount numerous sleep visions, many of which were prophetic.

In one case, on September 16, 1930, he was without a source of income and had no prospects for employment. In a dream he was told to go to another part of New York the next day to see two men, and, when he did as the dream directed, he was given an unexpected job. In other cases he dreamed of things that were about to happen. Around March 1, 1953, for example, he dreamed of "Catholic priests swinging lighted cressets in a procession," and on March 3rd he received in the mail an invitation to participate in a novena to St. Joseph.

In some instances the dreams did not become reality right away. His dream about World War II in which he was shown a map of Europe "greatly different from the present appearance," occurred on September 21, 1930, nine years before the advent of the war. In other cases the visions did not materialize during the composer's lifetime. Throughout 1951, for instance, he had many similar dreams about being a guest in a luxurious hotel "so grand that he didn't think they'd let him come in." But they did let him in, giving him a place of honor, and, while he was being honored he was shown huge stacks of records with his music on them, a beautifully published edition of the *Archaic Ritual*, choruses and orchestras performing *Troubled Island* and other of his works, and such additional wonders as color televisions "in which the screens were like large pictures on the wall" (March 24, 1951).

Yet another type of dream seemed to have no immediate relationship to life experience, but was symbolic in value. In some visions he was taken on trains into verdant valleys, or he was led through mud, mountainous terrain, or forty-mile tunnels to places with crystal waterfalls and brilliant lights. Sometimes his worn clothing was replaced with satin robes, and he was elevated to high places where he was taught the "images of life." Later, after awakening from these dreams, he felt refreshed and inspired.

It is obvious, therefore, that dream-visions were an operative part of the composer's life, and that he came to think of them as learning situations. In the same vein, a good number of his pieces of music were extensions of these learning situations, presenting manufactured dream-visions which were meant to aid his hearers in their progress through life. The *Three Visions* are certainly exemplary of such compositions.

In the first *Vision*, entitled "Dark Horsemen," where the sound of a horse galloping is brought to the keyboard, the image is one of death and of Divine judgment, coming to each individual person like the four horsemen of the Apocalypse. Yet this is not a view of death as a matter of finality, but a portrait of death as a doorway to the future. The composer believed that each human being dies and is reborn on earth many times in his progress toward the higher reality.

In the second *Vision*, "Summerland," Still gives the listener a glimpse, not of a "hot summer day," but of the occultist's concept of Heaven. The sense of Divine peace is so strongly conveyed that the piece has been a favorite ever since the orchestral version was performed by Howard Hanson and the Rochester Philharmonic Orchestra over NBC (October 28, 1937). The composer himself used to listen to the tape of this performance again and again to bolster his strength and courage during the tensions of daily living.

The final piece of the trilogy, called "Radiant Pinnacle," may well have the "Oriental cast" attributed to it by Miss Hinderas, but it also speaks of man's aspiration toward God. At the close of the work the spiritual aspirant falls back from his goal, not quite reaching the Divine height. In this way the listener is told that the spiritual man dies, steps closer to God in the afterlife, then returns to life through rebirth or reincarnation in order that he may learn new lessons of purity of heart and compassion. Taken all together, then, the *Visions* are an occult story of the human journey toward the perfection of the soul.

Thus the images and intentions behind the compositions of William Grant Still begin to materialize. And, though they were perhaps his own personal conceptions of life that are not shared by many of his hearers, even so, his concern for his audience was uppermost in the act of creation. When he was working on the later piano suite, *The Seven Traceries*, he noted in his diary, "I pray that the images will bless all who see, touch and hear them in whatever form they may be."

It might be thought by skeptics that the composer's clear concern for his human family and his unquestioning religious faith has made his music simplistic. Musicologists often comment that it did not, praising his "rigorous and brilliant orchestration" (*Micro Magazine*, November 6, 1955). The rare thing about Still, say many critics, is that his simple loves are rendered complex, yet intelligible, by the tapestry of his shifting melodies and harmonies. As Frank Fetta, conductor of the Marina-Westchester Symphony, remarked at a William Grant Still Festival in March of 1982, "In terms of individuality, complexity and variety, there is no other music like Still's."

Of course, music was unique with Still partially because he revered it as solidly as he treasured his faith in God and man. Once, at a social gathering in the thirties, he suddenly announced,

"Surely music came before the dance." Then, after a pause,

"Wait! Do I really think that, or did someone tell me so? But, on second thought, I believe it is correct."

Was he correct? Did music arise out of the primeval dust of the cosmos? Perhaps so. And yet, it doesn't really matter. What matters is that, through pondering the question, the outlines of an artist's life and achievement can be drawn.

Hopefully, the picture that emerges transcends future rumor and assumption. It must be admitted, however, that there is much of my own prejudice in the portrait. William Grant Still was a man who was much-loved by those closest to him, by those who can attest to his affectionate and personable nature, and to his humility and perseverance. But it is out of such love that the greatest truths about creative men must come--therein is the point of fusion at which the man and his work are inseparable. A man must love and be loved in order to bring forth his finest creations. And when these works are understood in the light of the artist's expressed affection for God or man, then it is unnecessary to separate "the dancer from the dance."

# "IN THE BEGINNING... :"
# THE GENESIS OF *ENNANGA*[1]

At what precise moment is a musical composition begun? When the first note is set down? When research provides sufficient knowledge for the piece to take shape? When long revision gives the work wholeness and purpose? Or, when the instrumentalist or vocalist takes up the score and breathes life into the creative body?

It is possible that every piece of music has many such beginnings, for all of these moments have the force of formation and forward motion. Indeed, where *Ennanga* was concerned, all of these moments were contributory, and, for that composition, the last moment, the role of the instrumentalist, loomed as large or larger than any other.

The prime instrumentalist in the story of *Ennanga* was harpist Lois Adele Craft. A prodigy born to music, Lois Craft was set on course by the great Salvi, whose tutelage she left behind to concertize successfully in the middle west and far west. Her career included a decade as solo harpist for the Kansas City, Missouri, Philharmonic Orchestra, and many years as the much prized virtuoso who enhanced the vocal displays of Eddie Fischer, Peggy Lee and Tony Bennett.

Lauded for her cleanness and fullness of tone, Miss Craft was everywhere well-received. J.D. Callahan of the *Detroit Free Press* sounded the keynote of the critical assessment when he said,

> Miss Craft is an artist of considerable beauty of performance. Her playing of the cadenza was a revelation of the tonal possibilities of the instrument. It was by turns warm and golden, with a quality approaching violin harmonies in its upper register. The work glowed with jewel-like intensity.

The *Kansas City Times* summed up the scope of the young lady's achievement when it said that she displayed "the capacity of the

---

[1] Reprinted here with permission of *The American Harp Journal* (9, Winter 1984, 15-17).

harp as a solo instrument--and revealed that the harp has melodic and pyrotechnical possibilities" (C.H.T.).

This high degree of artistry was bound to come to the attention of noted American composers. William Grant Still first heard Miss Craft's name when she was harp soloist with the Kansas City Philharmonic in the early forties. The conductor in Missouri was Karl Krueger, a leading admirer of Still's and a consistent performer of his music from the mid-1930s to the early 60s. When Still's *Afro-American Symphony* was done by Krueger in 1938, both audience and musicians were so taken by the third movement, the "Scherzo," that the Maestro was forced to interrupt the concert in order to repeat that section.

Inasmuch as *The Afro-American Symphony* contained a significant part for the harp, Lois Craft participated in the performance of this work when she came to the mid-west. Dr. Still could not attend the program, but there was talk of him among the musicians. The three first-chair instrumentalists spoke of having worked with Still in Los Angeles. According to them, "Billie," as he was called, was an awfully nice person and wonderful to work with, in addition to being the creator of "highly enjoyable music."

The young harpist was impressed to learn that there existed a major composer of serious music who was not only admired, but was also loved. How often are men of excellence also men of kindness and amiability? She hoped that one day she might meet this man--but her hopes were to remain unfulfilled for over fifteen years thereafter.

From Missouri, Miss Craft traveled to California, where she concertized for five years, after which she joined Fox Studios under contract in the fifties. Ironically, Still had also been at Fox during the forties, but he left the studios before the harpist arrived. It was not until 1956 that the paths of composer and harpist would begin to converge, for, in that year, Miss Craft began to appear as soloist in community orchestras, and Still began earnest work on *Ennanga*.

Yet the work that commenced in 1956 was not a matter of sudden impulse. The "quick craftsmen" notwithstanding, composition is a gradual process of evolvement and careful labor.

## "In the Beginning... :" The Genesis of *Ennanga*

Even before Still had heard of the artistry of Lois Craft and the Kansas City Philharmonic, he had been planting the musical seeds for his harp composition.

Still's knowledge of the harp came from his introduction to the instrument as an arranger for New York radio in the twenties, and from his spiritualist religious studies. From the Bible he discovered that the ancient prophets carried harps which they played while the Spirit of God visited them with prophecy. Further, the harp was a means to mystical healing, for David wrought magic with his harp to alleviate the melancholy of King Saul.

In the post-Biblical era, the composer found that many men of a spiritual bent were associated with the harp, including statesman and scientist Benjamin Franklin, who learned to play the harp and who invented the ethereal-sounding musical instrument called the armonica. Moreover, Franklin, like William Grant Still, entertained beliefs in life after death and reincarnation.

Following these researches, it was inevitable that Still should add a thorough understanding of the harp to his wide repertoire of mastered instrumental sounds. Already an acceptable performer on the violin, 'cello, oboe, clarinet and other such, he pursued investigations of harp technique through the 1921 edition of the *Modern Study of the Harp* by Carlos Salzedo (G. Schirmer, New York). He especially noted and circled methods for creating guitaric, plectric, metallic and timpanic effects, in the same way that he read and re-read instructions for making thundering, whistling and gushing sounds. On page ten he jotted a reminder that the "Aeolian flux" was "effective at a moment of excitement." For him, the unusual effects of the instrument helped to justify the maxim which was preamble to the 1921 text, "The Harp is to Music what Music is to Life."

Though these observations on Salzedo may not have remained uppermost in the composer's mind in the thirties and forties, certainly they were deep-rooted enough to germinate. Perhaps he thought of them when he came into contact with conductor Richard Lert, for Maestro Lert was married to harpist and writer Vicki Baum. Still surely admired Baum's art, and her training at the Vienna Conservatory of music. However, though Vicki Lert may have talked to Still about the harp, it was not she who was first involved with his harp composition; that distinction was left to Alfred Kastner, harpist for the Los Angeles Philharmonic who was also the teacher of Ann Mason Stockton, professional harpist.

Alfred Kastner and his daughter Stephanie first triggered the composer's resolve to write for the harp, suggesting that he ought to do so. Renewing, in his mind, his acquaintance with Salzedo, Still set down his first musical ideas, then sent them to Kastner's pupil, Ann Stockton, for her advice.

Miss Stockton received the music in the mail and looked over it. In a letter to the composer on February 4th, in 1957 or 1958, she said,

> I have gone through the revised copy and have made a few minor recommendations. The main one is in the cadenza at 13 (which, by the way, plays much more satisfactorily now) where instead of the trill I have noted an ad lib gliss--suggesting they follow the pattern I outlined. I hope this meets with your approval. Please don't hesitate to call me if my notation is not clear.

The composer did approve of Miss Stockton's suggestions, and readily acknowledged them on the fly-leaf of the music. Whereas the first draft of the piece had been dedicated to Stephanie Kastner, the second draft was inscribed to Ann Mason Stockton. The composer had gained new respect for the harp and for harpists.

But Still was not yet satisfied with the composition. He was well aware that there was more for him to learn about the wide range of sounds that could be produced by the instrument. When, in the spring of 1958, he attended a Los Angeles Community Orchestra concert, he saw, in the person of the guest soloist, Lois Craft, an opportunity to work with *Ennanga* more closely.

The composer and his wife, pianist Verna Arvey, approached Miss Craft after the concert. They praised her sensitivity and mastery; she expressed extreme pleasure and privilege in meeting someone so long-admired. Secretly she noted how gentile and gentle the composer was; privately Dr. and Mrs. Still commented on the lady's beauty, both inside and out. Dr. Still began to talk about the new suite that he had written for harp. It was replete with original themes inspired by African music, he explained, and he "recognized the native mood of it by naming it after the African harp called the 'ennanga.'" His voice was slightly animated--he was motivated by his work.

Miss Craft agreed to look at *Ennanga* and to try it out. Thus, at the end of March, 1958, Mrs. Still posted it to her. From the first, the harpist was taken with the piece; it "spoke" to her, she remarked later. In August she wrote to the Stills, "What a wonderful time I have been having with *Ennanga*. After some delay, I finally was able to 'get to work.' I find it exciting, beautiful, haunting, dramatic, plaintive. What more can one ask from a composition?"

Then the artist went on to propose a rehearsal of the piece. "I have a former pupil in Santa Monica that has kindly offered her apartment wherein is her harp and piano... She seems to feel it would be all right with no complaints from other tenants. It would be nice and cool--just three blocks from the ocean in its favor. ...I have a few things to confer with Mr. Still so a rehearsal rather soon will be most helpful" (August 16, 1958).

The trio, Craft, Still and Arvey, converged on the Santa Monica apartment to review the suite. Mrs. Still was the "Philharmonic at the piano," and they ran through it from start to finish. Though the composer was not a demonstrative or talkative person, his brightly-misted *eyes* conveyed genuine delight. Quietly he said,

"*Gee*...I didn't think that it would have such life and excitement."

The remainder of the afternoon was spent in improving the composition. The harpist discussed the use of color, resonance and technique to give the instrument and the piece a sustaining quality. In particular, she talked of the possibilities in the cadenza for amplification, and revealed the way in which some two-note chords could become many-note chords in order to make the harp sound, and to render the whole more soloistic. In one section she helped Still to insert harmonics over the melody in order to infuse it with sweep and vibrancy. Readily and willingly, the author rewrote entire pages of the suite in the light of Miss Craft's efforts to lift the work out of the even, pianistic mold.

What finally emerged from the converse of composer and

musician was a musical formation that made the best possible use of the unique potentialities of the harp for description and for fullness of feeling. Later on, the final draft was dedicated to Lois Craft, just as the first two drafts had been dedicated to Miss Kastner and Miss Stockton. These dedications were made, not only because the composer was grateful to these harpists for their help and friendship, but also because he wished music-lovers to recognize the importance of the harp in the total complex: it was a suite *for* harp with accompaniment, not a suite *with* harp accompaniment.

The importance of the harp and of the harpist to the work becomes clearer when it is realized that much imagination is required to perform it. Miss Craft has said of it,

> The composition presents vastly more than is at first seen. For me, the three movements speak of the development of life in the primitive world. In the first movement, with its percussive wildness, the listener gets a glimpse of the danger and rhythm of the jungle, the snakes and tigers and dense, dark undergrowth. The second movement is more spiritual, bringing into view the green beauty of ferns and grasses, the calm and peaceful water. The final segment brings out the magnificence of the environment, and the joy.

There is no doubt that the harpist's assessment of the work fell into line with the composer's intentions. (Once he commented that he was afraid that those who failed to understand the piece as well as she would be unable to play it.) As to the "jungle" interpretation of the composition, it is interesting to note that the composer had, throughout his lifetime, recurring dreams of lions and tigers and other beasts that became tame when he drew close to them. Also, more than once he dreamed of thick forests through which he had to pass before reaching some exalted place. He took these dreams to be symbolic of his own spiritual journey through life's temptations and dangers.

In regard to *Ennanga*, he saw it as a spiritual journey as well, a journey from primitive impulse, to the influence of God's natural harmonies upon human activity, and then to the final exaltation of learning and development. He believed, like Aristotle, in the undeniability of progress according to divine plan. He also believed that every creative act or product was an aspect of God's tutelage, and so he wrote at the end of *Ennanga*, as he did at the end of all of his works, "With humble thanks to God, the Source of Inspiration."

Perhaps it was the genuinely human yet spiritual quality, both expressed and unexpressed, that made the suite *Ennanga* so welcome among concert-goers. The piece had not had its première when Miss Craft first saw it--Miss Stockton had been scheduled to play it, but suddenly and mysteriously withdrew her appearance, claiming other commitments. She, in fact, never promoted or played the piece. It was first performed in one of Dr. Landau's composer's workshop concerts on October 12, 1958. The performance took place at the Westside Jewish Community Center in Los Angeles, with Lois Craft as soloist and Verna Arvey playing the orchestral part on the piano. Since that time it has had numerous performances in California and Nevada (with harp and full orchestra, or harp and string quartet, or harp and piano), and it has been recorded for Orion Recordings (Album OR 7278, or Cassette Tape 633). The latter album was made under the beneficent sponsorship of Joan Palevsky, a supporter of the arts in Los Angeles who has done much for the music of William Grant Still.

After hearing the Orion album, the Santa Barbara Music Club insisted that the work be brought to the Santa Barbara area, which it was, by artist Mary Jane Barton. This year, on February 5, 1984, Ann Hobson-Pilot's rendition of *Ennanga* received a standing ovation from a capacity audience at Howard University, Washington D.C.

Miss Craft says today that, though she has retired from the concert circuit, *Ennanga* continues to be an inspiration to her. "It represents something that was done for the harp as an instrument. It is an unfoldment, and carries a message to all of us who love music."

The harpist goes on to observe that one of the reasons she greatly respected Dr. Still was that he never let the message get lost. He worked on his musical ideas, seeking knowledge from all corners, until his work was perfected. He was careful and purposeful from start to finish. An example of his drive and conviction was evident at a particular performance of *Ennanga* when he was conducting the symphony orchestra. At one point in the score "the Concert Master failed to bring the violins in. Calmly Mr. Still--who was conducting, waved the orchestra off-- 'Beginning!' he whispered. His extreme calmness had its affect on the performers in this mishap, and so the audience was again treated to hearing those opening, impressive arpegio-chords that begin the third movement."

William Grant Still has since passed on, having died in Los Angeles of stroke and heart failure on December 3, 1978. But to Lois Craft and other harpists who have known *Ennanga*, his work has its own eternal "Beginnings!"[2]

---

[2] The American Harp Society Repository contains a first draft [sketches] of *Ennanga* [A] 245, harp part only; a final draft of the harp part, handwritten [A] 246; and a 31-page photostat of the harp part and the reduction of the orchestral score for piano [A] 247, as well as the letters [A] 248. However, sole rights to the reproduction of the final draft of the piece reside with Southern Music in San Antonio, Texas.

# WILLIAM GRANT STILL:
# A VOICE HIGH-SOUNDING...[1]

> We ride amid a tempest of dispraise.
> Now, when the waves of swift dissension swarm,
> And Honor, the strong pilot, lieth stark,
> Oh, for thy voice high-sounding o'er the storm, ...

He was a sometime friend to fame, yet a man unloved by fortune. In fact, a Los Angeles resident could have lived on William Grant Still's street for years without ever realizing that he was a person to be noticed. When the Still home was 3670 Cimarron Street in the central city--a one-story stucco fronted by a rectangle of ivy and a high wire fence--tourist buses did pass there occasionally. But the buses did not bring sightseers to view the Still residence; their destination was the comfortable, well-manicured household of Eddie "Rochester" Anderson in the cul-de-sac around the corner.

Jack Benny's "Rochester" was a visible celebrity, dressing in bright shirts and enjoying the attention of his fans when he walked down Jefferson Boulevard. Not so composer William Grant Still. The man of music was so much the opposite that once he was criticized for his lack of "image." When he dropped into a local newspaper office in his work clothes to seek information about a neighborhood appliance repairman, a reporter in the office recognized him. Shortly thereafter an item appeared in the Los

---

[1] Winner of a Distinguished Achievement Award from the Educational Press Association of America in 1985, "William Grant Still: A Voice High-Sounding" was first printed in the *Music Educators Journal* (70, February 1984, 24-30), while the interview from which the article was drawn came from a 1984 California State University, Fullerton, Oral History publication. The piece was later reprinted in the *Musical Mainstream* of the Library of Congress (8, July/August 1984, 4-13), and portions of it were reprinted in *Keyboard Classics* (5, July/August 1985, 6, 8-9), and in the *Phi Delta Gamma Journal* (48, Spring 1986, 10-12). It was copyrighted in 1987 by the Music Educators National Conference, and is reprinted with permission.

Angeles *Sentinel* which castigated the composer for appearing in public like a "Dungaree Dad."

Still read the newspaper story, mumbled something about "lack of understanding," then went on about his professional labors, his gardening and his carpentry. Even after he moved a few miles away to 1262 Victoria Avenue, he continued to be, paradoxically, domestically-inclined yet other-worldly, genial and yet reserved, known and yet unknown.

In 1968, a young man named R. Donald Brown, from California State University, Fullerton, came to the Still home to make one of the few taped interviews of the 73-year-old Doctor of Music.[2] During the interview, Still proved to be just as soft-spoken and self-conscious as he was accomplished and purposeful. He was troubled by a loose denture which interfered with the ease of his speech, and he stuttered somewhat when communicating extemporaneously; but, in spite of those problems, he did not need to be prompted to expand upon Brown's questions, and he said many of the things that needed to be said about his life and work.

The tape that was made on that occasion was forgotten in the files of the CSUF Oral History Department until the composer's death in 1978. It was found there by instructor Shirley Stephenson, who knew the Still family and was aware of the value of that bit of oral history. After being transcribed by Still's widow and daughter, it was returned to the files as one of the best expressions of the Doctor's attitudes toward his craft and toward the racial components in his music.

It is probable that the interview would stand on its own merits without comment. After all, the personal interview is to history what the photograph is to global events. But, like the camera close-up which obscures and fades its backgrounds, an unrehearsed conversation may fall short of the total picture of

---

[2] An interview with William Grant Still by R. Donald Brown, a community history project for the Oral History Program, California State University, Fullerton, November 13, 1967 and December 4, 1967. (To purchase a copy of this interview project, contact William Grant Still Music, 1109 South Plaza Way, Suite 109, Flagstaff, Arizona 86001-6317.)

thought and motive. What is in the mind of the man when he stammers or when his mind wanders? What are his true feelings about his racial heritage? What lies beyond the words, as well as beyond conjecture?

Much of the factual matter in the interview can be glossed over, dealing as it does with verifiable times and places in the composer's life. In response to biographical queries from Donald Brown, Still talks of his frustrated undergraduate years at Wilberforce University. His mother had sent him to Wilberforce to engage in pre-medical studies because she felt that he, as a Negro, could only find failure if he went into serious music.

Brown: Dr. Still, would you care to go over some aspects of your early education?

Still: I graduated from high school in 1911, and entered college, going at that time to Wilberforce University. ...I wasn't completely satisfied because I really wanted a musical education, and Wilberforce...didn't offer a course in music in their curriculum. ...[I] ached because I wanted [so much to study music]... I stayed there from 1911 to 1915.

...And then, after a couple of years, I received the legacy that my father left me. This [legacy] enabled me to go to Oberlin...[to study music. Then] the work was interrupted by the war and I enlisted in the Navy, served for the duration of the war, and then returned to Oberlin to continue working for a short period.

However, I did not earn a degree...at Oberlin. I left there and went on to New York [to enter] into professional work. But later on I was given an honorary Doctor of Music degree by Oberlin.

...Well, anyhow, that period that I devoted to professional work, particularly in New York, was one of great value to me. I was working largely with popular music--to an extent with it--but I wasn't confined to it, because when radio came in I was orchestrating for orchestras like Don Voorhees' orchestra. ...I learned to play many instruments, not for the purpose of being a proficient performer, but in order to capture the sound, [and to] have it so firmly implanted in my consciousness that I could bring it out and play with it and mix it. ...I was learning what to do, and what not to do, as far as instrumentation was concerned.

At this point Still goes on to describe his employment as an orchestrator for W. C. Handy, for Paul Whiteman, and for WOR radio and the Deep River Hour broadcast. He speaks also of his period of study with the ultra-modern composer, Edgard Varèse. He notes that this work with both popular and atonal idioms did much to expand his harmonic field of vision. When he became orchestrator for the Deep River Hour, his precocious arrangements made that program one of the best-loved and most innovative shows in its time. Of this broadcast he says,

Still: That [job] was the most remarkable opportunity that I'd ever had, because, while I had been working with orchestras that permitted me the opportunity to experiment, I hadn't been working with orchestras that were large enough to have complement like the symphony orchestras. We didn't have the bassoons and the English horns, and so on. ...[In the Deep River Hour, aired out of both NBC and CBS studios, we] had a very worthwhile orchestra. Splendid musicians! And I had a chance to experiment.

Indeed, Still's efforts were so varied and far-ranging during this period, that he had occasion to arrange a song for an unknown crooner whose career was uncertain.

Brown: You mentioned doing the orchestration for a song that Bing Crosby did.

Still: ...That was a song for CBS, for Columbia Records. We recorded that in New York. ...And, [a] strange thing: they didn't put Bing's name on it at all. ...He was just one of the "Rhythm Boys," and not the most important of the "Rhythm Boys" at that moment.

As Still talks informally about his role in the pre-adolescent growth of the mass media and of American serious music, it becomes clear that there is more to the unobtrusive musician than anyone would suspect from a passing acquaintance. Still was a man who ventured into the arts rather like the first mountain man

## William Grant Still: A Voice High-Sounding

to cross the Great Divide, eager to view the landscape and, at the same time, laying some important landmarks along a rugged but irresistible trail. His answers to Brown's queries trace the course of his journey:

Brown: Do you feel that the "Harlem Renaissance,"[3] or "The New Negro Movement," did not take place in the area of music?

Still: ...I don't know of anyone else [in America] who was branching into any decided departure, as far as musical idioms are concerned. My working with Várèse had opened up this new field [to me, but]...I think that most of the other Negro writers were writing just conventional things. ...(He mentions the work of composers such as Nathaniel Dett, Clarence White and Florence Price.)

Brown: Going back to your experiences with working for the Hollywood movie studios, were you unique in your capacity, Doctor? Were there other Negroes doing the type of work that you were doing?

Still: Bill Vodery came out from New York to do some work at one of the studios, and I think [that] he came out here and worked for awhile before I did, in the studios. ...I believe it was 1936--before I did any work for the studios.

Brown: ...I was wondering if there were other Negroes doing the type of work you were.

Still: ...At the time that I was? No. Not that I know of. Later on...Calvin Jackson came out...around the time of World War II...and I think [that] he worked out at MGM.

---

[3] The Harlem Renaissance is defined in the interview, thusly: "At the beginning of the twentieth-century, the Negro population of New York City was concentrated in a section of the city called Harlem. Although some Negroes looked upon Harlem as a place from which escape was desirable, others praised it as the center of a surge of literary and musical creativity called the 'Harlem Renaissance,' or, 'The Negro Movement.' Poets, novelists, dramatists and composers such as Claude McKay, Countee Cullen and Langston Hughes were part of this Renaissance, revealing a new interest in Negro culture and an originality of creative effort that supposedly had not existed before. White men like Carl Van Vechten provided financial support for the movement."

> ...[But, speaking of opportunities for Negroes] here in Los Angeles. I received a wonderful opportunity here, one that I had never received before, and that was of conducting a major symphony orchestra [, something] which hadn't been done before that, by any Negro. That was in 1936 at the [Hollywood] Bowl [that] I conducted...the Los Angeles Philharmonic.
>
> Brown: ...Were there any Negro musicians in the Symphony?
>
> Still: No, not at that time.

Here the dialogue touches on some of the prizes and commissions which came to the composer, including the Cleveland Symphony Prize, the Cincinnati Symphony Orchestra Prize, the National Federation of Music Clubs and Aeolian Foundation Prize, and the commission to write the theme music for the first New York World's Fair.

> Still: Some few things [commissions] have come in, but all were firsts, not because of any lack of ability on the part of other musicians, but [because] it just happened that I was in a unique position: the first to come along. For instance, [Nathaniel] Dett had not trained for orchestral [work].

He was indeed the first to come along in the American classical realm, at least as far as Negroes were concerned. At a time when the Institute of Musical Art (our present-day Juilliard School) would not admit Negro students, George Chadwick, director of the New England Conservatory, volunteered to teach Still free of charge. At a time when George Gershwin "used to come up and go to the little churches [in Harlem] to hear the music and pick up things," borrowing his themes from Negro musicians, Still created his own themes in all idioms. In his words,

> Still: ...[in 1930]...I began working on my first symphony, which was based on an original blues theme. Although I wanted to use music that would be recognizable as American Negro music, I did not want to use anything that had been written. I wanted to create my own themes.

It is clear here, and in the previous passages, that the composer is visibly proud of the honors bestowed upon him, and yet he fails to mention all of his "firsts" in the area of music. Researcher Miriam Matthews, herself a pioneer as the first Negro librarian in Los Angeles, has listed other hallmarks in the Still annals: "the first Negro in the United States to have a symphony performed by a major symphony orchestra, the first to have an opera produced by major company in America, and the first to conduct a White major symphony orchestra in the Deep South."[4]

Perhaps few other members of a minority race have broken so many barriers of race and culture through simple excellence and dedication to a chosen career. As journalist Frank Gagnard put it,

> Dr. Still faced his professional challenge a long time ago, and by winning it he also secured a place in musical history and American history. He broke barriers of race in symphonic music, not through revolution but by gentle, attractive persuasion (New Orleans' *Times-Picayune*, April 17, 1968).

It is unfortunate that our modern concept of racial progress seems not to include men like Still, Paul Laurence Dunbar, Colonel Young or George Washington Carver. Like Topsy we have no sense of pastness--we cannot see very far beyond those who carried placards in marches and sit-ins, singing, "We shall overcome." All too often we are made to believe that, prior to the civil rights unrest of the 1960s, all Negroes were under-privileged, disliked, segregated, oppressed and under-achieving.

The current preference for the term "Black," as opposed to the terms "Afro-American," "Colored," or "Negro," is one of the results of our ignorance of past milestones. Under the guise of good works, political activists tended to polarize the races, turning the mosaic of ethnic America into Blacks vs. Whites. The epithets, "Black," "Black music," and "Black culture," were widely-used in the last decade of William Grant Still's public life, as indeed they continue to be today, and yet Still deplored them. As the

---

[4] These statistics were part of Miriam Matthews' presentation at the dedication of the William Grant Still Community Center in Los Angeles, California on March 11, 1978.

## William Grant Still: A Voice High-Sounding

"Editor's Note" in the 1968 interview explains,

> Dr. Still never referred to himself, or to any other member of the Negro race, as 'Black.' In his opinion, the term 'Black' connoted separatism between the races, and suggested not only that there was a wide gulf between the White man and the Black man, but also that White and Black were, by nature, in opposition to each other. For him, such opposition did not exist.

In the same vein, Still worked against the fiction commonly touted that Negro culture developed primarily in menial, decadent or simplistic surroundings, that is, in the dives and brothels of Scott Joplin, or in the nightclubs of Duke Ellington. He disagreed with the notion that Negroes could not come to greatness through any other avenues than through popular music or athletics. He was frequently annoyed by the claim that the metropolitan foci of Negro musical accomplishment in the twenties and thirties were The Cotton Club in New York and the Club Alabam in Los Angeles, both nightclubs. He did not concur that the major source of Negro literary brilliance was the Harlem Renaissance, the small flowering of creativity and race consciousness in Harlem. He could quote lines from Dunbar's poems, "The Colored Soldiers," "We Wear the Mask," "When All is Done, and "Slow Through the Dark," to point out that Langston Hughes' lyricism and ethnic awareness had their royal antecedents.

Naturally no one would wish to discount the work of Joplin, Ellington or Hughes, just as no one would want to criticize the positive goals of the civil rights activists. Yet it must be noted that such men are only peninsular adjuncts to a vast mainland of enviable successes. It was never true that Negroes had to develop their talents slowly, by group effort only, and with a difficulty born of universally low circumstances. It was never true that Negroes did not have, before mid-century, the innate ability and individual creativity to stand alone and unparalleled. It was never true because men like Dunbar and Still stood as proof long before the sixties that it was not so.

Still's responses to several queries put forward by Donald Brown shed some light on common misapprehensions about the history of Negro culture. When Still mentions that he was, at one time, the recording manager of the all-Negro phonograph company called the Black Swan, Brown observes,

> Brown: I've read that one of the reasons that Black Swan failed was that it ignored, to a large extent, the Negro musicians and the Negro audience by emphasizing classical and semi-classical artists and recordings. To what extent do you think this is true?

The obvious implication here is that Negro audiences are not, or were not, sophisticated enough to appreciate classical offerings. Still avoids dealing with the biased assumption behind the question, because he feels that there was no undue emphasis on the classical at the Black Swan.

> Still: No, I don't think so. The effort was to have balance in their product, and not to go too far afield in either direction. For instance, Ethel Waters used to make things for us, [and] you know [that] she made popular things. There were some things that were serious that were done, [and] some lighter things.
>
> And, as far as Negro musicians are concerned, they did the orchestral playing, so they were not disregarded at all. As a matter of fact, they were relied on solely, as far as the playing was concerned. And...the recording artists were all Negroes too. [So, the notion that the Black Swan ignored Negroes] was a rather false idea.

Later in the discussion, Brown asks about the ingredients of Negro culture in Los Angeles, seeming to suggest that Negro musical arts had to exist either apart from the White community, or in a night club setting.

> Brown: What was the nature and extent of Negro culture in Los Angeles in 1934? ...Were there concerts out here by Negro artists for Negro audiences when you came out in 1934?
>
> Still: Well, ...there were not so many things that were just apart [segregated]. For instance, Roland Hayes came out ,..[but] his concerts weren't confined to Negro audiences.
>
> Brown: ...When you were out here in 1929, do you recall a

nightclub on Central Avenue called "The Alabam?"

Still: Yes. "Club Alabam" ...I went there several times.

Brown: What was their show like? Was it something like what was going on at the Cotton Club...[in New York?]

Still: I think [that] they were very much alike...

Brown: I was wondering what the nature of [the shows there] was. Was it primarily directed toward Caucasian audiences?

Still: No, I don't think [that] there was any effort directed toward any particular group. I just felt that they wanted to give an entertaining show that would appeal to any person. I don't think that it had any racial aspects of that sort.

Brown: I was thinking of what Langston Hughes says, that...all of the Whites would go slumming in Harlem, at the cabarets and so forth...

Still: I know that many [White] people did come to those clubs up there...

Brown: Yes. I was thinking of the Club Alabam. What proportion of the audience [in that club] was Caucasian?

Still: ...I don't know. I didn't go often enough to make any broad statement about how the attendance was divided up. I think that they had a large number of Caucasian patrons.

Brown: When you came back out in 1934, was that club still in existence? Do you recall?

Still: I don't know. You know, when I came back, I came back to work, and that's all [that] I did.

It is clear, then, that Still is not aware of any real importance of the Club Alabam, and of the Cotton Club, just as he is tentative regarding the Harlem Renaissance. Does this mean, therefore, that the composer has no solid feelings for his minority origins? Has he never suffered from the incidences of racial prejudice which inspired Langston Hughes?

He has indeed suffered, though he does not speak of incidences of bigotry in the interview, nor does he ever dwell on them excessively in private conversation. However, in a letter of

February 17, 1943 to Claude Barnett of the *Associated Negro Press*, he describes one of the more blatant confrontations with ethnic bias:

> Late in 1942 I was approached to act as Supervisor of Music on the Fox all-Colored film called "Stormy Weather," then titled "Thanks, Pal." I was told that the film had a very high purpose, and that it would employ some of our finest colored artists. That was the original plan. However, when I came to the studio the music director, Al Newman, began a systematic plan to discard every bit of work I did and to ignore my suggestions, on one pretext or another. (Incidentally, everyone else in the music department was fine; I met splendid, friendly, efficient courteous people there and Al Newman was the only one who caused me any concern in that department.) Naturally, I did not approve of Newman's ideas that in order to be authentic, Negro music had to be crude and Negro dancing had to be sexy. I know from experience that those are the sort of misconceptions that help to breed misconceptions in other people's minds and indirectly influence the lives of our thirteen million people. In addition, I felt that after having worked for so many years to build up a reputation, it would be suicide to let my name go out on the screen credits as taking the responsibility for music about which Newman had let me have nothing to say. I decided that I would not accept the studio's money any longer under such circumstances, and although it meant a considerable financial loss, I resigned after six weeks of work, on January 30th.

Was it Al Newman who--when Still first walked through the halls at Fox--exclaimed indignantly, "What? A nigger in *this* line of work?"

One wonders that experiences of this kind did not tend to shake the racial pride and personal confidence of this educated, sensitive man. And yet, they did not. Throughout his career, he found in Negro culture a prime source of ideas for singularly attractive compositions. As he explains to Brown,

> Still: Now, in the blues, I saw this: a unique musical creation of Negroes. ...I created a theme in [the blues idiom], and used it as a basis for this symphony [*The Afro-American Symphony*].
>
> ...I realized that the American Negro had made an

unrecognized contribution of great value to American music, particularly and more so in the blues than in the spirituals. ...[I felt] that they represented the yearning of a people who were reaching out for something that they'd been denied. ...[I felt that hope and sorrow in the blues], and I wanted to use that idiom. I wanted to dignify it through using it in major symphonic composition.

This is not to say, of course, that Still embraced the Negroid idiom, to the exclusion of all others. There came a time in his broadening awareness of the human family in which he began to use themes of other races as well:

Brown: Now, at what period did you come to the conclusion that you should broaden out from Negro music?

Still: From the Negro idiom? ...I would say almost about the same time that I came out here [to California]. You see, ...while I still intended to devote myself to giving expression, to a very large extent, to the use of the Negro idiom,...I did not want to confine myself to that particular idiom because I think [that] here in America we have so many idioms. The Indian music, the Creole music, and so on. I would like to write music that expresses America. ...

Outside of this interview, in notes concerning *The Afro-American Symphony*, Still enlarges upon this point:

In *The Afro-American Symphony* I seek to portray, not the higher type of Colored American, (who represents a decided departure or a composite), but the "sons of the soil," (who are not yet so far removed from the standards of their African forbears and of whom the idiom is characteristic).

...I am thankful that subsequent growth has broadened the scope of my vision, enabling me to see the narrowness and selfish aspects of the desire to be of service to my race only. I realize now that those who render the most valuable service to Colored Americans are those whose efforts are directed toward serving all of the people comprising the American nation. My most sincere desire at present is for my efforts to have sufficient merit to cause them to mean something to America.

It is necessary to reiterate the fact that, though Still left the blues behind to some extent, he did not give up the fight for racial equality. He simply concluded that, unless all races achieve respect and understanding, no one race can aspire toward humane acceptance. In speaking of his doctorate from Bates College, Still alludes indirectly to the poor treatment that he received from prejudiced servicemen in the Navy, and to his resolve to work against such injustice:

> Still: I felt very, very highly complimented to have received the degree from Bates [in the Humanities, because] I've always wanted to do everything [that] I could to build up better race relations. From the very beginning, in the time when I was in the Navy in World War I, I made up my mind that, when I got out...I would devote myself to establishing friendships, [and to] building good will. So, to have received a degree in the Humanities...seemed...to be sort of a recognition of those efforts, even though they were small. I never got out in a big way, but who knows what some little thing...would accomplish...on a larger scale.

He hoped to attain something on a larger scale. Yet he never participated in a sit-in, read *Soul on Ice*, or railed against the White people who pushed him off the sidewalk or called him "Nigger." He remembered always the fine Caucasians such as Howard Hanson and Leopold Stokowski who loved him and helped him. He knew that the only way to build respect was to remain constantly worthy, always positive in attitude, and continually productive. Unfortunately, while he lived, his ideals--like warm summer ponds--lapped all too gently at the shores of the American will and apprehension.

Even so, apprehension can cast a backward glance. In the 1968 interview, and throughout his fifty years in music, Still's voice was the voice of cultural and social growth, charging men to look back and then forward. He hoped to bring to public attention the idea that individual achievement and universal brotherhood are not separate entities. They are two parts of the some whole, for man's most irrefutable contributions to the quality of life are assured only when they are made in service to the family of man.

As the "Editor's Note" in the interview sums it up,

> He never wished to be known as a "Black" composer who strove only to "dignify his race." Instead, his goal--as well as his dream--was to create works whose compelling harmonies would dignify all mankind and would instill in all races a spirit of loving reciprocity and interracial understanding.

This, then, is the intention, the high-sounding motive behind the voice of the composer in 1968. Perhaps, through the interview itself and this comment upon it, the voice and the intention will become visible entities in the progress of a people.

# THE LITTLE LIFE OF
# WILLIAM GRANT STILL[1]

> ...We are such stuff
> As dreams are made on, and our little life
> Is rounded with a sleep.
>
> (Shakespeare, *The Tempest*, IV, I, 156-158).

For the poet, earthly existence is merely tributary to the broad, surging sea of dreams, the wide-water for souls outside of the physical. Shakespeare's respect for the life of the spirit in such passages suggests the degree to which many artists--poets, authors, painters, sculptors, composers and musicians--rely on that realm for inspiration and assistance, approaching their work as a religious calling.

Aside from the numbers of Baroque composers like Bach who were men of the church, there have been popular artists such as Jenny Lind and Hans Christian Andersen who have attempted to forget themselves "in the service of the Supreme." Poet and musician Sidney Lanier asserted that there were aspects of music and of poetry that were so close to God's laws that they were "a later revelation of all gospels in one" (Verna Arvey, "Famous Authors and Their Love for Music," *Music and Dance* [February 1960, 18-20]). In our century, perhaps the most memorable figure to acknowledge the spiritual nature of the arts was William Grant Still.

A Negro composer and conductor of serious music, William Grant Still (1895-1978), was the author of such endearing and enduring compositions that racial barriers could not always prevent his works from being presented to the public. He became, therefore, the first person of color to conduct a white radio orchestra in New York City, the first to conduct a major symphony orchestra in the United States, the first to direct a major symphony in the Deep South, and the first to have a symphony

---

[1] Accepted for publication by *Doorways to the Mind* magazine but was never published therein.

played by a leading orchestra and an opera produced by a major American company. During his lifetime he was described as "one of the very greatest living composers of the New World" (*Micro Magazine*, Brussels, Belgium, [November 6, 1955]).

In his writings and speeches, Still attributed his success to Divine guidance and love. A letter from him to Carl Murphy, then President of the Afro-American Newspapers [November 7, 1956], stated that becoming a composer of serious music demanded the same dedication that was required to enter the ministry, and that composing yielded similar spiritual rewards. Later, in a lecture for the St. Paul Lutheran Church Missionary Society of Los Angeles, on September 27, 1964, Still spoke of music and "spiritual consciousness." Music served "a spiritual purpose," he said, for, if it had emotional appeal, meaning harmony and beauty, it became "the channel through which God speaks directly to us."

Where this composer was concerned, the worlds of music and of the spirit were structurally in-mixed, layered and woven one upon the other as were the ancient cities of Troy. A discovery of the way in which these two worlds came to be significant in his career, co-mingled, and then influenced the course of events in his life, can be made by taking a look at his books of "Prayer, Praise and Dreams."

The composer recorded his dreams, his prophecies, and his prayers together in the same volumes, largely because he believed that the three were a unity, all of them being involved in communication with the Almighty. He thought of prophecies and dreams as a means for him to receive God's messages. He wrote, "That we may commune with God is a privilege beyond valuation."

Still began his records of dreams and religious observations in the 1920's, after a period of philosophical evolution and visionary experience. He had grown up in an extremely religious, yet traditional, home in Arkansas. He was intimately acquainted with the Bible, as he was with the hymns and spirituals of various faiths. He believed especially in the Psalms, the 23rd and 91st, and he had absolute faith in the Power of God.

When he moved to New York, he underwent a crisis of doubt and fear concerning his professional future. It was impossible for a Negro in that period to make a living in the field of serious music, and yet, the higher forms of composition were those that he wanted to deal with. Poverty stalked him as he struggled to support a family by making arrangements of popular songs. Lying alone one night on his thin-blanketed bed in Harlem, he felt compelled to make a decision: he determined that he would write the kind of music that he wanted to write, regardless of hardship. Further, he made a commitment to dedicate all of his future work to the glory of God, praying earnestly for His aid in every endeavor.

The instant that the prayer was uttered, he felt as if a Presence came into the doorway, gave him assurances, and lifted an enormous weight from his prone body. A warm wave of peace and of light seemed to elevate him from the bed, and he realized that a step had been taken in the right direction.

From that point on, Still became accustomed to sensations of "uplift" and exhilaration during certain moments of prayer, and he saw many visions, which he described in his journal of "Prayer, Praise and Dreams." In 1926 he wrote,

> In a vision, I beheld a mighty cloud of angels approaching me. They sang a song of overwhelming beauty unlike any I have ever heard; a song that I have been unable to recall although I am a musician and can generally retain with ease any melody that appeals to me. As the angels sang I broke into tears, and awoke to find myself sobbing with joy.

In addition to this angelic chorus, he was also visited by heavenly harmonies in other forms.

> God spoke to me. His was the voice of a violin; elegant, pure and soaring to the heights of celestial beauty.

> God spoke to me. His was the voice of a 'cello; soft, mellow, and soothing.

> God spoke to me. His was the voice of a trumpet; strong, clear and stirring.

The composer was so motivated by these incredible experiences that he began actively to seek them out. Through prayer and meditation he invited communion with, and inspiration from, the Creator, and found overwhelming success. In a brief space of time he completed *Sahdji*, the choral ballet which was lavishly premiered by Howard Hanson in May of 1931, and he finished the much-lauded *Afro-American Symphony*, the "first major piece of music written by a Negro to be played before an American audience" (Mary D. Hudgins, "An Outstanding Arkansas Composer, William Grant Still," *Arkansas Historical Quarterly* [Winter 1965] 312). He wrote,

> Since having learned the lesson of relying on God for inspiration and of giving unto Him thanks for what is accomplished a great change has come over me. Composition has become comparatively easy. Inspiration lies never beyond my grasp. The time consumed in completing rather lengthy compositions is surprisingly short. I find greater joy in working now that its sole aim is to glorify my beloved Father.

And yet, although his facility in composing had reached a high level of development, his ability to provide for the basic needs of his family was faltering. The Great Depression, by drastically altering the contours of the world economic landscape, had left him jobless. At once it occurred to him that the God who had nourished him musically might also do so physically. He prayed, and,

> In a dream God showed me that I would visit an office where I would converse with two men. Later I went (in the same dream) to a place where an orchestra was assembled. I was shown that some of the players there were formerly connected with Whiteman's orchestra, and that the orchestra was conducted by Don Voorhees. This week the occurrences of my dream actually happened as I had dreamed them, and, through the grace of God, the employment I have longed for and prayed for came. I asked no man for this work, but relied on my Father. He secured it for me [September 1930].

The realization of the events shown in this dream convinced Still that there was significance in dream-prophecies and psychic visions. On a loose piece of brown paper in his journal he announced,

> I am recording experiences that many would term "strange." But, to one who believes in God and has had repeated proofs of His power exerted in the interest of those who believe, they are not strange.
> 
> --William Grant Still, March 12, 1933.

The first entry following this announcement revealed that,

> Mrs. Becton predicts death for President Roosevelt and war for America. She also warned me to be careful with my car as there were indications of an accident. A few days later I was impelled by a force almost irresistible to have one of the tires removed and replaced by another. Since then I have seen that I have God to thank for giving me the leading anent the tire, for a serious accident was averted by changing it.

Immediately following this entry, Still recalled past visions that had come to fruition:

> Over one year ago I was given a vision that told symbolically of great success for my orchestral poem, *Africa*. God is blessing this work wonderfully and great success accompanies each performance of it.

Within a year from this notation, Still was encouraged, through spirit leadings, to move to California. Once on the West Coast, he met and eventually married the Jewish pianist and journalist, Verna Arvey, who shared his interest in spiritual matters. Her interest proved to be fortunate, for the years which succeeded his move and marriage were characterized by increasing demands on his time. While working on the opera *Blue Steel* for the Guggenheim Foundation, he was also producing numerous vocal, orchestral and instrumental works, including the song *Victory Tide* for the 1939 World's Fair. Moreover, because he now had six children to support, four by a former marriage, it was necessary for him to do orchestrating for the film studios in order to make enough money to survive. He no longer had free moments to make entries in his "Prayer and Dream" books. From then on, it was left to his wife to write down his dream visions and messages from psychic friends.

As time passed, his dreams continued to give him indications of things that were going to transpire. On March 31, 1952, for example, Mrs. Still reported that he dreamed of "a friendly Jewish man...at a courthouse...who explained to him that something was going to happen that had not happened before. Some people would be mad. Some man named Nathan was going to do something." The next day he found out that Nathan Feinstein, head of President Truman's Labor Conciliation Board, had made a ruling which allowed Truman to seize the Steel Industry.

On August 15th of the same year, the composer saw himself "trying to talk about brotherhood to a White Southerner who was badly disposed, and awoke crying." That morning he heard that President Truman had okayed the sending of Gershwin's *Porgy and Bess* to Russia, instead of his own inspiring opera, *Troubled Island*.

In many cases the dreams foretold performances of Still compositions. At one point, when the composer had reached a low ebb in terms of access to conductors and orchestras, he saw in his sleep that some of his music was about to be played [January 30, 1959]. On the same afternoon, a letter arrived from Maestro Isler Solomon asking to see several scores.

Interspersed with these prophetic dreams were those which seemed to be symbolic. During the latter he became a traveler, sometimes by train, sometimes on foot. He crossed tumultuous rivers, or murky, harsh terrain, in order to reach places of unspeakable loveliness--green locales brimming with bright streams and tall grasses. Once in a while there were children and dogs playing in the grass, or in shady corners he saw two-story plantation dwellings which he took to be part of his property. Frequently, when he arrived at such destinations, he was further led to high hills or temples overlooking the thick groves and fields; there he was given white robes, and was taught things of importance about earthly life. The chief lessons that he learned were these:

> That "reverses are blessings when He suffers them to come. I have learned to ask of God, and then to wait on Him."
> That "Tolerance curbs temper, and the godly man feels compassion for those who do him wrong."

That "It were better for me to have never been born than to live a life that contributes nothing of good to my fellow men."

Of course, when awakened from the gentle schooling of his night-journeys, the lessons were not always easy to learn. Opposition, both racial and professional, followed the composer throughout his years, barring him from many performances of his music and preventing him from getting his pieces recorded. His dark hours were reflected in his dreams, for he frequently found himself outside of noble concert halls, or on the steps of the Metropolitan Opera, unable to enter because, for one reason or another, he was not properly dressed, or he was ignored by the important personages inside. Even so, his frustration was almost always mitigated, for he was shown before awakening that presentations of his works were destined to go forward anyway, whether he was present or not.

In any case, whether he was inside or outside of concert halls, whether he stood in rolling fields or rode fast-moving trains, he was always the recipient of Divine inspiration. Once or twice he wrote down themes that he had heard while he slept, keeping these notations for use in his compositions. One such theme was this one:

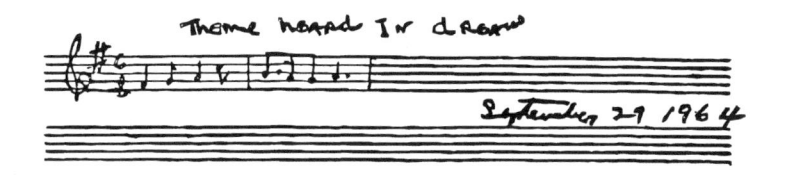

Usually, however, he heard spiritual melodies while he was awake and engaged in meditation or prayer. His gratitude for these harmonious gifts was so great that he never completed a piece of music without writing at the bottom of the last page, "With humble thanks to God, the Source of Inspiration."

God was ever the source of all that was good for Still; He was the Form and Substance of the composer's creativity. But, though the fuel flowed freely, the vehicle began to fail. A heart attack, the bitter rejection of him by his son, and the sudden death of his beloved son-in-law, all contributed to his physical and mental decline. Just before this decline became pronounced, on February 29, 1972, he clearly heard, in a dream, the tune, "The Song is Ended, but the Melody Lingers On." Unfortunately the years of prodigious output and mental clarity were at an end.

But the spirit and the melody are one, so both will linger, co-mingled, as the "little life" opens into the larger sea of awareness. William Grant Still will continue to have his influence musically, and thus, spiritually. And, even those who are not privy to his religious thoughts, will sense the impact of his faith through his life and work. Indeed, many people who speak of him after his death come very close to the essence of his achievements. As Ellen Wright, widow of author John Wright, wrote to the author in December of 1982, "John and I often said, if there was a Saint on this earth, it was your Father."

# THE LAST SHALL BE FIRST: THE CRUCIFIXION OF THE WORLD'S FAMOUS COMPOSERS[1]

> He [Pilate] knew very well that the Jewish authorities had handed Jesus over to him because they were jealous.
>
> --Matthew 27:18

In the thirties, composer William Grant Still, who was a serious student of metaphysics, consulted a psychic and asked when his music would achieve the success that he felt it deserved. The psychic replied gravely that Still's deceased mother, Carrie Still, had sent him this message:

Have courage, for you will have to struggle to the bitter end.

Unfortunately the prophecy came true. When Still died in a rest home in 1978, after years of disappointment and hardship, he left an estate that was too minuscule to probate. Some said that a man of his race might have expected difficulties; others, who were familiar with the lives of other musical giants in history, knew that, with Still, race was the excuse, not the problem. Wherever and whenever creative people write music, struggle is almost inevitable.

Deems Taylor, a fine composer whose own career anxieties are touched on in the Still biography called *In One Lifetime* (Verna Arvey, University of Arkansas Press, Fayetteville AR 72701, 1984), has written at length about symphonic composers who could not make a living from their creative efforts. In an article entitled "Most of Our Great Symphonies Were Written on Empty Stomachs" (*Up Beat I* [January 1939] 9, 16, 26), Taylor offers numerous facts about the sufferings of the greats in music.

Schubert, says Taylor, had to teach for a living, and, at death, left an estate of less than $40. Both a conductor and a teacher as well as a composer, Beethoven earned no more than a bank clerk.

---

[1] This article is previously unpublished.

Chopin's money came to him by virtue of his keyboard talents, not as a result of his compositional output, and Brahms supported himself by conducting and performing at the piano. Alexander Borodine was a chemist and medical doctor, while Rimsky-Korsakoff's primary occupations were those of naval officer and teacher of music. Edward MacDowell, who died of exhaustion, worked as a college professor and pianist.

Summarizing the situation, Taylor concludes that "one of the attributes of genius is the possession of sufficient strength of character to persist in spite of neglect. ...it is entirely possible for a composer to be world-famous during his lifetime, and still have to sublet the garret that the painter left when he got his first big commission (p. 26)." (Taylor's view need not be tempered by the observation that the painter may not always do so well either; Frans Hals, to cite one example, died in extreme poverty in the St. Jorisdoelen Almshouse in Holland.)

The implication is, of course, that those who do not care for sackcloth and ashes should avoid becoming composers and artists. Yet, the question remains, why can't creative men make an acceptable living by simply being creative? And the answer lies in the phrase, "professional jealousy."

There is a very real sense in which the person who wants to know how well he is doing in life should count his enemies rather than his friends. For every ten kindly and appreciative human beings on the earth, there is one who wishes to degrade and to destroy anyone who surpasses him in talent or industry. The moment that followers begin to gather at the feet of a Master, a Judas awakens to prepare for a betrayal.

The saddest element of the betrayal is, of course, that no one expects it. Many believe that backbiting and jealousy do not reach from the "peasant classes" into the ranks of professional and artistic men. The more educated and cultured a man is, the less he is thought likely to indulge in childish envy. However, nothing could be further from the truth. Jealousy among the educated is not less earnest, it is simply less condemned. The professional man who is envious slides serpentlike into the Eden of genius, and, with an adroit turn of phrase, or a studied coldness, or a cavalier verbal thrust, makes the dark seem light, and the good, evil.

Verna Arvey's survey of distinguished composers who were vilified by critics is really a survey of incidences of professional jealousy ("What Power Professional Criticism," *Etude* 75 [May-June 1957] 14, 40-41). Puccini, notes Miss Arvey, was "crucified" by what he called "the vile words of the envious Press." Certainly Puccini had reason to be bitter, for the critic, Berta, writing about *La Bohême*, characterized the opera as a "degradation." Berta's colleague, Carlo Bersezio, speaking also of *Bohême*, insisted that it was "deficient in form and musical color," and predicted that it would "leave no trace upon the history of our lyric theater." The same sort of antipathy greeted *Madame Butterfly* at its première, causing it to fail at the box office, while *La Tosca* was ruined by bomb threats and poison-pen letters.

Moreover, Puccini was not alone in his martyrdom. Beethoven was often castigated for his "newness," and the *Eroica Symphony* was labeled "shrill," "bizarre" and "incoherent." César Franck was ignored by the press, except when a minor journalist said that the composer Delibes was at fault for applauding a Franck composition. And, critic Johann Scheibe reported that Bach's compositions were "bombastic," "intricate" and "over-elaborate."

Happily, Beethoven, Bach, Franck and Puccini lived through the torture, but other composers who were victimized were not so strong. George Bizet was rumored to have been so upset by the harsh critical appraisal of *Carmen* that he died of a broken heart. At the première of *Carmen* on March 3, 1875, the press categorized it as a "confused work," by a "wild Wagnerian who made the motive unfashionable" and "dispensed with antiquated melody" (Arvey, p. 40). Having read the reviews, Bizet wept inconsolably, then passed away suddenly on June 3, 1875.

It is fortunate that most renowned musicians have learned something from Bizet's experience. Indeed, one American composer has cast a most irreverent glance at the critics themselves:

> After the performance you wait up all night to learn what the critics say. Now this is an interesting spectacle. Here you have worked nine months on a composition. You have tried to cut out all the bad spots.

Even at rehearsals you have made changes. But immediately the critic, from his position of superiority, can tell you exactly what's wrong with it (Arvey, p. 41).

Or, as Jean Sibelius put it, "Pay no attention to what the critics say. There never has been set up a statue in honor of a critic."

Of course, critics are not the only ones who are capable of professional jealousy. Casual musicologists and historians are often given to defamation of character and achievement. For example, Niccolò Paganini, a composer as well as an incredible violinist, gained a reputation for stinginess among historians perhaps owing to a negative story told by a taxi driver. Paganini was going to play a number on one string at a particular concert, and, when the taxi driver asked him for ten francs to deliver him to the theater for the performance, the artist declared,

"I will pay you ten francs when you drive me on one wheel!"

Then Paganini gave the driver what he thought was an acceptable sum for his services, and went on to the concert. Strange that this story should be better known than the fact that Berlioz received twenty-thousand francs from Paganini when he was in need (Nellie G. Allred, "How Paganini Triumphed," *Etude* LX [March 1942] 169, 199).

Indeed, the willingness of many people to believe the worst about any public figure may be an indication that professional jealousy is a pervasive human fanaticism. One composer, Robert Russell Bennett, has spoken at length about the "natural desire on the part of those who know them to scream out the less glamorous features of the hero's life" (from a letter to William Grant Still, July 9, 1945). Bennett's tale continues thus:

> Perhaps the best commentary on the term "fame" came to my notice recently. In the publishing office where I spend some time I got into the habit last winter of bringing in one of those paper horse races to which one touches a lighted cigarette and six little lines of spark crawl down the paper to a finish line, each spark representing a horse. I got everybody in the office to put up a dime and choose a horse, some fifty or sixty bets resulting. After the "running" I would take time to divide the pot among all those on the winning horse, and

payoff. As I left one large room one of the secretaries who had placed a bet of ten cents on a horse, turned to the rest of the room and said, "Is that the way the poor man makes his living?"

Yet Bennett's story is innocuous compared to the treatment received by the most idolized of all composers, Johann Wolfgang Amadeus Mozart. Documentation suggests that Antonio Salieri, court composer and conductor in Vienna at the end of the eighteenth-century, conspired to prevent Mozart's works from being performed and appreciated. Further, Salieri saw to it that Wolfgang could not obtain acceptable salaries for composing or teaching, to the extent that the young genius borrowed money to meet his needs during the last few years of his life.

Many scholars, to discount the notion that Salieri "starved" Mozart to death, assert that Mozart, after enduring some financial hardships, was able to enjoy a furnished apartment, good clothing and two servants at the end of his life. Furthermore, it is intimated that Mozart had to borrow in order to pay for these luxuries, not because he was ill-paid for his music, but because he was lax in keeping his household accounts in order. Perhaps, it is whispered, he spent money frivolously. No one has mentioned that Mozart, as an artist seeking royal patronage, was expected to keep up the appearance of wealth, and that he certainly did not have resources commensurate with his station or talent. A man of his achievements should not have been expected to spend time balancing figures in order to live as a recognized artist was expected to live--and as Mozart's enemies lived, certainly, in even greater luxury.

That Mozart's enemies did succeed in their persecution of the young composer, is clear in his letters. In messages to his father he wrote, "It is all off between the Princess of Wurtemburg and myself. The Emperor has stood in my way, for he cares for no one but Salieri" (December 15, 1781). And, "You wonder how I can flatter myself that I could be maestro to the Princess! Salieri is certainly not equal to instructing her in the clavier--all he can do is to try to injure me with Someone Else in this matter!" (August 31, 1782).

Later, on April 18, 1786, Mozart's father, Leopold, wrote to his sister, "'Le Nozze di Figaro' is to be performed for the first time on the 28th. It will be very significant if it succeeds, for I know that there are astonishingly strong cabals against it. Salieri and all his partisans will again endeavor to move heaven and earth. Duschek said to me recently that the reason your brother has all these cabals against him is that he is held in such high esteem for his great talents and ability" (*Letters of Wolfgang Amadeus Mozart* [London, J.M. Dent & Sons, 1928]).

Indeed, it was the high esteem in which Mozart was held that most incurred the wrath of Salieri. Therefore, when Mozart died mysteriously at the age of thirty-five, although no clearly-documented illness or chronic depression had led up to his final fevers and weakness, the court composer might well have been suspect. Suspicion, however, was not necessary: the victim himself made the statement that Salieri had poisoned him, and, after his death, Salieri confessed to the crime more than once in the presence of Beethoven and other reliable witnesses.

If the ungodly injustices done to Mozart had ended with his unceremonious burial in a third-class grave, his soul might still have found rest in the blessings that his music brought to his name. But later detractors and traducers have arisen to suggest that Salieri was probably senile when he said that he killed his rival, and that Mozart's accusation was brought on by the mental derangement of illness. One academician has even gone to a great deal of labor to convince everyone that Mozart's death was the result of unconscious suicidal impulses--impulses brought on by remorse over Leopold's demise some four years earlier (Thomas Holliday, "Amadeus: The Man and the Child, The Child in the Man," *The Opera Journal* XX [1987] 7-23).

In an article entitled "Mozart's Mysterious Death A New Interpretation" (*Ovation* 5 (April 1984] 19-27), Francis Carr presents circumstantial evidence to suggest that Mozart was murdered by Franz Hofdemel, the husband of Magdalena Hofdemel, the woman with whom Mozart was having an affair during the last three years of his life. Carr's pathological discussion and reports on the burial of the composer reasonably substantiate the assertion that the great man was poisoned, and that the facts of his murder were concealed from the public by the authorities in Vienna.

It is true that, in June of 1791, Mozart told his wife, Constanze, that he had been poisoned with aqua toffana, which was a blend of arsenic, antimony and lead oxide. It is also true that, in December of 1791, the symptoms of his malady at death tended to bear out his claim: "swelling of the body, inflammation of the joints, fever, headache and vomiting" (Carr, 24). The fact that there are no writings of his to reveal the tremulous hand of a poison victim, does not mean that no such writings existed. Any such papers might have been destroyed by conspirators, including any medical records alluding to signs of poison. Also, Erna Schwerin's contention that Mozart died of rheumatic fever is hardly conclusive; if a man had fevers, catarrhs, a sore throat or an abscessed tooth before the age of fifteen, it is no proof that he perished from a weak heart over twenty years later ("More on Mozart's Mysterious Death," *Ovation* 5 [July 1984 8-9). Dr. William M. Ober's theory that the composer developed "poststreptococcal glomerulonephritis," the culmination of childhood illnesses such as rheumatic fever, is similarly undocumented and unprovable.

Certainly it is unusual that Constanze did not attend her husband's funeral, and that none of Mozart's friends and admirers would help to pay for more than a third-class burial. It has been claimed that the mourners did not follow the body to the grave owing to possible inclement weather, or to the fact that Joseph II's laws restricted funeral observances, and yet those who were members of the upper crust might well have afforded, and might have been allowed, to take carriages to the site. Daniel Nagy's insistence that the stringent nature of the funeral could have been due to the government antipathy toward Masons ("Correspondence," *Ovation* 5 (July 1984] 9) is refuted by Carr, who observes that other highly-respected men who were also Masons received traditional Christian burials.

Following the composer's funeral, other odd events resulted in his third-class grave becoming a common burial ground, or a pauper's grave. Some have said that Constanze failed to pay the taxes on the plot, so that other bodies were interred with the composer; others have insisted that the cemetery attendants accidentally mixed up the plots, and therefore laid other bodies with that of Mozart. None of these explanations reveals any solicitude for the deceased following his death; none is evidence that there was no conspiracy against the composer.

Carr concludes that Mozart was not properly buried because he was murdered, and that the perpetrator of the crime was Franz Hofdemel. Carr presumes that Hofdemel was the culprit because Franz and Magdalena engaged in a violent argument the day after Mozart's demise--an argument in which the husband attacked his unfaithful wife with a knife, then cut his own throat. Though Hofdemel died, Magdalena survived; a few months later she gave birth to a son and named him Johann, after her deceased lover.

The case against Hofdemel is strong, but not convincing. If the man were jealous enough to commit murder, why would he wait so long? Magdalena, after all, was Mozart's pupil for three years prior to his death, and her husband had to have been aware of the adulterous relationship. If the authorities knew that a minor chancery official had killed a man who was well-known in Vienna and in Europe, why did they take pains to avoid an autopsy or an investigation of the death? Hofdemel had not the friends at court that Salieri had, so how did he rate such a cover-up? On the other hand, if the concern was for Mozart's reputation, surely Salieri's friends would have made every effort to see that Mozart's marital infidelity was widely-exposed, not entombed in a third-class grave.

Moreover, why did Constanze display disregard for her husband after his passing? Carr seems to think that she did so out of shame over Mozart's unfaithfulness, and yet, adultery was not uncommon in the upper classes of Vienna at the time. While there does exist a letter of love and longing from Mozart to his wife in 1791, it is not unthinkable that the man might have been sleeping with one woman while continuing to reassure another of his loyalty. Further, Constanze herself was involved in an affair with Franz Xaver Suessmayr, the man whose name was given to her son when he was born. And, why did Mozart accuse Salieri and not Hofdemel? Even better, why did Salieri confess to the crime, knowing that his confession would be taken seriously in the light of Mozart's statement that he had been poisoned?

If Hofdemel did poison Mozart, it is likely that he was persuaded to do it by Salieri, and that the act was so repugnant to his nature that the news of the composer's death drove him to violence and self-slaughter. It is interesting to note that someone intervened in the disposal of Hofdemel's remains, just as someone prevented an inquiry into Mozart's death; Hofdemel was not thrown into a pit with the other suicides--he was consigned to an unmarked grave and the date of his death was changed in the official government records. Someone in high places was at work. Who? Obviously a man in favor at court and one who had much influence, so much influence, in fact, that Constanza was rewarded for her silence by sudden success in promoting her late husband's music, and by Salieri's agreement to accept her son as his pupil. Significantly, when Beethoven was asked about Mozart in 1823, he said, cryptically, "in a monarchy we know who is the first" ("A Day with Beethoven" *Ovation* 5 [June 1984] 7).

Had Mozart not been the formidable Master that he was, it would be apparent to anyone and everyone that Salieri was a murderer who used his political strength to mask his vulnerability. Yet the envious and the faithless want history to believe, without any evidence to the contrary, that not one but two testimonies to the crime were false.

Chief among the faithless, most assuredly, is the playwright Peter Shaffer with his play, *Amadeus*. Not only does Shaffer tend to relieve Salieri of blame, but also, in showing that God is capricious and irrational in the bestowing of gifts of genius upon certain men, Shaffer portrays Mozart as an infantile, profane, erratic, empty-headed Thing. From all of the composer's letters, and from all of the reports of contemporaries, Shaffer selects those which reveal lapses into course language or juvenilia, and from this selection conjures up a character who is, undoubtedly, the most distasteful man to have stepped into any artistic arena.

The truth is that most of Mozart's salacious letters were written at the age of twelve to his cousin, and they were the product of his rather free-minded upbringing among family and neighbors who tended toward the vulgar and the boisterous (Herbert Kupferberg, *Amadeus: A Mozart Mosaic* [New York: McGraw-Hill, 1986]). These letters are far outweighed by the many later communications that were thoughtful and able; indeed, John Harrison points out that Mozart's letters to his father were not those of an immature child, but were from a loving and understanding son who treated his parent as a musical colleague ("The Concept of Father in Mozart's Operas and *Amadeus*," *The Opera Journal* XXII [1989] 3-9).

The reports of two or three of Mozart's contemporaries which suggested that he made sarcastic and self-righteous remarks about other musicians, and that he had his wild and impish moods (one woman said that he jumped over chairs and turned somersaults), do not obliterate the balanced assessments of the man: he was, also, capable of breeding and sensitivity, "tender," "affectionate," "good-humored," "eager to please," and intelligent (Holliday). Undeniably, he possessed one of the finest minds ever to have been housed in a human body--a mind incapable of the doltishness ascribed to it by Shaffer. In the words of Steven Lubin, his artistic output reflects "the life experience of a highly developed human being," and a man attune to his time ("Was Mozart Childlike?" *Ovation* 6 [January 1986] 16-18).

That Mozart was a man of his time is evident in the continuing popularity of his music. Because he was able to empathize with the fundamental needs of the common man, he "caught the beat of the masses" (Nola McGarry, Letter to Judith Anne Still [December 12, 1984]); because he had breeding and sensitivity, he was able to give palpable form to that "beat"--to reveal its shape and substance and to capture it for succeeding ages to touch and to savor. Assuredly, a part of the life behind his timeless formations was somewhat bawdy, impatient and impulsive: Shaffer cut that part away from his nature and held it aloft, as one would sever the ears and tail from the striving beast while the great heart still pulses at the core.

A similar dismemberment might well have been made of a man like Shakespeare, if a biographer were to concentrate only on the obscene references in the poet's work, or of many exceptional figures, were a playwright to hover near with pen poised whenever they swore, or swaggered, or pursued women. Many creative geniuses have left their frailties dangling for the jealous to grab; many of the profane passions of the mighty have become ragged hand-holds for the aspiring inept to hoist themselves upward.

Unfortunately, when mediocrity defaces the sublime, the result is beyond physical fatality; the wrong done by *Amadeus* to Mozart is greater than that perpetrated by Salieri. Salieri slew the man; *Amadeus* profanes the memory of the man and removes the assurance of balance and justice in history. Death, in and of itself, is not tragic simply because it takes a man to another place--it is tragic because it deprives the man of the ability to defend himself against detraction.

And detraction does continue in spite of death. Perhaps no travesty in this world will surpass that of *Amadeus*, although nothing is certain, given the number of human beings who enjoy quenching the last thirst of rivals with vinegar. It is safe to say that the future of musical scholarship promises many revelations about crimes committed against singular composers.

Without question, also, many of these revelations will have to do with the career of composer William Grant Still. Ironically, Still's private papers--(recently donated to the University of Arkansas at Fayetteville)--contain detailed research into the trials and death of Mozart. Still felt that he shared somehow in the mortal distress of the artist from Salzburg, because, he asserted, there existed a group of men in America who conspired against him. On January 1, 1953, he wrote in his diary,

> There are in these United States too many who think it only right for me to be denied the right to live. They connive to stop performances of my work, to pooh pooh my efforts, to keep us [he and his wife] from expressing ourselves through the press, to cause others to hold us in contempt, and to force me out of music. These are the people who turned my opera's success [*Troubled Island*, New York City Center, 1949] into failure. ...God forgive them! ...I'm glad that I do not hate them for what they do.

An earlier diary entry, on April 4, 1950, stated,

> We want recordings badly. The small group of composers who have gained complete control of record companies have seen to it that we have only the *Afro-American Scherzo* [from his *Symphony #1*] on records.

The uninvolved observer might even now be led to wonder why

no major recording companies issue albums of Still compositions, in spite of the increasingly successful performances of his music.

Regardless of whether a conspiracy against Still has existed, many were the incidences of heartache experienced by the composer at the hands of both White and Colored people. On one occasion he was looking forward to a performance of one of his piano compositions by the Negro prodigy, Philippa Schuyler, until, on the night of the performance, he discovered that a work by Aaron Copland had been quietly substituted for his own. On another occasion, Hall Johnson, Afro-American choir director, agreed to do Still's work at a West Coast concert, provided that one of his own compositions was included in the program. However, when the time came for the dress rehearsal, the execution of Johnson's piece was flawless, but the members of the chorus had not yet seen the music for the Still rendition. Professional jealousy and neglect know no racial boundaries.

In fact, there is some evidence to suggest that jealousy may, at one time, have influenced government projects. Among the notes written by William Grant Still's wife about his life, are these:

> During the War, the U.S. Government made a series of films on various subjects. According to WGS' understanding, he was scheduled to play a prominent part in the music for the picture dealing with the Negro soldier. However, Dimitri Tiomkin stepped in as music director and thereafter WGS was out. Not a single piece of his original music was used as background, though other Negro composers, such as Duke Ellington, were represented. Even in the sequence where music was to be played as the grave of the Negro soldier was shown, WGS' well-known *Afro-American Symphony* was totally ignored, and an excerpt from a Beethoven symphony was used instead.
>
> From time to time, whenever it was suggested that WGS be employed for any film, the studio music heads had definite answers. If it was a dramatic film they would say they couldn't use him because he was "too popular." On the other hand, if it was a popular film, they would say he wasn't acceptable because he was "too symphonic."

Outside of the realm of film music, however, jealousy took other forms. In a letter dated September 13, 1963, Still and his librettist wife begged the San Francisco Opera to look at one of their opera scores:

> You may recall that we sent you sketches of the stories of several in 1960, and that you returned them as not being suitable. One of them was *Minette Fontaine*, set in New Orleans. We were struck by the coincidence of another composer being assigned to write an opera for you soon after that, with the same setting, and somewhat the same name for the heroine. This is mentioned in the enclosed article by Patterson Greene, our *Herald-Examiner* critic.
>
> Since writing to you, we have had successful performances of our short opera *Highway 1, USA*, at the University of Miami--criticisms of which we mailed to you several weeks ago.

The San Francisco Opera never accepted a score by Still--would never look at a score by Still, even in the 1980s--and *Minette Fontaine* was left without a performance until 1984. It was not until October of that year that the opera received its première with the up-and-coming Baton Rouge Opera Company.

As with the music of Mozart after the composer's death, the music of William Grant Still is now finding its measured resurrection. His *Bayou Legend* has become the first opera by a Negro to be broadcast on national television, and the four recordings of his music issued by the composer's family are among the most popular in the nation. Performances and publications of, and about, his works have tripled since his death. The aura grows around this musician, just as it did around Puccini, Bizet, Franck, Beethoven, and all of the others who were tried and convicted by professional jealousy.

Perhaps professional jealousy is, after all, unimportant, since good works seem to survive all attempts to bury them with the doers. As a friend wrote to Still in regard to criticism,

> I visited the World's Fair and you cannot imagine the thrill it gave me to be enchanted by music that you had composed, and also to see your name carried among the illustrious musicians of America. You have done a great work and persons who have reached the zenith which you have can expect to be maligned unjustly. ...Remember that the most brickbats and sticks are found under the best apple tree.
>
> (Nimrod B. Allen, Columbus Ohio Urban League, Letter to William Grant Still [September 24, 1940]).

Certainly the brickbats and sticks do not matter. Not unless some purity of man's soul is sought, or some cleansing of the spirit is desired. If human cruelty transcends the single life, then repentance and expiation must overcome death. In the words of a psychic who was asked to speak about Still and his wife during the last dark years of the composer's career,

> [They have been] an uplift for more people than they will ever know. You may be sure that all are not rewarded nor are all punished in one lifetime.

And, truly, the lifetimes of too many men and women of the arts have been scarred by punishment. It therefore remains for the lovers of art and music to provide the rewards, through enlightened compassion for future genius and appreciative good will toward those who have been crucified for their creativity.

# WILLIAM GRANT STILL: SOLVING THE MYSTIC PUZZLE[1]

> What song the Sirens sang, or what name Achilles assumed when he hid himself among the women, though puzzling questions, are not beyond conjecture.
>
> (Sir Thomas Browne, 1605-1682, *Urn-Burial; or Hydriotaphia*, Chapter 5).

The irony of scholarship lies in the fact that the puzzling questions are never asked when the artist is alive to answer; it is death which calls up the questions from the catacombs, hoping to breathe new vigor into a seeming past. And then, all too often, the questions having been raised, are ignored, in order to hasten toward the academic egotism of conjecture.

While William Grant Still lived, he did not appear to be an enigmatic figure. He was a racial figure and a national figure, and, musically, he was a conservative figure. His critics were either noncommittal or idolatrous. The idolators never questioned; rather their comments were clean and outward bound:

> You will be interested to know that after my first rehearsal with the orchestra [of *Sahdji*], the members put down their instruments and applauded your work. ...I think myself it is a stunning piece of work and should make a deep impression.
>
> (Dr. Howard Hanson, Letter to William Grant Still [1931]).[2]

> Still is one of our greatest American composers. He has made a real contribution to music.
>
> (Leopold Stokowski, Baltimore *Afro-American* [April 21, 1945]).

---

[1] This essay is previously unpublished.

[2] This letter was written by Howard Hanson while he was preparing Still's ballet, *Sahdji*, for its 1931 premiere at the Eastman School of Music, and it was quoted by Miriam Matthews in her "Biographical Notes on William Grant Still," presented at the Dedication of the William Grant Still Community Arts Center, Los Angeles, California, March 11, 1978.

> The difference between high art and low art is not intellect but evocative, religious power. ...I want to...tell you how moved I was by your truly beautiful music--I was moved to tears (no less) and this is the highest tribute I can pay.
> (George Frederick McKay, Letters to William Grant Still [August 24, 1949 and January 24, 1964]).

> This American composer shows remarkable qualities which place him as one of the very greatest living composers of the New World. A sense of immediate observation; the taste for a rigorous and brilliant orchestration; spontaneity and sincerity characterize his compositions.
> ("Musiques D'Evocation," <u>Micro Magazine</u>, Brussels, Belgium, No.552 [November 6, 1955] 7).

Such commentaries reverberated loudly, softly, continuously and genuinely during the composer's lifetime, in varying ways and words. With the death of the artist on December 3, 1978, the tributes took on documentary seriousness, becoming fixed in earth like the white sequences at Normandy. Homage could not ask, or answer, the emerging questions.

Yet, there are puzzles to be solved in the career of William Grant Still. Musicologists begin to wonder why Still decided to repudiate ultra-modern music after making broad use of avant-garde techniques early in his career. Theologians ask how the composer reconciled his fundamental belief in God and the Bible with his deep interest in mysticism and the occult. Both musicologists and theologians want to know how Still's spiritualism impinged upon and influenced his creativity. What were his philosophies of life, art and religion?

The queries are made because the musician left no satisfactory compilation of his thoughts on musical forms and on the religious approach to music. While touching on the subject in lectures and in odd writings, and while hoping that he might find time to author a book on orchestration, he lived rather than published his philosophy. His life-energies were woven primarily into the composition of hundreds of pieces of music, both serious and popular.

Regrettably, the composer is no longer here to fill the empty spaces between reality and certain knowledge. But his voice is heard in the void by means of his personal papers and favorite books. The totality of what he read, discussed, wrote and believed is being sifted and sorted by the Still family so that it may be institutionalized at the University of Arkansas in Fayetteville, Arkansas. From this material, both published and unpublished, and from memories of Still's privately expressed opinions, come the ensuing considerations of art, life and the occult.

Although many of the statements in these discussions will not be ascribed directly to the composer, they might well have been his. They are drawn essentially from sources in his library, or from sources with an affinity to those in his library, and they follow as closely as possible the answers that he would have given had he been presented with the questions. It is through them that the imperatives which gave motive and shape to his undeniable accomplishments are called forth, like Lazarus, to stand full in the face of conjecture. It is through them that his mysticism and musicianship are made available to the inquiring public.

## Light, Sound and Substance: God's "Rubik's Cube"

William Grant Still was a puzzler in more ways than one. In his domestic role, he made jigsaw puzzles for his children with a coping saw, or worked crossword puzzles to relax after a long day's labor, and with his relish for crosswords came his affection for words in general. He never failed to look up the pronunciations of terms that he did not know, and he searched for names of operatic characters that "had music in them." Because he believed, with the Jewish people, that names could be sacred, or could contain the essences of the persons named, he learned to calculate the spiritual values of appellations via numerological methods. He made pictures with words and letters using a typewriter.

When apart from his typewriter, his dictionary and his puzzles, the composer played with colors. He decorated his scores with bright pieces of construction paper, cut into geometric shapes, or he painted opera sets and toys with glossy enamel.

Occasionally his leisure moments were spent leafing through *Midwinter* and *Holiday* magazines to savor the seasonal landscapes. If he could get away for a day, he drove the family to a cliff overlooking the Malibu sea, or to the yellow-green groves of Fern Dell in Griffith Park.

Had the "Rubik's Cube" been invented in Still's time, he probably would have taken pleasure in it, for it is this popular game which best images his views on universal structure, sound and color. The composer was convinced that all aspects of the universe were as closely interrelated as were the words of a language or the colors of the spectrum. In this belief he was supported by the writings of Benjamin Franklin, where they focused upon the interconnectedness of primary colors from opposing ends of the continuum. Franklin pointed out that, "after looking through green spectacles, the white paper of a book will on first taking them off appear to have a blush of red; and, after looking through red glasses, a greenish cast..." ("Benjamin Franklin's Discourses in Music," *The Etude* LV [May 1937] 296).

It is significant that Franklin, in addition to toying with the riddle of red and green, expanded the body of human knowledge in realms as seemingly unrelated as those of electrical energy and music criticism. His wide-ranging experiments and literary efforts constituted a hint that there may be some formative linkage between light and color, sound and music, energy and matter, and that somehow the human senses might profit by an understanding of this complex interconnection.

Certainly Still sensed the linkage. On many occasions he spoke of musical harmonies as "colors," and of inspiration as "light" from the Creator. Further, he thought of sound as substance, a substance that could be manipulated and molded. During an oral history interview for California State University, Fullerton, he said, "I learned to play many instruments, not for the purpose of being a proficient performer, but in order to capture the sound, and to have it so firmly implanted in my consciousness that I could bring it out and play with it and mix it" (R. Donald Brown, *An Interview with William Grant Still*, ed. by Judith Anne Still [CSUF Oral History Program, November 13 and December 4, 1967] 3). For him, music was a total system that came down from the Divine origin in gradations of form, moving from harmonic vibration and spiritual energy, to light, to color, to sound, to substance.

Modern technology has approached sound-light relationships part by part. Even before hearing-impaired Thomas Edison put his ear to a piano to "hear" the vibrations, it was realized that the blind could apprehend music through their tactile senses, especially through fingers placed on sound sources. Meanwhile, scientists had become aware that both sound and color were energy and were measured in waves. Today sound, that is, ultrasound, is used to "paint" pictures of infants in the womb, and there is heavy evidence that the power of the mind can be used to produce images on film (Television demonstration on "In Search Of," Alan Lansburg, Producer, Leonard Nimoy, Host, KHJ-TV, Los Angeles [September 9, 1983]). In the computer field, mathematicians are only just beginning to elucidate similarities in the basics of musical composition to the basics of computer processing. Both clearly have universal qualities (Grant Delbert Venerable, Ph.D., "The Taming of the Computer: Some Right-Brain Strategies," *Omnitrom Associates Newsletter*, Mill Valley, California [November 25, 1982] 5).[3]

Throughout nature, God's tapestry of matter and energy, sound, feeling and form are in-mixed, and sound is fundamental. Wind and water move in audible rhythm, the earth shifts and breathes, trees sway and whisper--each creating its own pattern of sound. Living creatures walk or move in cadence, and hearts beat in rhythm. In truth, there is no life without vibration (that is, sound), owing to the constant motion within separate atoms, and because of the fact that there is no matter or energy without movement, vibration or oscillation. There is, indeed, validity to the Biblical assertion, in the Gospel of St. John, that Creation began with a Divine "Word," or, with vibration.

The primal nature of vibration, and thus of sound, was central

---

[3] Dr. Venerable was a schoolmate of Judith Anne Still, Dr. Still's daughter, and thus a frequent visitor to the Still home in his youth. As an adult he studied to be a chemist and software professional, and later became Dean of Students at Lincoln University, Pennsylvania.

to Still's philosophy. He believed that the cosmos was created by a harmonic force called God, which, like the conductor of an orchestra, coordinated all of the separate vibrations in all matter and energy. Oddly enough, this notion of God as Music Master is the controlling purpose of a recent book by Robert C. Lewis, called *The Sacred Word and its Creative Overtones* [Oceanside: Rosicrucian Fellowship, 1986]. In this book, Lewis quotes the assertion of Pythagoras that, "The world was brought forth out of chaos by sound or harmony, and constructed according to principles of musical proportion."

Pythagoras was, then, perhaps the first to postulate the essentiality of sound on a large scale, and the first to suggest that everything in the cosmos, including heavenly bodies, moved harmoniously, and according to mathematical laws. The ancients and the men of the Renaissance objectified the theory of heavenly motion in their concept of the "music of the spheres." According to this concept, the planets and other heavenly bodies were said to create music by moving in their orbits, and the celestial harmonies which resulted from this intergalactic motion were so extremely refined that only souls with highly developed sensibilities could hear them. St. Francis of Assisi was one who was believed to have been blessed with the spiritual delicacy necessary to apprehend this eternal motion.

Twentieth-century occultists, such as Robert Lewis, whose teachings were read and accepted by William Grant Still, readily attested to the notion that the "music of the spheres" was a reality. Theosophist Evelyn Benham Bull taught Still that sound was silence "at the highest rates of vibration," and that sound both propelled the heavenly bodies and emanated from that propulsion. The heavenly harmonies which were thus created were the principal source of musical inspiration for the masterful earthly composers (Evelyn Benham Bull, *Music Therapy: Its Future* [The Theosophical Society, 1964] 1). Moreover, Bull spoke of this "rich, celestial music" in terms of light and color. These harmonies, she declared, were "more brilliant than the flames," and they were couched in shimmering colors such as electric blue, vivid crimson, emerald green and delicate rose (Bull, *Parent's Bulletin*, Theosophical Order of Service XXV [Spring 1960] 1).

Other occult sources, too, convinced Still that music and color were so intimately related that harmonies could radiate colors which were visible to spiritual mediums. In the course of a musical gathering in the home of Mrs. Marjorie Lange, widow of conductor Arthur Lange, psychic Eva May Carroll related a message from Arthur which expressed joy over the fact that every bar of the music being played radiated spiritual colors. Still and his wife were present at this gathering.

Neither Still nor Eva May Carroll explained the mechanics of the music-color reciprocity, but the way lies open to scientific discourse. Perhaps the relationship between the two artistic elements can be dealt with by positing that vibrations instigate sympathetic vibrations of energy-sources in the surrounding atmosphere, and that the atmosphere therefore emanates colors. In this same manner, during the process of combustion, friction causes fire, after which burning substances give off a variety of colors such as red, orange and blue, depending on the material being burned. Researches have demonstrated that very low or very high frequency sounds can act upon certain types of materials to cause the emission of light from those substances.

The spiritualist connection between color and music is dynamic, in that both music and color are said to have the power to heal. The Greeks purportedly used colors to cure illness, as did the ancient Egyptians, who had "their healing temples of light and color" (James Sturzaker, *Sound and Color* [Division of Music, Theosophical Order of Service, Burbank, California] 3). Present-day professionals also recognize the physiological and emotional effects of color, painting the interiors of hospitals and police stations a soft blue or green to provide a calming influence, or decorating fast-food establishments such as McDonald's with reds, oranges and yellows to prevent customers from staying too long. Physiologically, colors have the proven ability to raise or lower heart and pulse rates. Indeed, physical reactions to colors are so marked that fashion consultants are now monitoring these reactions to determine what shades should be worn with which skin-types, and which hues contribute to emotional well-being and personal beauty (Karen Kelly, Color Demonstration for Amway Corporation, Mission Viejo, California [September 14, 1983]).

Just as hues can be found which are "proper" to a particular person's skin, so too, according to the occultists, can colors and harmonies be selected which are sympathetic to the particular keynotes of vibration in the atoms which make up each human being. When the individual is exposed to sympathetic vibration and light, his existent physiological energy is enhanced and he is able to deal with disease or illness. Patients who are so treated are said to feel the heat of such energy in a "warm, vital glow" (Bull, *Music Therapy*, 34).

Beyond this reported "glow," of course, there is little direct scientific evidence to link sound, light and substance in the way that Still associated them. But, without a doubt, there is a pregnant similarity between light and sound. Light is energy from moving sub-atomic electrons, and colors are varying frequencies of light. Sound, too, is energy, or electromagnetic radiation. Both sound and color are oscillating waves of atoms, and both of them have period, length, frequency and amplitude. Light-energy and substance are seen to be cohesive in experiments in which certain types of crystals will emit electricity and color when pressure is placed on them.

That there is a scientific explanation for Still's mystically comprehended linkages in the cosmos, is suggested by Grant Venerable. Dr. Venerable has written,

> It was my deepening understanding of pure chemistry which led me to the spiritual basis of matter and the universal structure which replicates itself at all levels of thingness in the universe--whether the structure is implicit in a galaxy, a solar system, a living cell, a human organism, or in inspired works of music, art or literature. All possess a common organic chemistry. I've felt it as I have gazed into the night sky over Sonoma Valley...and [as I've] experienced the structure of mathematical group theory in Psalm 119. ...And I have glimpsed it in what many respectfully (and others derisively) call the "occult."
>
>             (Letter to Judith Anne Still [January 15, 1983]).

In a subsequent clarification of his ideas on the subject, Venerable said,

Faith is the SUBSTANCE of things hoped for, the EVIDENCE of

things not seen (Hebrews 11:1). That concept of the early Christian writer Paul is really the underpinning of all science. ...That is, where there is substance, there is simultaneously evidence for that substance. Where there is evidence, there is a *substantial* basis for what is apprehended by the senses. Not just the physical senses, mind you, but all the sensory capacities available to the human organism, whether understood or not by modern scientists. ...Without this faith (substance < ---  > evidence), the chemist cannot practice chemistry. The physicist cannot perform physics. The engineer could not build bridges and expect them to hold up.

Sound and light are indeed related--simply. The fact of their *separate reality* is only apparent. Their separateness is but a consequence of our neural wiring, the internal circuitry in our bodies. Sound and light are phenomenal evidences for the *same* energetic, vibrational quality.

Both sound waves and light waves are the same substance--electro-magnetic radiation. Highly vibratory energy waves (visible light) are the highest energy manifestation which the human body can withstand without sustaining tissue damage. ...Lower energy vibrations (low-energy waves) cannot be acted upon by the body's optical system. That organ which is capable of apprehending low-frequency waves within a fairly wide range is the "ear" structure.
    (Letter to Judith Anne Still September 23, 1983).

Significantly, these words have come from a man who is known for championing the replacement of computer data/information/word processing language with a more ubiquitous system of computer communication not unlike musical notation. Venerable has called the current computer language the "Achilles heel" of technology ("The Taming of ...," 1).

    In some manner, then, sound (that is, rhythm, music) and light (that is, color) are familial members of the harmonic universe. Perhaps this matrix is elusive on a planetary level, but, in the natural world, the bond is more visible. Once in a while music can even be revealed as an operative factor in the lives of the most unlikely species. Consider, for example, the whale.

    At the whaling museum in Lahaina, on the island of Maui, Hawaii, there are recordings which demonstrate that humpback whales are composers of songs. These sea mammals give forth deep, booming song-like sounds which are probably an aspect of a breeding ritual. Although all of the humpbacks follow identical rules of composition, each individual whale sings a song peculiar only to himself. Yet, in spite of the fact that each whale has his own melody, all of the whales from a specific part of the ocean use similar themes quite unlike the themes employed by whales in other areas. Further, if one whale composes a passage which is well-liked by his fellows, the latter will copy it and develop it. In this manner, the song themes of one season or one year differ from those of subsequent seasons and years.

It is important to notice that the development of musical composition on the sub-human plane is an evolutionary one--a growth process in terms of related patterns--much like the growth process of organic plant and animal forms. The same development occurred where consonant music was concerned on the human level. David Patterson's discussion of dissonance points out that the music of humankind has grown from the seeds of tones into patterns of melody, then into harmony and counterpoint, according to the rhythmic laws of nature and of consonance. Patterson asserts, therefore, that, like the evolution of the earth and of man, the evolution of music should be rhythmic ("The Dilemma of Dissonance," *Music and Dance in California*, Jose Rodriguez, ed. [Bureau of Musical Research, Hollywood, California, 1940] 14, 20).

Probably it is the deep-structure-relation between nature and music that inspires writers so frequently to use "outdoor" images to describe musical compositions. Pieces are compared to clear, flowing water, or to the wind across bleak plains, or to lush green pastures. The text on the album jacket of a Disc Company recording uses plankton as a metaphor for folk music, saying that such music is a "great and ageless mass of plant and animal life suspended in and moving across the seven seas regardless of political boundaries." Moreover, traditions of folk music are "broad, deep, musical channels, leading naturally out of patterns of work and play" ("The Ethnic Series, Folkways of the World" record albums, Disc Company of America [New York, 1947]).

The relationship between music and universal patterns, whether it be real or imagined, is sufficiently rooted in man and in man's world that he cannot ignore it without becoming self-destructive. William Grant Still repeatedly said that unmusical music was destructive, for it was adverse to the laws of creative process (Letter to Professor F. J. Lehmann of Oberlin College [October 18, 1948]). He was aware that, in nature, there was a consistent, purposeful force of creation which always balanced the uncreative; in the rhythms of life, death and rebirth, or of winter and spring, winter was never allowed to take over completely.

Just as eternal winter was impossible in nature, so too were dissonant composers destined for failure when they refused to express harmonic mutability. As a music student put it in a letter to Still, the power of Still's music lay in the "delicate balance" between "wild rhythms" and "warm melody" which brings the listener "rebirth--warmth, love, compassion--along with death and tragedy... ." It was music that defied destruction, in spite of the fact that "we live in harsh, dissonant times" (Bradley Parker-Faye, Letter to William Grant Still [September 15, 1974]).

Probably what this student was saying was that composers cannot hope to interest or uplift or influence men unless they strike universal chords, chords which, in all strata of existence, are rhythmic and harmonious. Furthermore, because all forms of matter and all living creatures are somehow related by patterned sound, it is reasonable to assume that all can be brought into closer communication through the creative use of harmony. Music and rhythm are in all men even as they are in all things, thus music can touch all men in some measure. As Dr. Venerable explains it,

> Highly organized patterns [of sound] which reflect algebraic principles of unity, which the mind of man interprets and responds to out of both individual and racial experience, are ultimately recognized as MUSIC. People from all cultures recognize and respond to common universals in music though individual musical idioms may vary widely from culture to culture.
> 
> (Letter to Judith Anne Still [September 23, 1983]).

The capacity of music for world-wide appeal and for the promulgation of love and understanding in all peoples is implicit in the often-used maxim that music is the universal language.

Mitch Miller referred to this adage when he observed that he had conducted orchestras in France and Mexico without knowing Spanish or French (Mitch Miller, Interview on "Over Easy," KCET-PBS-TV, Los Angeles, October 23, 1980). James Francis Cooke repeated the phrase when he told how violent disagreements at the Pan-American Union Conference in Washington, DC were transformed into amicable debates by the inclusion of symphony concerts in the schedule of conference events ("Music the Humanizer," *The Etude* LXI [January 1943] 3). Assuredly both Miller and Cooke would agree with Dr. Howard Hanson's declaration that music can and should be an "uplifting emotional experience," bringing the listener "into rapport with other human beings in the search for brotherhood" (*Parent's Bulletin*, Theosophical Order of Service XXV [Spring 1960] 10).

William Grant Still also believed in the efficacy of brotherhood, and he, too, looked upon music as a means to bring it about (*William Grant Still and the Fusion of Cultures in American Music*, Dr. Robert Bartlett Haas, ed. [Los Angeles: Black Sparrow Press, 1972] 138-139). His summary assessment of his work, then, considering all of the complex musical relationships in human life and in the cosmos, was that music was the tangible manifestation of the glue that holds mankind and the universe together. It was the structure which supported, the fuel which fed, and the guiding wheel which directed his purposes. Indeed, when Dylan Thomas wrote of, "The force that through the green fuse drives the flower," he might well have been alluding to Still's concept of music.

## Music and the Fusion of Cultures:
## Ways to Work the Puzzle

At this point the question may be raised: If musical principles empower the cosmos, what is the place of the rest of the arts? Did William Grant Still's beliefs apply to all that is cultural and enriching? In the composer's mind, they did. If it was indeed true that there were universal vibrations which were basic to all life and to which all men responded feelingly, then it also stood to reason that those universal rhythms would bring about some discernible interweaving of any of the areas of life which involved the senses.

Tangible indications support the premise. More often than not, it is discovered that the fields of art, music, architecture, craftsmanship, literature, statesmanship and husbandry are intertwined. When historians earmarked artistic periods with the terms, "Classical," "Baroque," "Victorian," "Romantic," and so on, they were delineating times in history when men of genius painted, wrote, composed and designed buildings in such similar styles that the styles and periods could be labeled as one. One period was enough of an entity that it could be characterized by a phrase such as "simple dignity," another by "grandiose soaring," another by "restraint," and another by "impulsiveness." The cultural output in one period was readily identifiable as separate from that of another period.

Of course it might be argued that artists and thinkers and builders at a certain point in time are overly-prone to imitate the works of those among them who are highly respected. A legitimate argument, surely, when the number of contemporary composers is tallied who have unquestioningly followed the lead of Schoenberg, Stravinsky and Hindemith into the school of atonality, guided solely by transitory reputation rather than by artistic excellence. And yet, there are other windows through which the mingling of the arts can be viewed.

Note, for instance, the fact that men and women who are outstanding in the arts are often adept at more than one form of cultural expression. Many poets have also been musicians, and vice versa, since the sound relationships--the rhythms--in musical passages and in poetic verses are much the same. Certainly, in ancient Greece, poetry and music were one, as it was customary for literary men such as Homer and Anacreon to embody their tales in verses that were sung to the lyre. The term "lyric" itself originated with the Greek harp-like instrument.

Verna Arvey, pianist, writer, and wife to William Grant Still, conducted a brief study of literature and music in which she observed a definite connection. She listed a host of authors who were, secondarily, instrumentalists, including John Milton, originator of the epic poem, *Paradise Lost*, who performed on the organ and on the bass viol, and George Eliot, who was a music student in Coventry before she became an acclaimed English poet and novelist ("Famous Authors and their Love for Music," *Music and Dance* 50 [February 1960] 18-20).

Beyond the verisimilitudes in verbal sounds and instrumental sounds, there are also linkages between music, painting and the dance. Catherine Jackson illuminated the relationship when she told dancers, "Music is the symbol by which your dance motifs are understood by all peoples" ("Music is the Universal Language," *The American Dancer* 4 [November 1930] 15). Verna Arvey, again, when speaking of music and art, might well have been referring to music, art *and* the dance when she said that both music and art used "rhythm, balance, design, spirituality, thematic character, counterpoint, line and unity," and that they both "caused an emotional" reaction in an audience "Great Painters and the Art of Music," *The Etude* LVIII [November 1940] 727).

The like natures of harmony, patterned movement and the graphic arts are surely clear, given the artistic bent of many musicians and the musical inclinations of a number of painters. Gainsborough had a habit of painting while listening to music, while Rachmaninoff focused his attention on a picture or a poem to stir his compositional imagination. A creator of murals, Thomas Hart Benton was also a collector of American folk songs and a performer on the harmonica. The consummate artist, Leonardo da Vinci, was a composer, singer and lute player of such quality that his melodious songs brought him into favor with the Duke of Milan (Arvey, "Great Painters...," 727, 778).

Naturally one cannot mention da Vinci without remembering that he was equally at home with music and painting as he was with science, invention and military strategy. And there were other men, after da Vinci, who were associated with music as well as with science, statesmanship, oratory, or military strategy. Miles Standish was not only a soldier and a daring Mayflower colonist, but he was also a bugler. Warren J. Pershing, a General in the first World War, played the flute, as did football coach Knute Rockne. Actor Lionel Barrymore performed at the piano, composed orchestral scores, and completed etchings which were highly-regarded and exhibited (Martha Galt, *Know Your American Music* [Los Angeles: Galt, 1946] 61-71). William Grant Still was not just a composer of music--he was, in addition, a carpenter, a gardener, a writer and a lecturer.

A considerable number of Presidents of the United States have prided themselves upon being music-lovers and musicians, including Richard Nixon, Harry Truman, Woodrow Wilson, Thomas Jefferson and George Washington. Washington played the flute and violin, and was lauded for being a most "elegant" dancer of the minuet. Jefferson was as much a musician as he was an educator and politician, having lived up to his identification as "a gentleman who could calculate an eclipse, survey an estate, tie an artery, plan an edifice, dance a minuet and play the violin" (Allen Roberts and Juliet Bridgman, "America's Musical Presidents," *Music Journal* XXXII [April 1974] 16-17, 36) .The avid fan of Chopin and of Mozart, Harry Truman was also "an accomplished amateur pianist..." (Anthony Leviero, "Harry Truman , Musician and Music Lover," *The New York Times* [June 18, 1950] 18).

A second lover of Mozart who was a leader in the scientific community was Albert Einstein. Einstein was one among several pre-eminent scientific men who adored music. Another was Benjamin Franklin, whose endeavors paralleled those of da Vinci in terms of scope and variety. He was "America's first musicologist, first printer of music, first inventor of a musical instrument, first publisher of music and first critic" (Edward J. Smith, "New Light on Benjamin Franklin as a Musician," *Musical Digest* 29 [November 1947] 10). His experiments with electricity led him to speak, prophetically, of the electronic age; his musical studies taught him to play the violin, harp and guitar, and to write songs. The now-obsolete instrument of which he was the inventor, the "armonica," was constructed with glass bowls of "graduated sizes" which produced an ethereal sound, seeming "to emerge from infinite space and to fade away into endlessness" (Smith, 10).

It is noteworthy that scientists and inventors like Franklin and da Vinci were also apt to be composers of music, for both composers and scientists probe the harmony of natural law and causality, the universal matrix in which the harmony of sound and color are basic operatives. When James McNeill Whistler spoke of music as "the poetry of sound," and of painting as "the poetry of sight" (Arvey, "Great Painters," 727), he might well have gone on to allude to music and to art as the poetry of science. Science and the arts are so closely tied together that they do appear to be governed by the identical principles of energy and matter--the same structured rules--that govern life's processes. Such are the principles which also directed the life and work of William Grant Still. In fact, Still's work itself has been identified as a "fusion of cultures," an identification of which he heartily approved (*William Grant Still and the Fusion of Cultures...*, Haas, ed., 203 pp.).

## The Structure of Music: Following the Rules

Because the scientific principles which governed the universe and related the arts to one another were highly structured, it was only natural for Still to believe that artistic principles should also have form and organization. In order for music and art to be worthwhile aspects of creation, they must have been developed with careful regard for the harmonic structure of the universal vibrations which underlay the universe. As Still announced in a letter to Professor F. J. Lehmann of Oberlin College, the basic "laws governing harmonic progression in music are as immutable as the laws of Nature" [October 18, 1948].

In spite of the contentions of the Nihilists and the Phenomenologists, the believers in artistic chaos, structure and form are the white-hot core of all human progress and enlightenment, as well as of material reality. Everything has an order and an energetic place in an order. For instance, the sequence of the letters in the alphabet when words are being spelled is of greater importance than the letters themselves (Haas, ed., 112). It is the order which provides the power to communicate. It is the order of the sounds which gives names the mystical essence so sacred to numerologists and to Jewish philosophy.

Proportion and design, then, are fundamental to art. As G.E. Kidder Smith puts it, "Creative genius equals excitement plus order" (Program on architecture, KCET-PBS-TV, Los Angeles [August 2, 1978]). Japanese artisans understand the value of this precept, especially in the art of bell-making. The makers of bells in Japan believe that the sound of a bell is the voice of Buddha, and therefore they have pursued a meticulous investigation of the method for creating the finest bell tones possible. The pursuit has revealed that it is a beautiful shape which makes a beautiful sound--thus, the perfection of sound is related to the perfection of form in a direct manner. In a sense, sound must have form and form is sound.

William Grant Still said much the same thing in his article called, "The Structure of Music" (*The Etude* 68 [March 1950] 17, 61). Form, Still asserted, was "the most difficult of all elements that go into composing." It was much harder to put things in order, the composer explained, than to toss them in haphazardly. "I have made it a habit to sit down and plan out the form of a new work right after getting the thematic material," then to add variations, episodes and transitions.

Reiterating the idea that form and sound were one, Still went on to suggest that the theme of a piece of music "dictates its own treatment and even its own form. Form follows function, say the architects. That is as true of music as it is of the other arts." Still then expressed regret over the tendency of his contemporaries to ignore the laws of harmony and to use "disjointed counterpoint" and "sickly, miasmatic dissonances." He deplored the fact that atonal composers did not develop themes, or that they began with themes that were not repeated during a composition; he was saddened by the rejection of melody and consonance, or the choice of random groups of tones or harmonic effects to reflect "the troubled world in which we live" ("The Structure of...").

Ultimately Still did not insist that composers return to the tonic and dominant harmonies of the classicists, nor did he insist that themes recur exactly throughout a composition. He simply advised that, if dissonances were used, they should be resolved, and that there should be dominant themes which were repeated in varying ways throughout a piece of music.

Still was not the only one to have made a case for symmetry and relationship, theme and development, in music. Daniel

Gregory Mason made his own plea in 1947, when he said, "a work of art demands by nature a connective tissue alien to Schoenberg's methods" ("Atonality on Trial," *Musical Digest* 29 [October 1947] 11, 15). Mason's use of the word "demands" indicates a sense of urgency in the matter of composition. And yet, the possible negative consequences of ignoring form in composing or painting have been largely disregarded by composers in this century.

Perhaps the structural imperative is less apparent in music, painting or sculpture than it is in architecture, manufacturing, or in similar fields of creation. Yet, if an atonal composer were to apply his random theories to the building of a bridge across a river, the result would be a mass of girders and cables at the bottom of the water, rather than over the channel. No one would dare to fly an airplane which was put together in a cacophonous manner, nor would a critically ill patient be anxious to lie under the knife of a surgeon who believed that his work should reflect the chaos of the "troubled world."

Fortunately the atonalists do not build bridges or heal the sick, nor are they capable of doing so. However, their efforts to disrupt the formative nature of music may have been as destructive in an intellectual way as the failures of the bridge-builders. Music, after all, is capable of architectural beauty and design on a spiritual plane, while great music is probably the highest level to which form can aspire. As the spiritualists explain it,

> All art constantly aspires towards music. It is the art of music which most completely realizes this artistic ideal, this perfect identification of form and matter. In its consummate moments the end is not distinct from the means, the form from the matter, the subject from the expression. ...Music, then, and not poetry, as is so often supposed, is the true type or measure of consummate Art (C. Jinarajadasa, *Parent's Bulletin*, Theosophical Order of Service XXV [Spring 1960] 2).

If music is, thus, the loftiest point of creation, the highest ideal of beauty, one might almost think of it as a spiritual quality which it is a profanation to turn from its purpose. Without doubt, William Grant Still thought of it in these reverent terms. It was, he said, "food for the soul," "the handmaiden of religion," and "spiritual consciousness." Becoming a composer, in his opinion, required the same dedication that was required to become a clergyman (Letter to Carl Murphy, President of the Afro-American Newspapers [November 7, 1956]; also, Speech for the St. Paul Lutheran Church Missionary Society, Los Angeles [September 27, 1964]).

Still's favorite occult writers continually emphasized the role of melody in the cosmos. Both man and universe, said Evelyn Bull, were created according to musical or harmonious laws; because all of matter is a "rhythmical distribution of energy," it follows that "the essence of being and of ourselves is sound and music" (*Music Therapy*, 2, 6, 8). In this way, it might be claimed that mankind is "music externalized," having literally become an "instrument made of intricately organized elements" (*Music Therapy*). In addition, each human "instrument" is linked to every other human being, because all levels of matter and of energy are interrelated under the dominant universal harmony. This universal harmony might be entitled God, as it was by Still, or Divine Wisdom, but whatever it is called, it is the Source of energy and vibration in the cosmos.

According to Bull and to Still, man cannot progress or evolve if he denies the structured, well-formed aspects of his nature. He must maintain form and equilibrium in himself and in all facets of his existence, including his music. In particular, his music should become motion plus "mental organization and emotional power" (*Music Therapy*, 1). It must have tonal form above all. The greatest music--that which expresses the infinite harmonies of the Source--is music which inculcates design and proportion as well as innovation and brilliance.

If man becomes involved with music which has no equilibrium, his own mental balance can be impaired. If the keynotes of human understanding and harmony remain unsounded, there is no renewed sense of an emotional tie with other beings across the globe, there is no union with the Divine Force. The apprehension of universal chaos and evil is enhanced, with resultant despair and disorientation. Such are the dangers of atonal music. If form does indeed follow function, in continual dissonance there is no function, and in the scheme of mutable life, that which is functionless is destined for annihilation. Nothing can exist which does not serve a purpose.

For composer Still, nothing of worth did exist without a purpose, and more, without a spiritual purpose. Music was "the channel through which God speaks directly to us" (Speech for the St. Paul Lutheran Church...), in other words, the "channel for the God-source to act upon the personality, synchronizing thinking, feeling and action" (*Music Therapy*, 3). Great music could carry humanity to the highest rung of attainment.

## Dissonance in Music: Giving the Wrong Answers

Regardless of his personal attitudes toward composition, Still realized that the majority of his contemporaries considered the arts to be a means of ego-gratification, not a means to improve human life. It was the lack of religious conscience in ultra-modern composers that most grieved the composer. Meanwhile, the atonalists prided themselves on their novelty, discounting Still's tonal works as being "lightweight and insipid" (*Time*, [May 28, 1965]). They reasoned that the chaos and confusion in their music was the reflected chaos, horror and suffering of post-War life; they felt that they were helping modern man to face the reality of his discordant world.

Still stood firm. Reality, he said, was spiritual as well as material, and perhaps more spiritual than material. Handicapped people well knew that it was possible to take away the eyesight, speech, limbs, pelvis, physical attractiveness and a good number of the organs of a human being, and to find that an essentially lovely personality remained. In spite of the gross, the grotesque and the cruel in life, much simplicity, gentleness and goodness endured.

For Still the function of music and art was to reveal the goodness of life, inwardly and outwardly, to every individual. A student of Far Eastern religions who attended theosophical meetings with Still in the 1930's, Nola McGarry, expressed the beneficial function in this way. She said, the purpose of art or music is to "help you to pick up on your inner feelings stirred up by the art," and thus to become "more sensitive toward yourself and others." The power of books and music, she went on, "lies in how well it affects the inner person, arousing feelings or perhaps even affecting a transformation of thought or feeling" (Letter to Judith Anne Still [December 12, 1982]).

Stated in other terms, the vibrations of great music stir the vibrations of the inner self to a form of attunement. As a listener subconsciously becomes used to the higher frequencies, his moods, mental attitudes and even his body chemistry can be altered. If enough people are affected, whole nations can change and grow, as Plato and Aristotle posited when speaking of the power of music. If enough people are affected, the global populace can be led to sway in time with the eternal rhythms of the universe.

On the other hand, if loud or disintegrative music is encouraged, if music comprises disorganized vibrations or excessive vibration, then a nation of irresponsible, disobedient and irreverent citizens is nurtured. Cacophonous serious music, and blaring acid or punk rock, are revelatory of the destructive nature of mankind, and, as such, have the power to destroy. Confused, dark music inspires confused dark thoughts and feelings, and may very well lead to suicidal impulses where emotional instability is present.

Even so, many members of the youth culture assert that they sincerely enjoy extreme musical forms, and that such music sounds the keynotes of their personalities. If they are telling the truth, their enjoyment probably stems from the fact that the malleable natures of youngsters, when they lack musical background, are readily molded by peer groups and media bombardment. They want to assert an identity that is unique from, and more forceful than, the adult identity. Once the character is shaped, it tends to perpetuate itself, accepting only those forms of art to which it has become addicted. Inimical emotions are developed to the point where young persons will actively seek entertainment which appeals to a sense of sensuality, depression or violence.

Persons who are trained to seek ugliness for its own sake often look down upon those who do not share their predilections. They are convinced that melodic, pleasing harmonies are weak, faulty and immature. As a prominent music publisher wrote to Still on August 23, 1956 (asking that his name not be made known), "The ultra-modern art promoters have the audacity to tell me that my ears have not been trained to become accustomed to this incredibly disagreeable stuff. I tell them that if I heard enough of these ugly sounds, I would acquire ears eight inches tall and covered with hair." In truth they are "disoriented minds wandering in a world of cerebral breakdowns," and engaged in a "wholesale artistic swindle" of the cultured public.

Fortunately the cultured public has begun to repudiate the "swindlers." Public-supported symphonies lean more and more toward the classical Masters as they discover that audiences will not come to hear dissonance. Describing ultra-modern serial music as "cereal music," critics Miles Kastendieck and Winthrop Sargeant have indicated that it has "the texture, contour, emotional impact and power over the human spirit of oatmeal" (*The New Yorker* [December 14, 1965]). Mr. Sokolsky of the *Herald-Express*, in comparing Beethoven to Aaron Copland, Stravinsky and Bernstein, reveals that he would rather be "transported to the infinite" with Beethoven, than listen to "a million GIs rubbing dungarees on washboards" (*Los Angeles Herald Express* [August 2, 1947]). William Grant Still was vigorously applauded when he spoke out against the atonalist who praised Roy Harris' duo-choral work, not knowing that the two choruses during its performance had been eight measures apart ("Some Thoughts on 'Contemporary' Music," Speech for the Southern California Music Teacher's Association Banquet, Williamsburg Inn [June 13, 1967]). The problem with the avant-gardists, one critic notes, is that they compose "from the head and not the heart" (Uncle Dudley, "The Poet Speaks," *Boston Sunday Globe* [July 29, 1956]). While they look askance at Neoclassicism ("the sterile scoff at fertility"), they forget that novelty is not originality. They manipulate tonal elements through esoteric scientific processes, they draw diagrams in the manner of Arnold Schoenberg, they juggle keys mathematically, and yet, "the magic is lost as soon as the tricks are discovered" (David Patterson,

"Dilemma of Dissonance," 17).

The real magic of music, according to Still, is in using the infinitely various possibilities readily available in the tonal system, without repudiating tone altogether. Each tone, after all, consists of itself and a rich series of related tones. And, as Mason points out, "What need is there of passing beyond...the tributaries of chromatics, modality, the whole-tone scale...shaped by the inexhaustible complexities and simplicities of rhythm?" (Daniel Mason, "Atonality on Trial," 15).

The complexities in simplicity are the more admirable when it is realized that even a single note has expansive potential. The first of the American music critics, Benjamin Franklin, was also the first to observe that some of the barest melodies become more complex because each note continues to vibrate in the auditory nerves of the listener long after the note ceases to sound. This is the same vibration that causes a lighted object such as a flame to be "seen" by the visual nerves for twenty or thirty seconds after the flame is extinguished. The phenomenon can be witnessed by the casual observer:

> Sitting in a room, look earnestly at the middle of a window, a little while the day is bright, and then shut your eyes; the figure of the window will still remain in the eye, and so distinct that you may count the panes.
>
> *(The Etude* LV [May 1937] 296).

Outside of the vibrations of single notes, there are triads, chords, keys and elements both dissonant and consonant. William Grant Still lectured throughout the country at the height of the avant-garde era in order to encourage other composers to "use all the means of musical expression that are available," not just the dissonant substances. Strident phrases are sometimes useful "to express some particular mood or subject," perhaps a "Storm at Sea" or a "Cyclone," as Meredith Willson suggested (Speech for the MTA Banquet [June 13, 1967]), but beyond that, they cause a composition to lose its identity. A composer should "feel free to...express himself in a consonant idiom, because there is beauty in consonance yet." Life has pleasure as well as pain, and to believe that the ultra-modern idiom is the only legitimate one is tantamount to "having a diet of just one particular sort of food" (R. Donald Brown, *An Interview with William Grant Still*, 19).

It goes without saying that the employment of all of the ingredients of music requires inspiration, the inspired process of drawing on spiritual energies to galvanize the mind into creative activity. The great composer draws on the rhythms of universal life to compose. He works with mankind's innate instinct for rhythm, and understands the mystical and basic aspects of the triad form, or three consonant sounds grouped together. As Mason describes them, triads are like suns in a galaxy, and around them revolve related chords and keys, and "intervals dissonant and active leading into others consonant and fit to rest in" (Daniel Mason, 11). Immutably fine composers do not disdain triads, nor do they fail to express fundamental human emotions and positive ideals; their artistry becomes, therefore, Matthew Arnold's "great thoughts, greatly expressed" (Lillian Baldwin, Letter to William Grant Still [August 10, 1956]).

William Grant Still was said to have such great thoughts because he recognized the primary need of human beings for consonant rhythms. In the words of George Westerman, "Great as might have been Composer Still's knowledge of music his work would never have received the wide acclaim that it has were it not for its melodic content which, in the final analysis, is the sine qua non of all music that endures" ("The Passing Review," *Isthmian Negro Youth Congress Bulletin* [December 1943]). And, finally, at some point in the future, it will be this endurance that settles the question of consonance as opposed to dissonance.

## Music and Physical Effect: Puzzler-Power

If dissonance can be a source of mental disorientation and sickness, then it must be that tuneful music can lead to psychological control and good health. Indeed, a study completed in 1949 determined that musicians live longer and are healthier than the rest of the population (Waldemar Schweisheimer, M.D., "Do Musicians Live Longer Than Others?" *Etude* LXVII [January 1949] 24, 54). But this study was only a small part of the collected evidence that music can be therapeutic.

So-called primitive cultures, with their musical medicine men, have never relied on scientific evidence to believe that rhythm and melody can heal (Roma Sachs Freedman, "Music from a Medicine Man," *Music Journal* XXVII [November 1969] 28). The American Indians have used music for healing as well as for exorcism and rainmaking; the Jivaros in particular adapted specific songs to the cure of specific illnesses (James Sturzaker, *Sound and Color*, 3). The members of many American Indian tribes have traditionally had a quiet respect for the power of sound and sensibility, a respect which came in part from their acute senses of sight and sound.

Charles Troyer, the composer who lived with the Zuni Indians while researching native music, observed that the Zunis could see the stars in the heavens at high noon and hear noises that were inaudible to him, even though he had a practiced ear. In writing about the work of Troyer, James Francis Cooke, musician and editor, concluded that people who live close to nature have a certain delicacy of sense because they avoid the physical and emotional stress of intemperate, civilized living (Dr. James Francis Cooke, "Broken Strings," *The Etude* LIII [January 1935] 3). In other words, there may be a link between health and an ear for sound.

In more advanced cultures, sound and rhythm are also put to the task of establishing control over the subconscious mind, and over the muscular responses of animals. Like the ancient Greeks and Egyptians, Hindu fakirs play haunting tunes to exert power over snakes and to gain rulership of their own involuntary bodily functions (George W. Ainlay, "The Place of Music in Military Hospitals," *The Etude* LXIII [August 1945] 433).

Happily, however, it is not necessary to travel as far as East India to witness the effects of rhythm on the body. In western cultures, the influential quality of music has been apparent in the most mundane daily labors. During World War I, when global commands kindled an interest in increasing human productivity, it was discovered that employees in business worked faster when listening to music on phonograph records ("What They Read Twenty Years Ago," *Musical America* LVI [November 10, 1936]

17). By the time that World War II was heavy in the air, industrialists and government officials were not satisfied with knowing whether music increased production--they also wanted to know how much. Both human and animal laborers were tested, until it was determined that 10% to 11% more work resulted when participants in the study listened to harmonious music. In addition, harmony "reduces the number of rejects, cuts down labor turnover and definitely improves personnel relations" (Paul W. Kearney, "Speed Up With Music," *Coronet* 13 [November 1942] 131).

A further revelation during the two wars was that music not only made people work faster, but it also "made them less fearful and less tense. When they were ill or injured, it brought them joy and comfort, and seemed to promote healing" (Ainlay, "The Place of Music...," 433, 468, 480). It was thus that military bands gained new respect as a means to boost morale, and instrumentalists like Jascha Heifetz were called upon to soothe wounded soldiers in hospital wards. When the subject of music as therapy emerged as a serious topic, it was readily agreed that music was capable of arousing listeners, of putting them to sleep, of inspiring courage, of alleviating worry, and, in crisis situations, of forestalling panic (Kearney, 131-134; Dr. James Francis Cooke, "Forward March with Music!" *The Etude* LX [March 1942] 149). It was well-known that music could stimulate every sort of human emotion, including negative emotions. In Budapest, the song, "Gloomy Sunday," was so depressing that it was blamed for causing many suicides whenever it was played. Apparently the suicide reports were sufficiently creditable to warrant a government ban on the performance of the tune (Dr. James Francis Cooke, "Superstitions in Music," *The Etude* LV [January 1937] 5-6).

Detractors remarked that music which leads individuals to suicide does so because those individuals are already prone to emotional despair, and not because songs can transform the wills of healthy persons. And yet, the influence of sound upon mind and body cannot be underestimated. That there is a connection between harmony and health has been established by investigations apart from those in wartime.

It was in the latter half of the eighteenth century that Andre

Erneste Modeste Gretry (1741-1813), himself a musician, began to study the physical reactions of persons who were listening to music. His recorded experiments, though amateurish, indicated that music could and did stimulate heart action as well as affect the circulation of the blood, in the same way that colors affected blood pressure (Florence Cooles Byrens, "Psychology of Music," *Music and Dance in California*, José Rodriguez, ed. [California: Bureau of Musical Research, 1940] 39).

Gretry's rather unscientific probings were followed by the more clinical procedures of Dr. Tarchanoff in 1888, and Dr. Warthin in 1894, two men who revealed that it is not just the heart which is affected by harmony--melodious sounds also stimulate the respiration and the responses of all of the muscles in the body. In sum, music alters heartbeat, pulse, blood pressure, breathing, and muscle tension, and extremely rhythmic music can actively coordinate muscle action (Gustav V. Gumpert, "'Musical Therapy'--Science or Quackery?" *Musical Digest* 29 [November 1947] 20-21, 33).

It was clear, therefore, that music could relieve tension, anxiety and worry. But what was the connection with good health? The relationship was exposed when Dr. George W. Crile found that fear and frustration acted directly upon the body, debilitating the physical condition of both animals and people (Dr. James Francis Cooke, "Music's Part in Fighting Fear," *The Etude* LV [May 1937] 291). Thus, if tension was a source of ill health and music alleviated tension, then music also worked to alleviate illness. That this therapeutic benefit existed was affirmed by such a man of medicine as Dr. Charles H. Mayo of the Mayo Clinic; Mayo credited his organ music for being an "invaluable" aid to easing his own personal frustrations and worries ("Music's Part...," 292).

Yet Mayo and Crile were not the only medical or scientific personages who delved into "musical psychology." Studies from World War II to the present have grappled with the association of harmony and health in various ways. At the University of Iowa Psychological Laboratories, information has been compiled on the physics of sound, and on the nature and constancy of responses to compositions of differing types (Florence Cooles Byrens, 38). In other parts of the country, medical researchers have determined that music can awaken comatose patients (J. D. Taylor, "Radio 1: An Unexpected Response," *The Lancet* No. 7729 [1971] 881), and that, when a certain part of the brain is electrically probed, the patient will hear music.

More impressive than these experiments is the test, now routinely performed by school children, in which one group of plants is treated to fine, harmonic music, while another group is subjected to dissonance, hard rock, or silence. The result is that the serenely serenaded plants grow larger and more lush than the others (William Grant Still's grandchildren successfully performed this experiment while in elementary school). In fact, a man once demonstrated on national news that he had grown a four-and-a-half pound tomato by serenading it, and, William Grant Still was able to grow vegetables in his yard that were several times normal size, possibly because his music room window opened onto his garden.

Assuredly, if plants are larger and healthier under the influence of rhythm and melody, then the evidence should point strongly to music equaling health for human beings. And it does. Investigations disclose that music not only promotes health, but it also aids healing where sickness is present, especially in cases of psychological disorder.

Two ladies who were forceful champions of music as therapy were Harriet Ayer Seymour and Evelyn Benham Bull. Miss Seymour, who felt that her musical entertainment of injured soldiers in wartime was effective in their recovery, established the National Foundation for Music Therapy. At the same time she served on the faculty of the Damrosch School, or the Institute of Musical Art (Juilliard), in which capacity she brought instrumental performances into more than one-thousand hospital wards. Miss Seymour's work on the East Coast was simulated in Southern California by Evelyn Bull, whose writings in occult philosophy have already been quoted. During the years that she played the piano for the afflicted, Bull filled out detailed reports on the affect of specific compositions on specific patients. She noted, for example, that repetitive music was singularly useful in curing insomnia, and that a patient with a thyroid condition felt well enough to avoid her shots after listening to sequential presentations of Chopin, Grieg and Grainger (Bull, *Parent's Bulletin*, 30; *Music Therapy*, 20, 30). Similar musical activity at Bellevue Hospital, New York, at County General Hospital in Los Angeles, California, at Indiana State Prison, at the Spastic's Home in Owensboro, Kentucky, at Phipps Psychiatric Clinic of Johns Hopkins Hospital, Baltimore, and at Michigan's Wayne County Hospital, has produced corresponding results.

It has been established that music can relax persons under the needle, particularly orthopedic patients, dental patients and blood donors. Violin performances have been effective in calming hysterical mental patients, and "sing-along" therapy has assisted psychiatrists in diagnosing personality problems ("Music Provides Insight into Minds of Disturbed," *Los Angeles Times* [September 15, 1963] C-7). Group music sessions help participants to adjust to life with other people and to work productively in society (Henry R. Rollin, "Music in a Mental Hospital," *Music Journal* XXVII [November 1969] 23; Louis John Bean, "Music at Indiana State Prison," *Music Journal* XXVII [November 1969] 3; M. Priestley, *Music Therapy in Action* [London: 1976]). Among youngsters, handicapped children of all sorts have responded to melody, including cerebral-palsy-afflicted youths, for "music often provides the only channel through which an otherwise unresponsive child can be reached" (Donna Worthington, "Therapy with Cerebral Palsied Children," *Music Journal* XXVII [November 1969] 19). Rhythmic tunes have served "to end the temper tantrums of children" (Bull, *Parent's Bulletin*, 31; *Music Therapy, Tension and Relaxation: A Symposium* [London, 1964]), and music instruction of rebellious young people has decreased juvenile delinquency (Gregorio Surif, "Terapéutica Musical para la Delincuencia Juvenil," *Armonía* II [May 25, 1961] 19). Hyperkinesis in young ones has been completely eliminated by the introduction of piano lessons into treatment (Barbara Wood, "Diagnosis? Hyperkinesis, Prescription? Music!" *Music Journal* XXVII [November 1969] 29). With young and old, both in and out of prisons and hospitals, music has offered a positive release for the emotions (*Los Angeles Times* [September 15, 1963]), and a guide for constructive thinking (Trafford William Argus, "How Music Helped Me to Avoid the Asylum," *The Etude* LIX [January

1941] 17).

The question might be asked, of course, how is music capable of encouraging positive thoughts and feelings? The relationship between sound and feeling is a little clarified when it is noticed that animals "produce sounds when emotionally wrought up" (Dr. Max Schoen, "Doctoring with Music," *The Etude* LX [March 1942] 202). Hence, sound is feeling audibly expressed. And, since music is organized sound, and is associated with feeling, it is also capable of organizing feelings. Schoen, in fact, suggests that "Music is the art of feeling" ("Doctoring...," 166). Furthermore, Dr. Ira M. Altschuler, a Detroit-based psychiatrist, indicates that music does not have to be digested by the mind to be understood. It acts "directly on the thalamus gland," he says, meaning that it tunes in directly on the feelings and emotions, bypassing the brain altogether (Kearney, "Speed up...," 133).

If music exerts such a powerful force on the non-intellectual self, and on the physical body, why then is it not employed in every case of bodily illness or mental instability? The answer lies in the cliché that each person marches to a different drum; it is difficult to know what pieces of music will be beneficial to which individuals, for responses to any forms of art are frequently subjective and unique. Moreover, within the range of a single person's likes and dislikes, there will also be compositions that appeal to him only at certain places and times. Someone who enjoys Sousa marches will not be pleased to hear them while he is calculating his income taxes; sleepy department store employees will probably lapse into semi-coma under the influence of a slow movement by Mendelssohn. When people are younger they will want more rhythm in their music than they will when they become older (George W. Ainlay, "The Place of Music. ..," 468).

Differing times and places have their peculiar vibrations, as do diverse peoples, families and individuals. Music which has a quality of vibration which is unsympathetic to that of a particular individual will not aid that individual. For some, hillbilly ballads will bring the utmost joy and comfort; if such ballads are played while these people are ill or depressed, they will experience cardio-vascular stimulation. But if listeners to the folk concert do not enjoy hillbilly tunes, the result can be nervousness, irritability and the planted seeds of neurosis. For handicapped children whose vibrations and rhythmic abilities are impaired, a nursery melody may be more helpful than a Bach fugue. The varying needs of patients suggest that group therapy using musical performances may not be as beneficial as individual therapy (Gustav V. Gumpert, "'Musical Therapy' ...," 20-21,33).

On the other hand, there are some indications that a common thread runs through the enjoyment of music worldwide. The applicability of music as a universal language has already been noted. Also, some case studies of responses to music have revealed that similar thoughts and emotions are evoked in almost all hearers by certain types of music. Soft melodic folk songs are most likely to call up feelings of warmth, security and mother-love, unless of course those songs are associated in the listeners' minds with ugly experiences (Ainlay, "The Place of Music...," 433). As a general rule, chords stimulate action and passion, while single notes lead to quiet and contemplation (Bull, *Parent's Bulletin*, 25). If patients are monitored for responses during music therapy, treatments may be geared toward identified reactions.

All individual differences aside, there is a solid center of character and feeling in some compositions that can be translated into emotional response by the majority of people. It is owing to this principle of evocative transmission that the ideas and emotions of a race of people, or a culture, or a nation, can be passed down to succeeding generations by means of music. It is further owing to this principle that music tends to transmit or evoke the personalities--the energy and color--of those who created it (Bull, *Parent's Bulletin*, 24). As a member of the audience remarked to William Grant Still's daughter after a festival of the composer's music,

> "Having heard his music, I know that your father must have been a loving and a gentle man" (Judith Anne Still, "Turning Pages," *The Sounding Board*, Marina-Westchester Symphony Society Newsletter [April 1982] 4).

If it is possible, therefore, for music to communicate the personality of the composer, and of the composer's race, culture and nation, then it is also possible for harmonies to transmit healthy emotions and a sense of stability. If it is possible for music to evoke mental health, it may also be possible for it to promote physical health. William Grant Still was convinced of this evocative power of music, and he was supported in his belief by collected research and by his concept of music as the motivating force of the cosmos.

## Music and Infinite Power: The Puzzle Assembled

While it is clear that the emotional force of music has an affect on those who need mental support, it is less clear that it can reverse the inroads of non-psychosomatic disease. Even so, there is a structure of therapeutic action in harmony that has physical consequences, and that structure owes its power to the structural harmony of the universe.

In William Grant Still's scheme of things, the universe was created by sound, or vibration--"the Word was God"--and this cosmic rhythm continually sustains and rehabilitates all aspects of reality. It cannot be denied that the universe operates according to laws which are musical in nature, laws of energy and rhythm, laws of proportion and ratio. As Bull explains it, all of creation forms "a hierarchy of sound adjusted to the vibratory needs of each living thing." In other words, there is a single, eternal tone which constitutes all things, and each individual person has his own minuscule part of that vibration, both contributing to it and modifying it (Bull, *Music Therapy*, 11, 13, 38).

On the human level, each living thing is an instrument in a pervasive, cosmic orchestra. Each human is a universe in microcosm, made up of vibrations and overtones which are assembled in the same mathematically rhythmical and hierarchical manner as the cosmos. There is a superior vibration for the soul, or ego, and a subordinate one for the personality, or outer self. The thoughts, feelings, actions, individual habits and personal characteristics of the individual are components of a tonal, rhythmic pattern or spectrum. These parts vibrate "clockwise in mathematical ratios," to the whole "chord which expresses the soul" (Bull, *Music Therapy*, 5,8). Each person vibrates at a different level of frequency and has his own personal vibratory wave length (James Sturzaker, *Sound and Color*, 5).

Regardless of the total vibration which expresses the soul, there are possibilities for tonal expansion within the personality. The component parts of the outer self range from low to high in a spectrum of tones, and include a wider range of tones than the range to which that person actually responds. Highly developed persons have all of their component parts unified at the upper end of the spectrum, moving toward Divine harmonies. In beings of limited development, illness or lack of spiritual awareness blocks off the higher tones (Bull, *Music Therapy*, 29). Music can remove this blockage and aid progression in the direction of the upper ranges of the spectrum.

Ultimately the purpose of human life is to advance toward spiritual maturity, and music can motivate this maturity. When growth is fostered, the spiritual tone of an individual is developed in "rhythmically patterned melody, chordally expressed" (Bull, *Parent's Bulletin*, 35). When the person reaches spiritual perfection he embodies a "single note of indicated development" which harmonizes with the single tone of the cosmos. The cultivation of good music makes the individual sensitive and responsive to the spiritual world by awakening feelings of harmony and a subtle kinship with fellow humans everywhere (Bull, *Parent's Bulletin*, 34-35).

Music is capable of advancing spiritual perfection because it is vibration, and vibration has the ability to be transmitted. One vibration can augment another, or overpower another. Thus, when sound reverberates, the essentially vibratory energies of human beings respond to the tone by vibrating in sympathy. Too much reverberation is dangerous; it is commonly accepted that high levels of noise destroy the nervous system and eventually cause death. But sound that is melody and not noise can impose a positive vibration on the mind, emotions and body, and therefore change mood or body chemistry (Bull, *Parent's Bulletin*, 25; *Music Therapy*, 6, 13). Energy is focused, perceptions are structured, feelings are trained; finally, rhythm is clarified, altered, synchronized and tuned, as an instrument is tuned (E. R. Clay, *The Alternative: A Study in Psychology* [London: 1882]

167).

If it is difficult to believe that music can have this elemental effect, it might be worthwhile to consider the effective transmission of rhythm in other areas purely physical. It is known that women who live together in families, dormitories, prisons and other female complexes, tend to adapt themselves to the menstrual cycle of one central female in the group. That particular woman's menstrual vibration is so strong that it causes the rhythms of others to gravitate toward it, and, after a time, to vibrate in sympathy. Less tangible evidences of sympathetic vibration occur in cases where, for example, a pet dog chooses one person in a family as its master or "favorite" (William Cooper and nephews, *Dog Owner's Digest* [Chicago, Illinois] 4), or where deer and snakes draw near to the musical "charmers" of East India.

Where physical health is concerned, the issue is one of adjusting the ratios of vibration between the mental, emotional and physical parts of the self. Sickness disrupts the rhythm, as when a cancer cell operates according to a deviant frequency and runs amuck in terms of growth. Such deviations from the correct ratio of parts in the tonal pattern of a person "causes a shifting of inner emphasis" (Bull, *Music Therapy*, 8) .This shift can be treated by music, for music helps to reintegrate the self through sympathetic vibration.

The fact that some people do not respond to music that is considered spiritual or mature, is explained, again, by noting that individuals tend to like music which has a tonal pattern and keynote of vibration most like their own. When a musical selection matches their tonal value, they achieve a sense of power and invigoration. When a musical selection is in opposition to their tonal make-up, they become agitated and frustrated.

In many cases, however, a dislike for good music is the result of an overemphasis upon a limited number of the tones in the personal scale, and especially upon the discordant or atonal portion of the spectrum. Where individuals do have a wider spectrum within themselves, they can be assisted to expand their sensitivity to higher vibrations by being consistently exposed to broader ranges of rhythm and cleaner musical structures. Spiritually, emotionally or physically handicapped persons who respond only to simple or disjointed rhythms can find their responses improved and refined. As Bull puts it, "No note (Tone) can resound without affecting in some measure the patterns of the whole" (Bull, *Music Therapy*, 6).

The process of exposing persons with limited spiritual consciousness to higher levels of vibration, or great music, is a form of patterning. In the same way, brain-damaged children are patterned to rebuild brain function by means of reactivating motor function. When parts of the body are moved, the brain is taught to re-establish control over such movement; when the small bones in the inner ear are moved, the mind is schooled in the appreciation of rhythms that act upon it. Like processes occur in numerous activities of self-betterment, including that of improving the handwriting: graphologists have demonstrated that the personality can be improved by upgrading the handwriting (Paul de Sainte Colombe, *Grapho-Therapeutics* [Hollywood, California: Laurida Books Publishing Co., 1966] 339 pp.).

By the same token, unfortunately, reverse patterning is possible. A young person who is led by peer pressure to listen only to cacophonous sounds--acid rock, punk rock, heavy metal, and other extreme rhythmic forms--will eventually become conditioned to respond only to that sort of music. Children can be taught to enjoy atonal compositions. Moreover, degenerate rhythms encourage degenerate sympathetic vibrations in audiences, evoking reverberations which pervade the system of body-emotions-mind. It is owing to this persuasiveness that, in the past, the youthful drug culture has seemed to be so intimately bound up in the passion for extremist rock music. Possibly the drugs themselves are less detrimental to young people than the strident, dark music with which they are associated. Music is just as destructive in some forms as it is therapeutic in others.

In searching for music that is therapeutic, harmonies must be sought which will stimulate the healing processes in the body. As with faith healing, music therapy is a matter of "playing the music of healing in the body itself" (Television demonstration on "In Search Of," Alan Lansburg, Producer, Leonard Nimoy, Host, KHJ-TV, Los Angeles (August 1, 1983]). A faith healer, whose aura or corona of energy can be photographed, possesses a vibratory power that, like music, helps to put disjointed rhythms of the body back into order, and therefore brings about the elimination of physical problems. The body's own potential for rhythmic order is brought into play in the cure of disease.

That serious diseases are cured with "vibrations" has been substantiated only recently, in September of 1983, in a study of terminally ill cancer patients. In many cases, patients with only a few weeks to live were completely rehabilitated by ministering to their emotions through sympathetic vibrations. The miracles were brought about, said the experts, because "emotional vibrations...trigger responses in the adrenal cortex that boost the effectiveness of the immune system" (Marilyn Fuss, "Cancer Survivors Believe in Power of Positive Feelings," *Los Angeles Times* [September 20, 1983] V-I, 8).

Of course William Grant Still could not have known that studies after his death would give credence to his belief in psychic healing. And yet, in a very real sense, the books that he read, and the thoughts that were part of his conceptual framework, anticipated current research. His excursions into the work of Bull, Sturzaker, Crile and others were carried forth largely for his own edification, growing out of his desire to assemble the parts of his world into an understandable and colorful whole. He delighted in his reading, in the same way that he savored his colored landscapes, his crossword puzzles and his numerological discoveries. And, ultimately, he found a place for all of the color, the language, and the occult teachings, in his music.

There was an element of futurity in Still's philosophy of music and of man--an element of relatedness and purpose--that rushed ahead of his purely musical labors, clearing the historical way for a mystical, mental resurrection. He conceived of himself as a man among fellow men, a man who was forever developing, maturing and moving toward the spiritual realm. No stone would block the door to the tomb when he passed. In other terms, he was a master puzzle-maker, one who asked the questions and answered them in order to create an intricate web of thought--one who made up the puzzle then invited those who followed him to fill the spaces.

# TURNING PAGES[1]

The 1982 William Grant Still Festival, sponsored by the California Arts Council and the Marina-Westchester Symphony, was a page in the process of awareness for me. The sense of realization began to come when I started to look for the score and parts of the *Festive Overture*. Mother had been ill, and my children and I had "helped" her so avidly with her cleaning and organizing that even she didn't know anymore where some things were.

As I flipped through the leaves of books, letters, scores and albums, I felt glad that I didn't have to find the music for all of the selections on the program. Frank Fetta and the Marina Symphony were doing most of the gathering of sheet music in libraries and among published works. It was no small undertaking, yet they had shouldered it with superb competence and good will. I had the will but not the competence, so my attention wandered from my task. From a stack of books I took a small, wine-colored volume, a diary for the year 1930. The handwriting was unmistakably my father's.

I began to read, and was touched by the tale that unfolded of the composer's struggle to find work in New York in the Depression Era. With winter and Christmas coming on, he had a large family to feed and clothe. While making occasional arrangements of popular songs whenever he could secure such work, he was also writing *The Afro-American Symphony*. The entries went like this:

> September 11, 1930 - Worked in cellar. Preparing for winter. We have not yet gotten our coal for I am still without a job.

> October 30, 1930 - Started working on Afro-American Symphony. Things look dark. I pray for strength that I may do just as God would have me. ... I must not lose faith. I must not complain.

---

[1] This article was written for, and published by, the Marina-Westchester Symphony Society, California, in *The Sounding Board* [April 1982] 4-5. It is reprinted here with permission.

November 3, 1930 - No money comes in. But God will take care of me. I must bide His time.

November 5, 1930 - Raining. Gloomy. Thanks to God I received some splendid ideas for the Afro-American Symphony last night.

November 11, 1930 - I am conscious of development musically. But this development has gone hand in hand with spiritual development. If I can but get closer to God I know that He will supply all in which I am now deficient. Since I have been looking to Him for inspiration composing has become easy. So much so that at times ideas come as rapidly as I can record them.

November 26, 1930 - Don [Voorhees] gave me nothing to do this week. God will look out for me. At times I feel weary and am inclined to long for the end. God forgive me. I must go on,...

December 4, 1930 - ...It looks now as though my earnings will be small. ...

December 9, 1930 - ...But I will not cease trying for I know God has not deserted me. I know that we must struggle to obtain the worthwhile things of world. Is it then not the more necessary to labor for the greatest treasure in Creation?

December 19, 1930 - I pray that the kiddies will be happy Christmas...

As I read these entries, they called forth from my memory thoughts of my father's often gentle, often child-like nature, coupled with his sadness over material defeats and his pleasure in family life. All of these qualities were in him in 1930, and yet the diary expanded my vision to encompass the totality of his career. I had been in his company from 1942 to 1978; now I could see the broad base of his life, his long diligence, and the fact that, in spite of the gravest hardships, he remained humble before God.

I remembered how, eight years ago, the long struggle conquered his body and mind, and how, in 1978, he slipped quietly from lack of awareness to coma to death without knowing whether or not any of us were there with him. I grieved then, because it seemed wrong that he would no longer be here to display for the world his gentility of spirit and immense affection for God, man and country. But now, the diary was telling me that there was no reason to grieve, for there was something in the composer that was larger than mortality.

Ultimately, the William Grant Still Festival confirmed this realization about my father's accomplishments. Among the many welcome comments from members of the audience was the statement, "having heard his music, I know that your father must have been a loving and a gentle man. His music sounded as if he were a very kind and likable person." Hearing comments of this sort, I saw that, regardless of Depression or death, William Grant Still will endure in his music. People will hear his works and know feelingly that he was a man who would have been a friend to them.

Of course, without accomplished and sensitive musicians like those in Marina-Westchester--musicians willing to put their soundly beating hearts into the body of the composer's notations-- there will be no enduring friendship in the years to come. The musicians, too, are a step toward awareness and warmth of understanding, and they, along with the pages of a diary, the memories, the man, the music and its mission, have rendered the past intelligible and the future creditable.

# THE GLEAMING OF A RANDOM LIGHT[1]

One of the things that came with us when we moved from California to Flagstaff was a box of diaries and special books. In that box is a weary-looking volume published in 1907--its cover torn from the binding and some of the pages loose--entitled *The Life and Works of Paul Laurence Dunbar*. On the pre-title page are some penciled figures, and, in blue ink, the signature, "William Grant Still."

This was my father's favorite book of poetry. Often I saw him reading it around 11 p.m., lying on his bed in his pajamas and a blue terry cloth robe, his reading glasses balanced forward on his nose. Sometimes he read the best poems to my mother, sometimes to himself. He had brought Dunbar's works from Wilberforce, Ohio, to New York, and then to California, and until his death, kept the brown volume next to his bed for nighttime enjoyment.

William Grant Still kept Dunbar in the center of his life even when his studies of Shakespeare, Milton and Whittier were abandoned. He had started reading poetry at the age of 12 in Little Rock, Arkansas, because his mother, who was a teacher, encouraged him, and because it was the thing to do in upper-middle class Negro society in the post-Civil War South. Historians and filmmakers (those who brought *The Color Purple* to the screen) rarely document the high degree of literacy and culture achieved by Colored people in the late 19th and early 20th centuries. At the Lotus Club meetings (gatherings sponsored by Negro literary societies), Still heard Dunbar's poems recited, along with those of Shakespeare and Tennyson, Wordsworth and Keats. Still never forgot Dunbar.

When the composer came "up from the perfumed bosom of the South" to Ohio, he bought his *Life and Works of Dunbar*, and took it with him from that time on. He marked several of the

---

[1] This short piece appeared with the program notes for the November 9, 1988 performance of William Grant Still's *Afro-American Symphony* by the Flagstaff Symphony Orchestra (Arizona). It is reprinted here with permission.

poems with red or blue pencil for possible use in his compositions, and one that he especially noted was, "Ships That Pass in the Night:"

> Out in the sky the great dark clouds are massing;
> I look far out into the pregnant night
> Where I can hear a solemn booming gun
> And catch the gleaming of a random light
> That tells me that the ship I seek is passing, passing.

There was a sonorous yearning in these words that spoke to my father's spirit. Dunbar had wanted his prose poems to be recognized among the literary annals, but the world was only willing to accept him when he wrote in Negro dialect; most people liked the image of a minority that was poor and uneducated. And, it was the same in music: Still was unable to get his works recorded because Americans were not ready for an ethnic composer who wrote something finer than blues and jazz.

Both Dunbar and Still felt passed over to some extent, but modern ages are beginning to vindicate them. The friendship that Still has now found in Flagstaff, and in the Flagstaff Symphony, is a part of the process of vindication. As more and more Still works are performed and recorded, the multicultural understanding and emotional kinship of peoples is echoed and reechoed through the music. Furthermore, the other cultural strains in the Still family--the Spanish, Choctaw, Scotch-Irish and Jewish--find a place and an expression of force and worth. Dunbar and Still now have a good home in Arizona where, as the poet put it,

> O'er all that holds us we shall triumph yet,
> And place our banner where his hopes were set!

A page from William Grant Still's personal scrapbook.
Captions are written in the composer's own hand.

William Grant Still and his wife, Verna Arvey, and their children, Duncan and Judith Anne, at the piano in 1944.

William Grant Still making toys for Judith Anne and Duncan in 1944.

William Grant Still and Verna Arvey with their children and their dog, Shep, in Los Angeles, 1944.

William Grant Still and Verna Arvey at work.

William Grant Still and his family listening
to a broadcast of Still's music in 1944.

William Grant Still proofreading one of his compositions.

Judith Anne Still and William Grant Still in 1972.

**ESSAYS ABOUT THE COMPOSER'S
COLOR AND CULTURE**

# PREJUDICE: AN ACQUIRED DEFICIENCY[1]

One Sunday in 1971, the "Dean of Negro Composers," William Grant Still, went to Mission Viejo, California, to watch his grandson play in a Little League game. Mission Viejo was an upper-middle-class planned community outside of Los Angeles, where suspiciously few minorities lived, and where some of the residents had expressed a desire to live "far away from Niggers." At the Little League game that day there gathered a sea of White faces, and even Still's wife, grandchildren, and I, his daughter, were as White-skinned as the rest, and seemed to be a part of the unanimity of the crowd.

Still had not been settled in his lawn chair for too long before a small boy, not yet five-years-old, wandered over to him and looked intently into his face. Then the child ran a pudgy finger along the top of the composer's burnished hand as it rested on the arm of the chair, and he piped,

"Mister, can you turn green, too?"

The venerable brown face began to peel open like a blossom in time-lapse, and soon the Dean of Composers was laughing so hard that his chair almost collapsed under him. After a few minutes he wiped tears of pleasure from his eyes and declared breathlessly,

"God Bless the children. They are our only hope."

Bless the children, indeed, if they remain, through life, able to see skin color as color only, and not as an aspect of social status. It is the shame of civilization, however, that all too often the innocence and loving acceptance of the very young is debilitated by the adult malady of racial prejudice.

The hardihood of the racial strain of prejudice owes itself in some part to the forcefulness of the survival instinct in living creatures. In a certain sense, everyone is susceptible to the condition of bigotry, in that, at one time or another, each of us has felt an aversion to a particular type of person, or has thought of himself or herself as better than another group of

---

[1] Portions of this piece have appeared in the *Sonneck Society Bulletin*.

individuals. In minimal doses, and in special cases, this sense of avoidance and superiority is a positive force. Society will not survive unless we are impatient with those who commit crimes, abuse the blameless, and those who cultivate ignorance, indigence and negativism. There should also be a concerted effort to combat alcoholism and other addictions, although any aversion to people who suffer from substance abuse should manifest itself in a sense of compassion, not in feelings of self-congratulation or elitism.

Some inclination to prejudice is, by the nature of things, an ingredient of patriotism, and of any allegiance to tradition or religious dogma. Precedent and tradition are part of the same mind-set: the decision to like or dislike according to form, proportion, position, color, touch, sight or sound. We do, in fact, have a tendency to venerate ideology and nationalism as aspects of a higher form of human love and loyalty, while personal love is thought to be of a lower order.

Yet, it may well be that the prejudice involved in dogma and regional pride can impair their value. The metaphysical ("New Age") philosophers believe that the highest form of love is love of other beings; in other words, spiritual love is the altruistic attraction to others, and the appreciation of human life, life-energy and the creative forces of nature. This type of love, they insist, is above reason, precedent and tradition, and has no basis in the past, in national pride, or in societal laws (N. D. Willoughby, "New Age Alchemy in Action," *Rays* 79 [June 1987] 219-222).

The huge emphasis upon reason and material and historical knowledge in modern civilization is the result, the metaphysicians explain, of the lack of evolvement of the back-brain of the homo-sapien, wherein spiritual love is seated. When ancient humanity first began to lean toward materiality and perceptual thinking (the tenants of the frontal brain), the front-brain was given to rapid growth and to the imposition of its concerns upon the spiritual sensitivity of human nature. It was through this uneven evolvement that the penultimate species has become more human than spiritual, and more reasoning than reasonable (Richard Steinpach, "The Lord Gives to His Own in Sleep," *Gralswelt*

[Stiftung Gralsbotschaft, May/June 1976]).

But whether or not it is true that front-brain concerns are over-indulged in modern life, the prejudices involved in tradition, patriotism and material goods are usually injected into our daily activities as cohesive and positive conditions that strengthen and perpetuate, rather than attack, the health of civilization. Just as susceptibility to certain conditions in youth, and triumph over those conditions, will bolster immunity to more serious diseases in adulthood, so nationalism and religious faith usually contribute to a strong society.

Even so, when aversion to others in other places or races involves a hatred of a group of people--without each person in that group having done something reprehensible to deserve that dislike--then that aversion leads to the pestilence of bigotry. And, when a person hangs on to that bigotry in the face of better knowledge, he becomes a danger to his fellows, and to the mental, spiritual and emotional health of his community.

The weak tissue wherein prejudice finds a septic plot for growth is in most of us, just as we have within us the antibodies which can ward off unreasonable hatreds. It is in our weakness that we foster selfishness, arrogance and abuse of human rights, or permit the existence of the Ku Klux Klan, the American Nazi Party, apartheid, and religious terrorist groups.

It is surprising that so little is done to counteract the activities of prejudiced groups, and that no widespread programs exist which encourage an understanding of prejudice and its dangers to civilized progress. Millions of dollars are invested in a cure for cancer and AIDS, while comparatively minor sums are applied to anti-defamation and similar causes.

Not only are there few who fight prejudice, but also there are few who study it from an analytical point of view. Gordon W. Allport was one of the first, and one of the only, academicians to approach prejudice from a laboratory point of view, and to publish his findings in his book, *The Nature of Prejudice* [Addison-Wesley, 1954]. It was he who first noted that there is a certain type of personality that is more susceptible than other types to the infection of bigotry, and he labeled this personality, "authoritarian." That is, the biased person is likely to be one who seeks domination over others, or who desires to be admired above all others.

Because the authoritarian personality likes to believe that everything he owns, or does, or is part of, is better than any other thing, activity or group, he is prone to be super-patriotic, excessively religious and dogmatic, and dangerously fearful of anyone who might challenge his supremacy, or his feelings of "specialnessness." In spite of his religious inclinations, however, this person is quick to set aside his awe of Divine consequences when an inordinate hunger for power is involved, and thus the leadership of the Inquisition in the Middle Ages ignored Christian precepts in the operation of its machines of torture. When this personality is also glutted with covetousness, a similar destructiveness follows, as when the German Nazis coveted the property, labor and lives of the Jews in Europe.

Ironically, the very virtue which the prejudiced person desires most--self-esteem--is the quality which he most lacks. The low self-esteem of the authoritarian person is the source of his mental affliction: he dislikes himself, and seeks to transfer that self-hatred to another group, hoping that the dislike of others will obliterate his sense of inferiority, insecurity and inadequacy. He is afraid that he will be attacked owing to his weakness, so he looks about for a visible threat to justify his fear, and, seeing nothing, he manufactures a scapegoat. Better to criticize many others than to suffer self-criticism. Better to blame others for his troubles, or mental frailties, than to shoulder the blame himself. Better to be feared than to fear. As William Grant Still said of the White critics who are biased against Negro composers,

> These opponents are not only biased people, they are scared people. When they hear music by a Negro composer that is successful from an audience standpoint, they become desperately afraid. They have seen Negroes rise to prominence in so many fields; they hope it won't happen in the creative world.
> ("Negro Performers Brightened the Decades," *Pittsburgh Courier* 3 [September 17, 1960] 7).

## Prejudice: An Acquired Deficiency

For the prejudiced critics, and others like them, bigotry may be a disease that they are not strong enough to avoid, having not been fortified against it by stable childhood upbringing, mature guidance of role models, and a sense of personal integrity. Resistance to bias must be bolstered by parents, peers, educational or religious mentors, or by an outer society replete with humane friends, employers, legislators and media personnel.

When we are children we are not fraught with racial prejudgments, but we lack immunity to self-indulgence and intolerance in general: we have no difficulty, if wrongly influenced, in fomenting antagonism toward those different than we. In my childhood, my elementary school friends and I teased, taunted, ostracized and disliked the new boy in class who was grossly overweight. The boy had done nothing to deserve our cruelty: he simply looked different. It did not occur to me at the time that my parents, who were intermarried, were different than other parents; it was not until I became friends with a girl in school who was also obese that I realized the insanity of the group-torture of "the fat boy." Moreover, it was not until I was forced to deal with a weight problem myself that I became aware of the pain that the objects of ridicule endure.

Not only is pain involved in being a societal scapegoat, but also, there is considerable discomfort attached to the overcoming of prejudice. Being in a society configured with many individual realities which, although various, nevertheless intermingle and touch one another, is a stiff challenge. To think of each person singly and not as a member of a group--to treat people as individuals--is work: it is painful labor, just as dieting and learning require an arduous regimen. Stereotypes and prejudices are easy and comfortable. If one human being can react to another simply by seeing what color he is or where he is from, he can dispense with the difficulty of having to find out what the other person can do, what he knows and believes, and what kind of person he is.

Furthermore, it is through experiential pain that we gain an understanding of, and an empathy for, others. Suffering often enlarges our humanity, and, frequently, the inhumane have never suffered. When we have known the hurt of being shunned for an untenable reason, we suddenly develop compassion for others who have been vilified. Perhaps if members of the Ku Klux Klan were forced to ride in the backs of buses, or to patronize substandard restaurants and hotels, or to be racially abused and degraded, they would abjure their mistaken loyalties.

To side-step the pain, or to avoid learning lessons from painful experiences--to deal easily with the multiplicities of people and information in modern life--we stereotype, classify and generalize, we lock ourselves safely into categories, we put ourselves into dark cells of apprehension where infection grows. Yet, somewhere between the blocks of concrete the bright foliage must intrude. And, sometimes the foliage in the cracks is annoying to us: it is as exasperating to have our neat habits of mind disrupted by alternate ways of thinking as it is normal to try to simplify and to be selective in our human contacts. As with sugar diabetes, it is quite normal to like sugar, but if we eat too much of it we will give ourselves diabetes, acquiring the malady through unwise, self-indulgent habits.

It is through bad habits of thought that the stereotypes and biases of our day have surpassed the racial prison and have invaded every area where human beings can think themselves to be better, or more fortunate, than others. To the question, "What if people didn't have skin?," people respond that they would then develop hatreds against varieties of bone structure, muscle tension and eye color. Anyone who is different in some way is susceptible to being considered inferior or handicapped.

The irony of bias is, of course, that all of us are, in manifold ways, different from each other. In the words of Bree Walker, TV newswoman who has ectrodactylism, or disformation of the hands and feet, "We're all handicapped somehow," but we must not allow our supposed handicaps to become real ones ("A Letter to My Daughter," *Guideposts* [March 1989] 2-5).

> Some people feel they are too heavy, others hate their hair. Some people feel they were born with the wrong social background, and they let those misconceptions cripple them.

> What matters is what God sees in the inside: how we treat others, the spirit in which we work and play, our attitude toward facing life's challenges.
>
> Your true friends will be those who see through to the inside and accept the physical difference. ...Being a good friend means you have to look deeper for the truth.
>
> (Walker, 2, 4).

When people do not look deeply for the truth, biases breed and multiply. In our world there are prejudices in abundance, especially those against the handicapped, against various racial and national groups, against devotees of certain religions, and against women. In spite of the laws against sexism, there are women who receive less pay than men for doing the same work, and many are discouraged from entering fields of endeavor where males pre-dominate. For example, Mrs. Middlebrooks in Jackson, Tennessee, was a female automobile dealer when there were no women car dealers in Jackson, and, owing to her sex, she was prevented from obtaining her own dealership for a long time. Not only did she encounter bias in the outside world, but she also experienced it in her own family: one of the things that she remembers from her early years was the disapproval in her family when a Presbyterian relative married a Methodist.

It is only by virtue of the constitutional guarantees of religious freedom in the United States that differences in worship have not grown into dangerous antipathies. Americans feel themselves to be much more tolerant than those in the Middle East and in Ireland who slaughter "unbelievers" in the name of the Lord. Yet, to say that we strive for tolerance in our culture is not saying much, for it is frequently pointed out that the act of "'allowing' something inherently implies the right to forbid" (Clifford Goldstein, "Why I Find Religious Toleration Intolerable," *Liberty* 82 [Jan.-Feb. 1987] 8-10). To tolerate a minority is to suggest that the minority exists by permission only, and that the majority group has the power to rescind that permission.

In actuality, no group has the right to "permit" the

freedom of any other group. As Goldstein puts it, faith is a personal attitude toward Creation, and race is an aspect of Creation; no man is so "complete in wisdom" or so Godly in ability that he can usurp the right to tolerate Creation in all of its manifestations and inspired responses. "Toleration," adds Goldstein, "is what allows Jews their few synagogues in Russia, or Baptists their few churches in East Germany" (p.10).

Not only is tolerance not a viable alternative to prejudice, but also it is not always a habit of mind that we can maintain in its purist, most uncorrupted form. When Alex Odeh, a Palestinian, was murdered, his death was given little attention by the media and by the same Americans who had indulged in verbose outrage over the death of Leon Klinghoffer, a Jewish hostage on the *Achille Lauro*. Upset over the unfairness of public opinion after the incident, Daniel Fox, a Jewish lawyer, and other Jews, participated in the effort to raise funds for the widow and children of Odeh; Fox and his fellow Jews took pains, also, to remind the media and the public that the anti-Defamation League of B'nai B'rith and the American-Arab Anti-Discrimination Committee have the same goals, attitudes, sensitivities and concerns (Daniel Fox, "Dinner for a Dead Arab," *Liberty* 82 [Jan.-Feb. 1987] 3).

The unjust religious attitudes and instances of discrimination against women in the United States are aspects of the narrow habits of thinking that continue to fulminate beneath the forthright exterior of our society. They exist alongside less harmful stereotypical beliefs, such as the notions that Italians and redheads are hot-tempered, or "fiery," that Mexicans are "lazy," that blondes have more fun, and that females in general tend to act according to emotion rather than reason. These petty, debasing ideas are akin to those in Chaucer's day, when gat-toothed women were perceived to be more sexually free than other females, and dark-haired, dark-skinned women were thought to be less refined than the pale, blond variety. Fortunately, it is not likely that either the petty stereotypes, or the religious and sexist malignities, will increase in this country; in fact there is every indication that they may be forced into remission, given heavy doses of public repugnance over the religious atrocities committed in other parts of the world, plus regular injections of anti-chauvinist opinion. The debasement of women continues, but it is decreasing. Less easy to cure, however, are racial animosities, of which prejudice against the Negro is the most tenacious aspect.

In the United States, the infirmity of Black-White hatred differs from other misjudgments in that its history is at least as long as the history of the nation itself. The antipathy for the Negro gained its initial impetus from the profitable African slave trade, and gathered its epidemic strength when the subjugation of the Afro-American appeared to be necessary to the life support system of half the country.

When the Civil War splintered the disallowance of the Negro into myriads of subliminal stereotypes and unspoken codes of behavior, racism became so vast and complex a subject of concern that it was rarely acknowledged or studied. Today, the study of racism, with a view to determining our progress toward fairness and the directions that should be taken in the future, is so large a topic that a focus is obligatory: perhaps the following consideration of the racial battles in the life of William Grant Still, and an overview of Still's opinions on race (and those of his wife and daughter) will offer some suggestions as to where we have been and where we are going, or should go, in the upward climb toward equitable relationships.

William Grant Still's father, William Grant Still, Sr., may well have been a martyr in the earliest struggles against bigotry. Born of a Scotch-Irish slave overseer and a female house slave, Still, Sr., became a school teacher in Woodville, Mississippi, and was one of the first to say that colored teachers should be paid as much as white teachers. The elder Still was also a cornet player and the town band leader, and it was doubtful that he was paid at all for serving as Director of Music in Woodville. When he was murdered in 1895, at the age of twenty-four, rumor had it that he was the victim of certain White people in town who thought that he was too handsome, too smart, too well-off, and too vocal "for a

Nigger" in his day.

The younger William Grant Still was taken by his mother to live in an interracial neighborhood in Little Rock, Arkansas, far away from the dangers of life in Mississippi; but the pleasantness of his upbringing could not always shield him from antagonism: he was pushed off the sidewalk and called "Nigger" in downtown Little Rock, and he witnessed White mobs with guns hunting down a hapless colored man who was wrongly accused of a crime.

Still decided at an early age to go into serious music, and yet Negro music was in its infancy at the turn of the century; both Whites and Blacks looked down upon the blues and spirituals, and Negro musicians of every sort were outcasts socially, even among their own people. Serenading bands of Colored musicians were paid only a few coins for their performances, stage show artists were not invited into "nice" colored homes, Scott Joplin played the piano in a brothel to earn a living, and no Negroes were admitted to the all-White symphonic and operatic arenas.

When Still did get a job in music with W. C. Handy's band, he traveled from Tennessee to New Orleans, becoming acquainted with intolerance in many of its worst ramifications. He saw other Blacks beaten and lynched with slight provocation, and often he, too, suffered from hunger and deprivation owing to his race. His own account of some of his daily experiences from 1915 to 1918 ran thus:

> Handy's orchestra played the length and breadth of the South. Larger cities had accommodations for us (segregated, of course) but in some of the smaller communities there were no places for Negroes to stay. Once, in wintertime, we stayed in a mountain home where the floors consisted of rough pieces of wood with the openings half an inch apart. The wind blew through these openings and it was just as if we were outdoors. It was cold even in bed. They gave us grits and sowbelly to eat. I'll never forget that experience.
>
> Our traveling was done in Jim Crow cars. These cars, which were usually only half-cars, offered very little that was comfortable or desirable. Cinders, smoke, unpleasant odors and a

feeling of humiliation because of having to pay first class fare for third rate accommodations were our lot.

One early morning, our train made a short stop in Rome, Georgia. We had gone all night without food and all of us were hungry. There was no place for us to eat. We asked and were told that if we would go around to the back of a restaurant and come in the kitchen door, we would be served. None of us wanted to do that, partly because of the humiliation and partly because we were afraid of missing the train. We got back on and had to ride up past noon, without food.
(Speech at Lincoln University, Pennsylvania, *Music Department Bulletin* 2 [August 4, 1969]).

In the twenties, Still stopped traveling with Handy's band, and went to New York to arrange music, to write music, and to play in Eubie Blake's "Shuffle Along" orchestra. In those days Negroes were not allowed to live outside of Harlem, and oftentimes unable to find professional jobs and acceptance away from their home base, they were now-and-then visited by--and victimized by--White folk. White composers went into the night clubs and theaters in Harlem to find musical inspiration, helping themselves freely to rhythmic creativity at its most fecund source. Gershwin, for example, borrowed much from the Harlem musicians, including the opening notes in "Summertime," which he took from Handy's "St. Louis Blues," and "I Got Rhythm," a song made up by Still (Verna Arvey, "Afro-American Music Memo," *Music Journal* 27 [November 1969] 36, 68). Other composers simply bought songs from poor Negro music-makers for the price of a meal, put their names on them, and acquired a fame that they carry with them to this day.

Not only were the Negroes victimized by the Whites, but they were also demeaned by their own internal jealousies and self-seeking enterprises. Just as the Africans themselves had participated in selling their own people to the slave-traders, so Hall Johnson was not above sabotaging a fellow Negro composer if he thought that it would do him some good, and Will Vodery put his name to many of Still's orchestrations before the deception was discovered. Racially speaking, there was a caste system among the Negroes which operated as an extension of the system of segregation: the purple-black-skinned Afro-Americans were ostracized by the brown-skinned Negroes, who were shunned by the coffee-and-cream-colored Negroes, while the white-skinned Afro-Americans passed over the color line and moved quietly out of Harlem.

In the midst of this matrix of social hostility, the accomplished and intelligent Colored people tried to bring their achievements to the attention of the outside world. They would have had little success if all White people had been adverse to their progress--happily some Whites in high places were willing to help them to obtain recognition. Conductors like Leopold Stokowski, Howard Hanson, Sir John Barbirolli, Arthur Judson, Karl Krueger and Eugene Goosens played the music of Still and Dawson, and protected their right to enter the world of serious music ("Negro Performers Brightened the Decades," *Pittsburgh Courier* 3 [September 17, 1960] 7). Some lesser lights among the White populace also assisted, as when the White musicians in the "Deep River" radio orchestra in New York insisted that Still be allowed to conduct, even when one of their number threatened to quit if they persisted in their demands. (The dissenting musician did leave, but later returned when he saw that Still was more than competent as a conductor.)

It was through the efforts of these helpful Whites that Still's music was heard across the globe, and that he became the first Negro to write a symphony that was performed by a major American orchestra (1931), and the first to write an opera that was produced by a major American company (1949). In addition, he became the first Afro-American to conduct a major symphony orchestra in both the North and the Deep South. If he had stopped there, it would have been enough, but he was a pioneer also in his personal life: he fell in love with and married a White woman. In 1934 Still had tired of living in Harlem, and had moved to the freer intellectual climate of California. However, although some interracial mingling was permitted on the West Coast, it remained both illegal and socially taboo for the races to intermarry. Therefore, in 1939, when Still decided to wed his publicist, the Jewish pianist-journalist, Verna Arvey, he and Miss Arvey were forced to travel to Mexico to obtain a license and to have the ceremony performed.

The reaction of both Whites and Negroes to the marriage was immediate and bitter. One of the Arvey's relatives was openly rude to her new husband, while another would only see her (after she married) in the parking lot of his hotel when he passed through town. A Negro who knew Still, but not his wife, spread the rumor that Arvey was a tramp who was running a house of assignation. A friend to both Still and Arvey was told not to invite them to her wedding because, "In years to come, all people will remember is that you had a Colored man at your wedding."

The primitive attitudes toward intermarriage in those days were, probably, to be expected, given the widespread acceptance of segregation. Neighborhoods everywhere were either White or Black, even in socially-relaxed California, and there were vigorous protests if Afro-Americans tried to move into white settlements. So rabid were the demonstrations over any threatened integration, that, when Mr. and Mrs. Short, an interracial couple in California, bought a home in an all-White area, their house was burned down around them and the wife and children perished in the flames. The authorities refused to investigate the Short case, even as the media declined to cover race riots in other parts of the country. Indeed, the silence of the media and the police over racial events contributed to a vast present-day ignorance of the triumphs and tragedies of the period. When Still became the first Afro-American to conduct a major American orchestra, none of the White newspapers would cover the story.

The refusal to reveal the truths about race, and about interracial relationships, caused misconceptions to develop. One of Verna Arvey's aunts warned her niece not to have children with her Colored husband because any offspring born of the marriage would be social outcasts and psychological defectives. "Think of the poor, helpless children," the aunt implored, tearfully. Undoubtedly, in later years, she was amazed to discover that the Still's son and daughter did not grow up to be mentally deficient misfits and criminals. No concept existed in those days of the well-balanced interracial family.

So perverse was the notion of the emotionally deprived mixed-race child, that the Los Angeles Bureau of Adoptions tried to persuade the Stills to adopt a Negro child that had been born of mulatto parents who were passing for White. The parents had rejected the baby because it was dark-skinned, and the adoption bureau felt called upon to find an intermarried couple to accept it. The myth existed then, and still exists today, that a child cannot find a sense of personal identity unless its parents are of the same race as itself.

This myth may persist for many years hereafter, until there are enough interracial children who are vocal enough to refute it openly, assuring society that identity comes more from love and stability in the home environment than from the appearance and cultural predilections of the parents. Children who do prove to be adversely affected by being of a mixed race--and I have known some of these children personally--have usually been emotionally unstable since birth; in other words, they would have been disturbed by any difference between themselves and others, anything that would set them apart from the social mainstream. It is not environmental differences that cause instability, but the instability itself that makes the differences unsettling.

Indeed, so unimportant is human diversity in determining emotional health, that race ought not to be a factor in shaping the course of adoptions. When minority children are adopted by White parents, they need not be thrust among people of their own race in order to develop a personal identity. Exposure to a minority racial heritage and cultural traditions can contribute to the enrichment of a child's life and thoughts, but it is not absolutely necessary to the avoidance of anxiety and emotional deprivation.

Certainly there was no deprivation in the Still household, in spite of the mixing of the races. Those who had warned the

Stills not to marry and who had predicted disaster, were silent and disbelieving when the years rolled by and the marriage remained warm, viable, and replete with loving concern. Instead of being repudiated by their friends, the couple kept their old friends and made hundreds of new ones. As Norma Gould had told Verna Arvey in 1939, "Your friends won't let you down, and there will be plenty of them."

William Grant Still and his wife discovered that prejudices could be obliterated if people were encouraged to interact with members of other races who were on the same level in terms of interests and intellectual abilities. As Still said, "You cannot continue hating an entire group of people if you have learned to deal with members of that group on a personal basis." The best way to conquer the disease of prejudice was, ironically, not quarantine, but human exposure and social intercourse.

Although exclusivity was to be avoided, the Stills also warned against indiscriminate cordiality toward all people. Verna Arvey noted, "We knew a wealthy society lady who thought that she had to invite the Negro service station attendant and garbage man into her home just to show that she wasn't prejudiced. It would have been all right if these men had been on par with her in terms of interests and abilities (not in terms of income), but they weren't. The presence of such men at the lady's parties did nothing to show that the races could relate to each other either mentally or socially."

Eventually this wealthy woman met William Grant Still and his wife, and learned that it was possible to be discriminating, not discriminative, in associating with those of another race. Ultimately she was part of a growing enlightenment in the United States, in which individuals began to mingle with other races on a personal and enriching basis.

Apart from individuals, however, and in professional circles, the enlightenment was still slow in coming. Even though Still had orchestrated such popular stage shows as Earl Carroll's "Vanities" and "Rain or Shine," none of the twelve major studios in Hollywood would hire him to score any film other than "Stormy Weather," starring Lena Horne and Bojangles Robinson. Still needed the money from the work on

"Stormy Weather," but, after a few months he resigned from that job in order to protest against the stereotypes that the film perpetuated. The directors at Twentieth-Century Fox had told him that they wanted his music to be "more sensuous" for the film, and they insisted that Negro bands in the twenties did not play as well as Still represented them. Still said, "I told them they had. I guess I knew. I had played with them (Stanley Williford, "William Grant Still: Time to Discover a Musical Giant," Los Angeles *Sentinel* [February 8, 1973])."

The bigotry in the film studios was surpassed in the world of opera. Although Still's opera, *Troubled Island*, became the first opera by a Negro to be done by a major American company, it was not without a struggle that it came to the stage. Still's story of his efforts to find acceptance for his operas was revealing:

> I sent an opera to a leading opera company and it was returned because *Troubled Island* was racial in theme. So I wrote another opera, *Bayou Legend*, non-racial, but before sending it to the director I took pains to outline the plot and explain the manner in which the music was handled. Shortly thereafter my letter was returned with an injunction not to bother sending the manuscript, nor any other for that matter.
>
> I didn't know until I read in *Music on My Beat* that this opera company refused to consider operas on racial grounds, whether because of subject matter or composer (J. Douglas Cook, "Visits to the Homes of Famous Composers #3," *Opera and Concert* [November 1946] 8).

When *Troubled Island* was finally produced in New York, the critics conspired to pan it and to close its doors prematurely, so that scant attention was paid to Still's operas from then on. In 1983 an effort to mount a William Grant Still opera was met with the comment, "You mean to say that Niggers can write that kind of music?"

Aside from his operas, the treatment of Still's music in the recording field was similarly reprehensible, for the "Dean of Negro Composers" never had an item listed in any of the catalogues of the phonograph-recording companies (J. Douglas

Cook, 26). Even though his compositions were included in the CBS "Black Composers Series," a series of albums which was initiated as a grant project, Columbia Records declined to reissue the Still works on a separate disc, regardless of the fact that the Still part of the series had sold out rapidly, and had been among the top classical recordings in the nation.

The leadership in the classical recording industry, and in the major opera companies, was biased against the composer in his lifetime, and remains so today. And yet, by the time that Still was in his seventies, he had seen racial strides made on levels other than professional. The quality of life of the Negro had been improved by the passage of the Civil Rights Act in 1964, which was the aftermath of public demonstrations, sit-ins and marches--the "shock therapy" applied to prejudice by political activists in the fifties and sixties. Where once there had been no hotel rooms available to W. C. Handy's band members, where once Still and his wife had been denied rooms at both White and Colored hotels and motels, and had been prevented from living in a White neighborhood, now accommodations and homes were legally open to everyone. Where once Artie Shaw's bandsmen had felt called upon to create havoc in a restaurant which refused to serve their Negro vocalist, Billie Holliday, now eating houses, restrooms and schools were convenient to people of every color.

On the surface, progress had been made, and the legal steps taken would insure integration in public facilities in future years. The present day finds the public growing in enlightenment, with some dark crevices remaining to be illumined in the private sector. The barriers established by the large, professional companies, are, as we have seen, unsurmounted, as are the hidden obstacles created by unlawful discriminatory practices. For example, certain august fraternal groups, which have been required by law to establish minority chapters, still maintain all-White chapters that non-Whites may not join. A member of one of these all-White chapters in southern California admitted recently that, should a Negro attempt to enter the ranks, some excellent and lawful excuse would be found to exclude him. In some states groups and private schools still exist which are dedicated to the "protection of their own" from non-White elements, and I have discovered one of these private schools flourishing in my home state of Arizona. (A teacher from the latter institution, who shunned my company owing to my racial heritage, was, ironically, full of self-pride over having learned to accept the homosexuality of one of his sons.)

Of course, the state of racial attitudes in this country, despite occasional corruption, is far ahead of that in other areas such as Australia. Nothing can be more untenable than the system of banning the immigration of dark-skinned persons, regardless of the political, strategic or economic excuses that are made to protect that system. There are always those who can bring forward excellent reasons for slowing the approach of a needed reform; indeed, in the pre-Civil War days there were pro-slavery orators whose eloquent reasoning might have swayed the slaves themselves. Not until slavery had become a distant memory, did it appear that no amount of logic or consideration for political priorities could have justified the forced repudiation of an entire group of people.

Our outrage over Australia's racial attitudes, while important, of course, should not take precedence over our concern for our own national disorders. Not only do some intolerant institutions and businesses continue to operate in this country, but also, in the realm of education and in the information that is passed on to the public by the media, we have taken some steps backward. School children have been integrated, but their cultural heritage has not been; little effort has been made to include the history of the Afro-American and of other minorities in the curriculum and textbooks of the educational system. Students in the colleges and universities who haven't had time to enroll in Black Studies courses remain ignorant of the tremendous accomplishments of Negroes in the past. Moreover, the Black Studies curriculums themselves are frequently inadequate.

Ignorance of the past triumphs of their own people has led the black militants to denounce "Whitey" for having prevented the Afro-American from realizing his potential. Some White people, who relish the image of the inferior and non-achieving Black man, are all too happy to push the Negro militant to the forefront; the media gives him platforms from which to harangue the citizenry, and represents him as *the* spokesperson for the race.

Further, the media tend to treat all minority groups as groups only, rather then as associated yet variable individuals. Newspeople habitually ask men like Cassius Clay and Jesse Jackson "how Blacks feel" about this or that issue, as if all Afro-Americans vote and think alike. The conservative political opinions of Negroes such as George Schuyler, Tom Berkley, and J. A. Parker are ignored by the news commentators. When Black issues are discussed, the focus of the discourse is usually on unemployment, teenage pregnancies, poverty and ignorance; with this focus in mind, the general public is encouraged to think that Negroes are less responsible than Whites, and more prone to joblessness, avoidance of proper schooling, and to indulgence in their sexual passions. (A critic, reviewing William Grant Still's opera, *Minette Fontaine*, in Baton Rouge, observed that the dance sequence was not "orgiastic" enough, or, in other words, not sensuous enough [David Foil, "Dobish's Career is Soaring," Louisiana *Morning Advocate*, [October 26, 1984]).

Negroes themselves, infected by the militant mania, and by television stereotypes, often claim that they must have more government welfare programs to help them to climb out of their disadvantaged state. In the 1980's, however, it was discovered that an increase in government aid to Negroes did not alleviate the problems, rather it led to an alarming rise in Negro crime, Negro unemployment, Negro illegitimacy and Negro drug abuse. Statistics revealed that, if things went on in the same way, by the year 2000 "70 per cent of Black families will be headed by single women and 30 percent of Black men will be unemployed" (J. A. Parker, "Finally, Concern About the Growing Black Under-Class," *Lincoln Review* 6 [Winter 1986] 1-6). Not surprisingly, also, when the government cut some welfare assistance for minorities, the Negro unemployment rate fell to its lowest level since December of 1980 (J. A. Parker, Lincoln Institute Letter to the Public, [March 16, 1987]). When it was assumed that the Afro-

American was well-qualified to support himself, he began to rise to the occasion and to prove that he was not in need of a societal crutch.

Certainly the end result of years of discrimination, followed by years of misguided leadership, followed by years of welfare assistance, has been the loss of Afro-American self-confidence. As Dr. Carolyn Quin, professor at a predominantly Black college in Tennessee, puts it, Negroes in the South are "hampered by extreme feelings of inferiority" (Carolyn Quin, conversation with Judith Anne Still [October 12, 1986]). Outside of the South the situation may not be much better, for it has been observed that the Negro, regardless of his origins, lives in an "environment of despair," in which he "finds it difficult to believe he can enter a field in which he can earn a satisfying living on an equal footing with other Americans" (Harry Trimborn, "Talented Negroes Find Few Barriers in Musical World," Los Angeles *Times*, Editorial Sect. [June 24, 1968] 1,6).

One of the side-effects of a sense of inferiority among Negroes is that it can lead to reverse prejudices: there are many Afro-Americans who strive to dislike White people as much as they believe Whites to dislike them, and who struggle desperately to set themselves apart from the predominant culture. I once heard a Negro Ph.D. from a Southern California university announce loudly that "we-all have more fun than those other folks," that is, White people. Other Afro-Americans are convinced that the most important contribution of their race to civilization has been in the development of blues and jazz, and in athletic exploits. A recent curriculum guide for a course in Black music covers only blues, gospel and jazz musical forms and exponents, and nowhere mentions symphonic Negro composers such as Coleridge-Taylor and Chevalier de Saint-Georges. The universally preeminent Afro-American inventors, soldiers, scientists, doctors and entrepreneurs receive less attention from their own people than the sports figures and popular singers.

The militants justify the exclusion of the most distinguished Negro doers and thinkers by their allegiance to "Black Pride."

It is asserted that Black people should be proud of aspects of their culture that are peculiarly their own, and that they should shun those things that are part of the White man's world. Black pride means a disdain for anything belonging to "Whitey"--even traditional schooling, standard English, and classical music--and an inclination toward the total separation of the races. What these proponents of racial pride do not realize, is that bigoted Whites are more than delighted for Negroes to cut themselves off from the mainstream.

The historian Donald Dorr, who is an expert on Black-White relations in the ante-bellum South, has suggested that "Black Pride" is really a device of the Whites designed to keep Blacks "in their places." Dorr has written a fable in which he creates a "fictional" society made-up of two opposing classes of people, the dominant yellows, and the subservient blues. The blues, in Dorr's pretend world, can be kept subordinate as long as they can be identified by their color, but when they mix with the yellows to produce green people--people superior to both the yellows and the blues--the yellows feel threatened and attempt to expel the green class. The yellows then deny the existence of the greens,

> ...merging it by fiat with the subdominant blues. Any stray debris can be easily disposed of (as, for instance, by outlawing yellow-blue marriages). Now the green race is subsumed within the blue class (whose jealousies of the green race have made them eager to cooperate with the yellow), and this accommodation can be rewarded by suggesting empty formulas--blue pride, for example--to which the remnants of the green class will be forced to adhere and which merely strengthen the color identification which is the yellow class's passport to continued dominance. This distinction can be reinforced by furthering the blue race's self identity with blue television shows, blue universities, blue hair styles--all with the admonition that "blue is beautiful." Chiefest of all, the idea of specifically blue music can be floated, music in which--to the exclusion of all else--the blue race may be allowed exclusive pride and with which it "identifies."
>
> (Donald Dorr, "The Hoax," an unpublished article, [1987]).

If "Blue Pride"--or, "Black Pride"--in the United States has been promoted, as Dorr suggests, by the authoritarian Whites, it is one of the most successfully engineered incidences of mind control ever put forward in this country: Negroes everywhere subscribe to the concept of racial pride, and the Black militants, while no longer rioting in the streets and on college campuses, have, with the aid of the television camera, convinced the public that there should be separate courses in the schools dealing with Black art, music and literature.

When composer Still was encountered by the proponents of Black music, he found them to be "insincere, ignorant, hypocritical," and insane in their efforts to separate black from white again (*Music Department Bulletin*). The Black culturists upbraided Still--as the White critic, Olin Downes, had done forty years before--for not always using racial themes in his music. Still responded by calling it a new brand of prejudice to insist that Negro composers could only reflect their own heritage. He added, "Music is bigger than that" (J. Douglas Cook, 29). In another context he asserted, "A real artist...writes as he wishes, to express whatever idea he plans to get across," and why shouldn't a Negro be allowed to be a real artist? (Letter to Burt Korall [June 14, 1968]). As to the militant veneration of jazz, he commented that authentic jazz is to be esteemed, but it is not "the only or even the most important form of Negro musical expression" (Boris Nelson, "William Grant Still Celebrates 75th Birthday," *The Toledo Blade*, Ohio, [November 22, 1970]).

Negro music, explained Still, which was a fusion of African and other elements beyond the ingredients of jazz, was one of the great contributions of the United States to the arts of the world ("Africa and the United States: Images and Realities," Report of the 8th National Conference, U. S. Commission for UNESCO, Boston, [October 22-26, 1961] 65). But, while it was a valuable artistic accomplishment, this sort of music could not sustain its impact unless its proponents could learn to blend it with the music of other races beside their own (Charles Wisenberg, "Negro Impact Minimal," Los Angeles *Times* 4 [October 28, 1966] 11). The Negro needed to master all of the minority idioms (Creole, Spanish, American Indian, and so on) in order to foster an appreciation for cultural richness in the concert-going public, and to convey the idea that varied groups could learn to live together in mutual admiration. How would the Afro-American be able to convince the world of his racial worth, if he did not accept and promote the worth of other races?

Moreover, courses in Afro-American music ought to require historical, analytical and comparative study, and to inculcate a knowledge of Bach, Mozart and Beethoven, and all other composers who have made a valuable contribution to music and who have displayed genuine gifts. Said Still, "Now that the doors are opening to us, it would be tragic to have them again shut in our faces because those who enter are not yet truly prepared" (*Music Department Bulletin*). When all are prepared, then advancement should be merely a matter of merit, irrespective of color (Still, Letter to Burt Korall [June 14, 1968]).

This concept of preparation and universality should, according to Still, apply to all courses in Afro-American studies. In addition, courses in minority culture and history "should be made attractive to White as well as Colored students," and should be part of the total curriculum in the schools. In other words, "the most effective solution to current racial matters is one of education--not only education of the masses so that they can take their places as responsible citizens, but also education of both races to the very real contribution made by Negroes who have already forged ahead (William Grant Still, "Program Praised," Los Angeles *Times*, Letters Section [November 21, 1966]). The Negroes who had forged ahead prior to the fifties and sixties were, like Still himself, "decent...citizens [who] prefer to reach our goals through friendship and accomplishment, and to respect our fellow citizens, even as we ask them to respect us" (William Grant Still, "Excellent Cartoon," Los Angeles *Herald-Examiner*, G [October 30, 1966] 4).

In regard to the militant stance in general, Still insisted that it was a mistake to destroy good public relations by generating hatred, not love. Racial violence, he said, led to fear and distrust among both White and Colored people. It was not "Uncle Tomming" to make friends, not enemies, and "One can make friends and still keep his dignity; one can make friends and still assert his rights." We needed "Black Can Be Beautiful" to give us identity and pride in our racial heritage (*Music Department Bulletin*), yet "Black is indeed beautiful, but only as white, brown or yellow are beautiful, when we make it so" (*The Blade*). It was necessary for all to work together harmoniously, for, what was good for the nation, was also good for the Race. "We must never let ourselves be 'duped' into a separatist philosophy" (*Music Department Bulletin*). In sum, "As I am now 74 years of age and have been a Negro for all of the 74 years, I did not need people fifty years my junior to tell me what it is, or should be, to be a Negro (Dominique-René de Lerma, *Black Music in Our Culture* [Kent State University Press, 1971]).

For Still, what it meant to be a Negro was what it meant to be a decent human being. To say that the Black experience and the White experience were separate and incohesive was, to him, elitist, inhumane, incorrect, and, in itself, prejudicial. He was joined in this opinion by scholars such as Dr. Benjamin Alexander, who noted that we all have melanin, or pigment, and therefore we are all people of color:

> Since our physical differences are the result of environmental needs that (over millions of years) caused mutations or genetic changes, they do not provide us with an appropriate or a scientifically correct rationale for calling ourselves Black or White.
>
> ("Are We Black?," *Lincoln Review* 7 [Fall 1986] 49).

In the perspective of both Alexander and Still, there were multitudes of Whites and Blacks who shared common goals, lifestyles, attitudes and feelings; they could have, without a doubt, formed families and would have had no trouble understanding and participating in each other's traditions and concerns. They may have had certain qualities, aptitudes and predilections which were part of their racial make-up, and yet their peculiar qualities were not so far removed from the human condition as to be beyond the appreciation of, or the adoption of, other peoples.

Numerous proofs of the truth in the assertions of Still and Alexander can be found, but one only will be mentioned here, and that is the case of Mrs. Barbara Knox, the Colored waitress in the "Quickie Grill" on Santa Monica Boulevard in Los Angeles. Knox came west from Oklahoma City in the fifties, and, in spite of a deep-rooted fear of White people, she went to work for Mr. and Mrs. Shulkin, the Jewish owners of the "Quickie Grill." After thirty-three years Knox had become so much a part of the Shulkins' family that the Shulkin grandchildren thought of her as their aunt, and the Shulkins themselves bequeathed their business to her upon their retirement (Bob Sipchen, "A Friendly Takeover at Lou's Grill," Los Angeles *Times*, View Section [August 18, 1987]).

Clearly Barbara Knox and the Shulkins, like Still and Arvey, have been living testimony to the flaws in the separatist philosophy of modern-day pro-Blacks. Isolationism and racial pride essentially ignore the fact that Colored peoples everywhere possess all of the civilized, educable attributes of other races, and that they can achieve masterfully--in spite of racism--through dignified effort and through the excellence of their standards. Negroes do not need to be cut off again from the mainstream, nor do they need welfare assistance; rather, they require a complete education, and an awareness of their own illustrious heritage, from the birth of civilization in Africa to the significant inventions, acts of heroism, artistic triumphs, and intellectual milestones that are the unsung legacies of the race. Furthermore, they need to abjure the politically antagonistic and improper term "Black people," and begin to use a more appropriate word, such as Dr. Alexander's phrase, "the golden people," or, simply, "the colorful people."

Had Still lived, he would have persisted in his verbal campaign to turn people away from the idea of "blackness," and the language of "Black Pride," toward brotherhood. Still's belief in the necessity for brotherhood developed, not because he had capitulated to White supremacy, but because he had found that educational refinement and constructive effort could cure the prejudices of both Whites and Negroes, and that empathetic human interaction could turn the White man's world into a place wherein all might live harmoniously.

Of course, this world of harmony and peace and compassion had not yet been established in 1978 when Still passed on. He and his wife, Verna Arvey, had suffered much, had done much, and had left much still to be done. Even so, the composer had created a large body of musical compositions which would speak to the public for years after his death. As he put it,

> All my compositions are for all people. I intend them to say something to everyone...Americans and Africans and every person alive.
> (Doris Reno, "I Compose with Pain I Enjoy,"
> *The Miami Herald* [October 29, 1961] 19-E).

It is the sense of brotherhood in his music that J. Douglas Cook praised when he spoke of the composer's "floodtides of spiritual creativeness" that "lift human thought a notch higher in its quest for the all-Embracing Truth about itself" (J. Douglas Cook, 8).

In fact, the spiritual Truth to which Still subscribed went beyond the earthly plane of prejudice and cruelty. Still's personal religion taught him that, if the color of our skins, our personal wealth and status, or our nationalities were important, we would not, when we die, leave our bodies and nations and treasures behind. The soul--which has been scientifically "identified" by its weight at the point of death--can take with it no more than its attitudes, feelings, apprehensions and values. We all go "skinless" into the eternal, with only our attitudes to recommend us: visionaries and mystics since ancient times have warned us that there are no segregated societies beyond death, and that prejudice, and unreasonable hatred of others, is the only material infirmity that clings to us in the afterlife, hanging upon us like an albatross, and turning the suffering we have caused back upon us in the ethereal realm.

It is the hope of avoiding spiritual suffering that directs our purposes on earth: the immortal object of daily existence is not to gain wealth or status, but to learn how similar we all are underneath the borrowed clothing of place, race and culture, and beyond the defects of personal selfishness and bias. The purpose of life is to help one another to advance toward higher knowledge, and to respect and to appreciate the rich differences in all peoples.

We are not isolated, unrelated entities of a superior or inferior nature; rather we are integral parts of an immense and breathtaking picture, a panoramic display which improves in color and meaning if it reflects the fraternity of all races and nations. Without that fraternity, the invisible artist, life, succumbs to a malaise. His affliction, prejudice, is an indisposition that has been acquired from people who are emotionally and morally decayed; it is a defect that can be further transferred to the young, and then perpetuated in stereotypes presented by the media. And more, it is an ailment that destroys the texture of civilized concourse, and distorts the richness of the portrayal of ourselves as human beings striving toward perfection.

Still affirmed, in spite of the discrimination from which he had suffered, that the perfectibility of men and women was not an impossible dream. He was certain that a day would come when we would live together in "brotherhood and understanding," in " justice and kindliness," in equitableness and "fair play" (*The Blade*), and he thought that this day was as near to us as the least of us wanted it to be.

If Still had been the only one to dream the dream of human compassion, if he had been the only one to suffer from bigotry and to maintain his empathy for others in spite of oppression, the progress that has already been made toward brotherhood might not have been made. Fortunately, Still's urgings toward a cure for social corruption have been echoed by many other public figures in many other parts of the world. Dr. Jack Schwartzman, for example, who fled from Russia in the 1920's to escape the Communist tyranny, wrote of his flight from his birthplace and described his sorrow at leaving his homeland, which, at the time, was full of the smell of spring lilacs. At the end of his narrative he said,

> Men are men the world over, be they black or white or yellow or brown or red; be they Christians or Jews or Moslems or Hindus or Confucianists; be they royalists or anarchists or revolutionists or humanists or Communists; be they Frenchmen or Americans or Indians or prisoners or musicians or politicians.
>
> How wonderful it would be if the world of men were to accept diversity, and to welcome it! The earth is ablaze with the colors of flowers and fruits and foods and customs and languages of men. All things are different; therefore, all things are alike in their various magnificence.
> ("Lilacs," *The Freeman* 36 [September 1986] 337).

The high purpose of both Schwartzman and Still was to expose "the reason for man's own existence on earth" (Schwartzman, 337)--to teach that the life-force (for some, God) is in all things, apart from individual prejudices, and that the freedom of each of us to be what we are must be fostered and protected. "What the Lord hath made, let no man put asunder."

The freedom to be what we are, to make our way forward, will be maintained in a healthy society, unless the illnesses of selfishness and bigotry are left among us uncured. But, even though sickness exists among us, or festers unnoticed, the things that we learn about Barbara Knox, Alex Odeh, Mrs. Middlebrooks, Mr. and Mrs. Short and William Grant Still may well combine with the innocent acceptance of our unblemished childhoods to guard our mental and spiritual well-being from any acquired deficiency.

# WHY BLACK ISN'T BEAUTIFUL[1]

And finds, with keen, discriminating sight,
Black's not so black--nor white so *very* white.

(George Canning "New Morality,"
*The Anti-Jacobin*, 36 [1798] l. 199).

Recently, when my late father's biography was being edited for publication by the University of Arkansas Press, a Black historian who saw the manuscript complained that the author (my mother) had always referred to Afro-Americans as Negroes or Colored people, rather than "Blacks." The word "Black" ought to be used, observed the historian, for to ignore the currently-accepted term was tantamount to "waving an academic red flag" in the face of the Black community. Black was beautiful. The slogan had powerful implications that could not be ignored.

Powerful implications indeed. When the slogan first gained currency in the 1950's and '60's, my father warned against its subliminal urgings. He indicated that "the term 'Black' connoted separatism between the races, and suggested not only that there was a wide gulf between the White man and the Black man, but also that White and Black were, by nature, in opposition to each other" (R. Donald Brown, *Interview with William Grant Still* [California State University at Fullerton Oral History Program, November 13, 1967 and December 4, 1967] i).

William Grant Still felt that no dichotomy existed, or should exist, in the field of race relations, and he was joined in that feeling by several of his contemporaries, including such men as Frederick Hall, a Negro composer and eminent Doctor of Music at Dillard University. Mrs. Hall, in a letter to me dated November 8, 1981, said that Dr. Hall "has always thought as your father about the use of the term 'Black.'" Leon Zuckert, Canadian composer and instrumentalist, commented that "Negro denotes a people, and I don't understand why the Negro people should be ashamed to

---

[1] Requested for publication by the *Lincoln Review*, Lincoln Institute, Washington D.C., 1989-1990.

use that word" (Letter to Judith Anne Still, April 24, 1985). In Ethiopia, the Emperor Haile Selassie, speaking for a culture in which the word "Black" meant "slave," registered an imperious refusal to be called "Black."

But if some people have repudiated the term, just how did "Black" come into prominence as the accepted designation for the Negro race? The lexical choice is certainly strange considering its negative origins. According to J. A. Rogers, the title which has the benefit of a dignified history is clearly that of "Negro." The name Negro comes, not from the Latin Nigra or Nigrum, but from Nigrito or Nigrita, the word for the "people of the great river"-- which were "the oldest known branch of the human race" (*100 Amazing Facts About the Negro*, Second Rev. Ed. [New York: Futuro Press, Inc., 1957] 14). Other ancient names for the Negro were Nehesu or Nubian, and the terms widely used in Europe, which were Ethiopian, Moor and Black.

While it is true that the *Oxford English Dictionary* does not bear out J. A. Rogers' research, it is also true that any dictionary is a reflection of the prevailing standards among educated persons of the time, and that education does not necessarily preclude prejudice. There is every reason to affirm a pre-Roman source for the word "Negro," particularly when it is realized that some of the splendid civilizations prior to the Roman Age were "Colored" civilizations. Even the most casual observer of the likenesses of King Tutankhamen will have to admit that the ancient Egyptians were Negroes.

Yet the establishment of the term "Negro" as an illustrious designation goes beyond ancient Egypt. There is also evidence to suggest that the word "Black" is "positively a White man's word" (J. A. Rogers, 40). Coming from the Anglo-Saxon "blaec," Black "has the most horrible meanings. See any large dictionary" (40). Or, as Dr. Halford H. Fairchild, of the University of California at Los Angeles, puts it,

> Race names have long been influential in the level and maintenance of racial attitudes. Europeans were quick to label Africans "Black," because the term enhanced the perceived differences between Africans and Europeans, and because the term "Black" was heavily loaded with negative connotations in the English lexicon.

# Why Black Isn't Beautiful

(Synopsis of Dr. Fairchild's presentation for the University of California at Los Angeles faculty seminar on Afro-American studies [February 5, 1981]).

Without doubt, in the post-Civil War days, Negroes felt that being called "Black" was an insult ("Negro History Week.," *The Negro History Bulletin* II [February 1939] 34). The slaves were called "darkies" or "Blacks," the freedmen were "Coloreds," the post-World War Colored people became Negroes or Afro-Americans, and, in the fifties, the word "Black" was exhumed from its slave origins. In spite of all efforts to purify the term, it maintains its negative associations. Dr. Benjamin Alexander, the Colored chairman of the Joint Board on Science and Engineering, says that the term Black is "used consciously or unconsciously to indicate that we are inferior." Thus, "whenever society wants to take a good word and make it negative, it too often only has to add the word, black, as an adjective," as in "black list," "black market," "black mail" and "black death" ("Are We Black?" *Lincoln Review* 7 [Fall 1986] 47).

Dr. Alexander's accusations are supported by polls taken for the Los Angeles *Sentinel*, a Negro newspaper, and for *Jet Magazine*, also an Afro-American publication. In these surveys it was found that 33% of all Negroes wanted to be called "Afro-American," while only 10.6% preferred "Black," and 10.6% liked "Colored." The other 45.8% chose "Negro" and other assorted terms such as "Exotics" and "Mixed Americans" (*The Sentinel* [August 8, 1968]). A similar survey of White Americans produced similar results, when an investigation by Dr. Fairchild discovered that the word "Black" carried with it many negative connotations which were not ascribed to other labels such as "Afro-American." Only 9% of White university students polled thought that Afro-Americans were lazy, 28% viewed Negroes as lazy, and 35% saw Blacks as lazy (Dr. Fairchild's presentation at UCLA).

The question must again be asked, if "Black" has always been used to convey a sense of ill-feeling, why did it gain favor in the 1950's and 60's during the time of racial ferment? The leaders of certain right-wing Negro groups lay the blame in the laps of political radicals whose advocacy of "blackness," it is claimed, is part of a shrewdly orchestrated leftist propaganda campaign.

Clay Claiborne, National Director of the Black Silent Majority Committee (2714 West Avenue, San Antonio, Texas 78201), traces the Communist leanings of the Black Panthers and the Black Nationalists with the help of FBI documents and militant newspaper articles. He quotes Michael Laski, member of the Central Committee of the Communist Party, as saying that his group spent two years agitating to create the Watts riots ("'Right On'...to What?" Black Silent Majority pamphlet [1974]). During this agitation, the use of key words such as "Whitey," "Black power," and "pig," gave focus to the insistence that the two races could not avoid involvement in a class struggle. The normal evolution of the language of race was interrupted by the sweep of organized anarchy.

J. A. (Jaye) Parker, the Afro-American president of the Lincoln Institute (1001 Connecticut Ave. N.W., Washington, D.C. 20069) makes similar accusations against leftist minorities, and says that the "bare facts about the use of the term 'Black' should be brought to the attention of the American public" (Letter to Judith Anne Still [August 6, 1984]). In a mass-mailing written during the spring of 1984, Parker states that 150 black "ultra left-wing" groups are conspiring to make the public believe that Negroes present a united front against the government's administration. Denying the fiction that hardship makes Negroes militant, Parker adds that he climbed out of abject poverty to become an award-winning insurance salesman, and one of the most popular talk-show hosts in Philadelphia. He entered politics as a teenager in the mid-1950's, became a leader of the Young Americans for Freedom in the early 60's, and headed the Reagan Transition Team at the Equal Employment Opportunity Commission (EEOC). Today he is a leading proponent of the free enterprise system.

Both Parker and Claiborne are living proof that all Negroes are not oppressed and militant. How then has the image of the angry Black man become so widespread? Surely some of the culpability can be ascribed to the media, as the press and television have given wide coverage to race riots and to the

## Why Black Isn't Beautiful

opinions of men like Eldridge Cleaver, Huey Newton, and Malcolm X, but little attention to the work of J. A. Parker and Clay Claiborne.

My mother, Mrs. Verna Arvey Still, in a speech to the Pasadena Interracial Women's Club on February 5, 1964, declared that constructive and successful efforts to promote good race relations are not given their due in the media. "It seldom seems as interesting to talk about people who are getting along together," she said, "as it is to gossip about those who aren't." (Mother, who is Jewish, could never convince book publishers that her interracial marriage to a Colored man was a success; "Your story won't sell," they told her privately. "The public won't believe it, and neither do we.")

However, the role of the media in bolstering the negative associations of the militant word, "Black," goes beyond the simple refusal to believe. In 1983, a media critic complained that, after nine years on television, the comedy show "The Jeffersons" was being neutered by removing its "blackness" (Mary Helen Washington, "As their blackness disappears, so does their character," *TV Guide* 31 [July 30-August 5, 1983] 4-9). What did the reviewer mean by "blackness"? "Blackness," she explained, involved coarse references to White people, the use of the word "Nigger," Afro-hair styles, frequent allusions to roaches and the ghetto, and lower-class roles such as the caustic Colored maid or the youth who was convicted of shop-lifting. According to Ms. Washington, the view of the Black person should be one of an oppressed figure being forced to climb out of the ashes in order to live acceptably in an alien world. Television writers must admit, she adds, that most Blacks aren't "living in a high-rise dream world of mink, ultra-suede and corporate investments" (Washington, 9).

The assertions made by this *TV Guide* journalist are representative of a pervasive attitude in the media toward Negroes. It is presumed that Afro-Americans who appear on television talk-shows must be interested in the ghetto, Africa, the West Indies, or "Black culture." Martin Luther King is touted as a liberator of a subjugated race which has accomplished nothing because it has been consistently barred from accomplishment.

Black movies or situation comedies must always express "Black life," which is, inevitably, low-class. Both White and Black media critics told Brock Peters that his production, "Five on the Black Hand Side," would be unsuccessful because it dealt with a middle-class Black family. The same warning was given to Bill Cosby when he proposed his upper-middle-class comedy. What a shock to the people who read the public mind, when Peters and Cosby were vindicated.

News commentators invariably believe that any Black politician, Republican or Democrat, can speak for all Negroes in regard to crucial issues. No White politician would be asked, "What is the feeling of the White community about the present administration?," and yet, time and again, liberal Black candidates for office are asked to speak for the conservative Colored populace.

In 1985, the Center for Media and Public Affairs, located in Washington, D.C., revealed a startling disparity between the opinions of Negro "leaders" and the views of average Colored people. The Center polled 105 heads of the major Black political and civil rights groups, as well as 600 randomly sampled Afro-American laymen. The men touted by the media as spokesmen for Black people claimed that Negroes in this country were not making any progress; they said that they themselves had been victims of bigotry, and they supported busing and preferential treatment for minorities. By contrast, average Colored people said that they had not been victims of discrimination, they opposed busing and preferential treatment, and they felt that Negroes in this country *were* making progress (Linda S. Lichter, "The gap between Black leaders and Black laymen," The Orange County, California, *Register* [September 26, 1985]).

In a like vein, the Los Angeles *Sentinel* poll revealed that most Afro-Americans "believe that Cassius Clay-Muhammed Ali made a mistake when he refused to submit to the military draft, that many American Negroes believe that Adam Clayton Powell was as much a victim of his own arrogance as he was of racial prejudice, if not more so; and that most American Negroes want *more* police protection not less" (*Sentinel* [August 8, 1968]).

Strange that these opinions are rarely expressed on television,

## Why Black Isn't Beautiful

in the movies, and by the press. In the media, the Negro is often the object of stereotyping, and, most often, the dark side of the race problem in the United States is emphasized. News reports dwell on the fact that one out of every two Black children live in poverty, and that Negroes are one of the largest sources of crime in the nation. "White guilt" is a theme frequently reiterated--the purported poverty, violence and illiteracy of Negroes is seen as a result of the devastating affects of slavery, lynchings and race riots. It is thought that White people should give Colored people an edge in education and the job market because "Whitey" has been guilty of heinous crimes against minorities.

To say that today's media overemphasize the ugly side of the race question is not to imply, certainly, that minorities have no cause to be indignant over injustice. Indeed, there is reason to be concerned about the resurgence of visible racial animosity in the United States. Nazi groups are reappearing, while the Institute for Historical Review is attempting to deny the truth of the Holocaust. William B. Shockley has gained the attention of many by promulgating the belief that Blacks are genetically inferior to Whites, and the Ku Klux Klan is finding new sources of energy in all parts of the country.

It is absolutely necessary to reply to the vocal White people who continue to insist that Negroes have had nothing to do with the development of American culture and history. My father often spoke out on the subject, particularly in the 1940's when the self-styled patriot, Reverend Fifield, announced over the radio that minority groups would have to be put in their places. On February 25, 1946, William Grant Still wrote in a letter to Fifield,

> As a Christian, you surely know that Christ did not give the world to any single group of people. And you know that the greatest lesson He brought to earth was that of the brotherhood of man and the Fatherhood of God. Can you then deny anyone whom God has created the right to exist equally with other men under His supervision? I am wondering, too, to which minority groups your remark referred. Was it the Negro, the Jew, the Mexican, the Catholics, or to the people of other nations who have now become Americans? Or was it to the Anglo-Saxon who is now in the minority all over the world, yet who has been aggressive enough to

deny basic human rights to many other peoples of darker skin?

That Negroes have too often been prohibited from enjoying their basic human rights is true. What is not true is that the situation is pervasive or unalterable: "White guilt" and "Black deprivation" are both mythological concepts. Because many Negroes may have been poor and ignorant in the past, it is not to be concluded that all are deprived, or that conditions will continue to keep them in poverty and ignorance. Because, in bygone days, too many Whites enslaved or lynched Negroes, it is not an axiom that all White people remain guilty for these injustices. If a man had a parent who was an alcoholic, should he also be classed as an alcoholic even though he avoids liquor? Because there were witchhunts in New England over 200 years ago, should present-day descendants of the early Puritans feel responsible for the hanging of witches?

If most White people were racist, our Negro achievers would never have been able to make the strides that they have made toward historical immortality. Though my father suffered because of his color, he was grateful to White men for making large orchestras and publishing houses available to him, and the list of Caucasians who helped him included renowned figures such as Leopold Stokowski, Howard Hanson, Karl Krueger, Eleanor Roosevelt and Mayor Fiorello LaGuardia.

Without doubt, guilt must give way to awareness. As a result of the unemployment situation caused by the Great Depression and trade unionism, Negroes are now one of the largest sources of crime in the United States; and yet, there are indications that this crime is directed more against themselves than against White people. A Black Silent Majority Committee pamphlet [1974] reports that seven out of ten crimes committed against Blacks are committed by Blacks.

And, Negroes are not necessarily poor. At the close of the period of racial unrest, Charles Gould of the *San Francisco Examiner* stated that,

> A recent official report shows that since 1960 the number of Negro families earning more than $7,000 a year has increased more than 100 percent. In just four years the number of Negroes hired for

professional jobs had climbed 35 percent.

We have more than 300 Negro millionaires in our nation. We have more Negroes acting as judges...more in Congress...more in state legislatures...more in our city halls...and, more in positions of power than all the Communist nations of the world combined.
(Reprinted in the El Toro, California, *Rancho Reporter* [August 5, 1970] 2).

Gould's words were borne out by Henry Hazlitt, who collected statistics to show that the Negro middle-class has grown in size in the last forty years. Between 1949 and 1969, the increase in real family incomes of Negroes outstripped those of Whites by 47%. Hazlitt also noted that, although unemployment of Negroes was always higher than that of Whites, the income of employed northern Negroes was 99% to 107% of the income of employed northern Whites ("The Story of Negro Gains," *The Freeman* 21 [November 1971] 694-698).

Not only are not all Negroes poor, but they are also not all uneducated. Moreover, they were not uneducated in the 1950's and 60's. Hazlitt reports that, from 1957 to 1967, Negroes gained 1.4 years on the Whites in years of school completed (Hazlitt, 695). Statistics from J. A. Rogers reveal that, "In 1957, the White population of New York was 1.3 more illiterate than the Negro one." Over 500 Negroes had doctorates in 1950, and over 230 taught in leading White universities. The distinguished Colored M.D., William A. Hinton, was a professor in the Harvard Medical School and was recognized as a world-wide authority in his field (Rogers, 3, 45). Dr. Benjamin Alexander's records report that "there are over 600 descendants of slaves who are millionaires; there is one Supreme Court jurist, 20 United States representatives, 90 State senators, 300 State representatives, 200 mayors, 2,500 councilmen or aldermen, 500 county officials, and more than 6,000 who hold elective office in this country" ("His Truth Is Not Marching On," *Lincoln Review* 6 [Winter 1986] 12).

If the education of Afro-Americans in the United States is compared to all races in other countries, their progress becomes clear. Rogers tells us that Negro literacy since 1870 has risen 85% in the U. S., while 62% of the world's population is illiterate. The peoples of Europe and Russia are less able to read and write than Negroes of this country, and Colored people of the North, East and West are more literate than Whites of the South (Rogers, 5, 23). Charles Gould notes that "Today the average Negro in our nation is more likely to go to college than the average citizen-- White or Black--in England, Germany, Belgium, Denmark, Italy or Spain" (Gould, 2).

Clearly the hardships have not prevented courageous and hardworking Negroes from becoming educated, to the extent that the tales of achievement are too numerous to recount. For example, Mrs. Frances Graham of Milwaukee, a divorced Negro mother of five children, worked her way to a Master's Degree after reaching the age of twenty-six. Ultimately she became a curriculum counselor, purchased a $40,000 home, and made plans to open a skating rink for inner-city youth (*The National Insider* 25 [August 25, 1974]). Twenty years before Mrs. Graham's degree was acquired, William Grant Still wrote in his diary,

> Phoned Bill Jones' boy to compliment him on being admitted to the California bar. I feel happy when I see fine young Colored Americans of that type, for they can do much to help bring nearer the day when all racial barriers will have disappeared (January 15, 1953).

Of course Still was cognizant of the fact that it was not a new trend for Negroes to be educated and successful. Minority accomplishments have been a matter of record throughout American history. Donald Dorr, historian and musicologist, has discovered during his researches that a large number of Negroes and Mulattos in the 1880's were literate, especially those living in Wilkinson County, Mississippi, near the farms of Milton and Duncan Still. Even in the days of slavery Negroes were often educated. A document unearthed by Dorr indicates that two children born to a slave and to Thompson Stille, a White slave-owner, were bequeathed to Lewis Stille on condition that Lewis teach them to read and set them free when they reached the age of thirty (Undated letters from Donald Dorr to Judith Anne Still [1983]).

In 1863, the slave George Wesley Allen was set free in

Alabama, and his first act upon gaining his freedom was that of finding someone to teach him to read. After much private study he built his own school house and became a teacher himself. Later he became, also, a preacher, a Congressman, and a co-founder of Tuskegee Institute, a teacher's college for Negroes. As time went on he helped to educate his brothers and sisters and his children, all of whom received degrees and became professional people. His formula for achieving success, he said, was "hard study, sacrifice and self-control," plus a firm belief in God and a faith in "the dignity of human personality" (A. K. Kenney, "The Legacy," *Columbus Magazine* [June 15-July 15, 1959] 4).

Actually, while George Allen was incredibly gifted, he was not an isolated phenomenon. In discussing the Creoles in Louisiana, Dalt Wonk touches on the fact that many free Colored people in pre-Civil War New Orleans were well-schooled and cultured. He says, the Colored Creoles were "educated, refined, extremely literate, aware of the latest styles and the currents of their times," and they "put a great strain on the theory of Negro inferiority that underpinned slavery." He adds, too, that relations between the races in New Orleans, though restricted by law, were actually freer and more intimate under the surface than they are today ("The Creoles of Color," *New Orleans Magazine* X [May 1976] 55).

Thus, if Negroes have a long acquaintance with education and accomplishment, why is this acquaintance-ship not generally known to the public? As it has been pointed out, the mass media are partially responsible. Dr. S. I. Hayakawa said in 1970,

> The other day, I saw to my great horror that Stokely Carmichael was given an hour interview on one of the networks. This, when there are distinguished people like Andrew Brimmer, the first Negro to serve as governor of the Federal Reserve Board, available.
> 
> Brimmer will do more in one week for advancement of the Negro cause and for the advancement of all of us in general, than Stokely Carmichael will ever do in his lifetime.
> 
> (*Mission Viejo Newspost*, Editorial Section, [August 26, 1970]).

Hayakawa's view is more vigorously stated by Bert Underwood, the novelist, composer and violist who was the first

Colored man to play with the Detroit Symphony. While alluding to his novels, Mr. Underwood says that his works deal with "the better days for the educated Colored, i.e., before the media and middle Whites got into the picture of telling us who we are" (Letter to Judith Anne Still [April 24, 1985]). He explains that,

> When my book *A Branch of Velvet* came out ten years ago, the *New York Times*--and others--insisted I use the word 'Black' in advertisements and I refused, saying Colored and Negro had been dignified and there was no reason to change. Even a celebrated author exchanged a long dialogue on whether people of Color preferred Black or Negro. I thought he was one of our most enlightened writers, but in the end the kind of people I knew were completely unknown to him. He told me I would be pleased with Colored characters in his next book, but when I read of a family out of Philadelphia who supposedly were free of slavery for several hundred years still talking a thick dialect of the slums, and living in disgraceful circumstances...I realized that writers like others have difficulty picturing Colored persons of culture and background; so I decided I would continue to write on this subject, and you can believe it, most publishers will shy away from my books and my subject.
> 
> (Letter to Judith Anne Still [April 8, 1985]).
> 
> Today we are in terrible danger from television and the media short-cutting history down to a convenient "lie" which even Negro people believe! ...they forced this horrible word 'Black' on people without referendum--they control the spoken and written word in America. ...To me it was like asking the Jewish people in Europe to sew yellow stars on their armbands...
> 
> (Letter to Edmund Opitz [June 13, 1985]).

Underwood's case against the media is strongly made. Beyond the media, however, much of the blame may also be placed at the feet of the academicians and proponents of the fine arts. White and Negro professors in the universities, and Negro writers and artists in the world of culture, actively promote the concept of the abused and revolutionary Black, or the image of the violent and sexually blatant Black.

George H. Lewis, academician, is self-assured in his conviction that "Black music celebrates sex with a directly physical beat," and it reveals the Black "community's shared perspective," a perspective which is different from that of the "straight white world" (George H. Lewis, "This Bitter Earth," *National Forum* LXII [Summer 1982] 26, 28).

Mr. Lewis' assessment of the Black community and its culture is similar to that of many Afro-American writers and artists. During a Writer's Day Conference at Mount San Antonio College, California, on February 9, 1974, Ishmael Reed, Negro poet, novelist and author of *Mumbo-Jumbo* and *Conjure*, spoke of the Black experience as being unproductive, dissident and atrophied. America is a mirage to the Black man, asserted Reed--Blacks are always thirsting vainly for the American dream, while the stench of offal remains in their nostrils.

Later, on April 5, 1974, the Twenty-Fifth Annual meeting of the Conference on College Composition and Communication presented a group of scholars who painted a portrait of the black writer in America. The Black writer, decided the learnéd professors, was like other Blacks in that he was depressed by unemployment, poverty and street violence, and in that he was motivated by anger toward protest and confrontation.

When the panelists had finished drawing these conclusions, Thomas Gabriel, a dignified Colored graduate student from California State University, Dominguez Hills, rose to address the group. He spoke, he said, out of respect for his twenty years of experience "on the streets," to erase the false notion that most Colored people are pitiful victims of bigotry and oppression. Black life in the main, he continued, is no different from White life. Negroes (like Shylock) work, eat, sleep, love and laugh like other human beings, and any significant variations between them and others are individual rather than collective. Negroes have sought for centuries to prove to White people that they have similar goals and abilities, only to be told by academicians that they are still second-class citizens.

Gabriel's observations apply not just to the CCCC panelists, but also to the poetry of Ishmael Reed. The irony of Reed's view is that the stench of offal is nothing that he experienced himself: he was a self-taught drop-out who grew up in a comfortable home. As it was not fashionable to be a well-fed Negro in the artistic vein--as publishers were not interested in stories about his simple childhood--Reed wrote verse about the despairing Black, full of the penniless anguish that scholars expected to find in Black literature.

Reed's publishers and readers never thought to question the fact that the Black man had a corner on the market of anguish; had they done so, they would have been forced to admit that all Blacks are not despairing, and that the despairing White man is equally as pitiful as the despairing Black. White authors such as John Steinbeck and Jack London were severely criticized early in their careers for their portrayal of life among the lower classes, yet Ishmael Reed was expected to deal with the subject of deprivation.

This fallacious expectation that "Blackness" means despair is in fact a form of prejudice. "Blackness" is accepted as the only reality, and Black literature is separated from regular English and American literature courses in the curriculum, as if to say that Black culture should be isolated from the mainstream. If students do not enroll in Black studies programs, they learn nothing of Negro achievement or creativity. James Baldwin, Richard Wright and Malcolm X are discussed in high schools and universities because they are thought to best represent the Black man in his role as a bitter dissident, and the White man as a repugnant racist. Meanwhile, impeccable, non-militant Colored writers such as Paul Laurence Dunbar, Countee Cullen, George Schuyler, Frank Yerby, Alexander Dumas and Alexander Pushkin are glossed over or ignored. Composers like William Grant Still, whose works are not "sexual" and whose beliefs do not include a hatred for the "straight white world," are frequently discriminated against for being "Uncle Toms."

The prejudice against Negro excellence inherent in the term "Black" is ultimately destructive, for to ignore talent is to destroy talent. Students of the fine arts are told that the themes and ways of expression of Negro writers, musicians and painters are different from those of other artists, and so they reject works of genius which do not reflect the perceived differences. Art, music and literature which do not fit the image are identified as being irrelevant or lacking in cultural distinction. Young developing artists do not rely on their own creative instincts as they search for styles and themes--rather they imitate the misconceptions taught them by the advocates of "Black culture."

The promulgation of the misconceptions is inescapable. In an anthology called *The Black Aesthetic*, by Addison Gayle, Jr. [Doubleday, 1971], Hoyt Fuller says that "The two races are residents of two separate and naturally antagonistic worlds." He rejects all European traditions and suggests that Black art must be revolutionary and committed to its blackness. Fuller's ferment is reflected in a record company slogan, "Jazz is black and must be kept that way." To that "axiom" Leonard Feather replies in the Los Angeles *Times*,

> ...a statement such as "opera is Italian and must be kept that way," ...could have prevented Marian Anderson and Roland Hayes and many...White Americans, from taking part in the interpretation of a form that has surely transcended its national origin.
> (Calendar Section [October 3, 1971]).

What Leonard Feather is really saying is that genius knows neither cultural boundaries, nor social restrictions. It is powerfully given without concern for the appearance of things, and it expresses themes which are common to all peoples. There is much unrecognized genius in Negro literature and art, and genius is rarely voiced in terms which are predominantly cheated, despairing, gross and violent.

Etta Moten, the Negro singer and actress, says that poverty has only become a deplorable condition of Afro-American life since the "Ghettocrats" have taken over. She says that, as a child, she did not consider herself poor, even though she only "had one dress for each season." Her mother saw that she spoke English eloquently and sang beautifully, because "that was the way things were done then. But now, we have these 'Ghettocrats.' These people who make a business of being poor and telling a poor-mouth story. We had too much pride for that" (James A. Standifer, "Reminiscences of Black Musicians," *American Music* 4 [Summer 1986] 195).

The Colored opera singer, Anne Brown, expands on Etta Moten's comment when she observes, "The trend today is to do your thing as well as you can and don't bother about the rest being good, and maybe compromising a few principles along the way. That's not my idea...[you must] give everything you've got if you're going to be an artist and have real greatness as your goal" (Standifer, 197).

Speaking in a vein similar to that of Moten and Brown, my parents, in a 1973 interview, deplored the loss of recognition which had come to William Grant Still as a result of militant propaganda in the 1950's and 1960's (Fran Zone, "Interview with Mr. and Mrs. William Grant Still," [February 24, 1973] unpublished). It was a shame, complained my mother, that William Grant Still had become just a Black composer whose works were played only during Negro History Week, when at one time he had been regarded as being on a par with Bach and Sibelius. My father interjected that this diminishment of reputation had come from the fact that there were "too many limitations" in the word "Black" (Zone, 21).

Proceeding to explain my father's remark about limitations, my mother commented,

> This black, black, black thing is going to be a dead-end street eventually...My brother was teaching in the University of Mississippi...in the scientific field, and I said, "Have you had any difficulty with militants?" and he said, "No, we haven't yet been asked to teach black biology." ...If you get to the ultimate in this black business, that means that nobody but Black people can play a black composer's music, and nobody but Black people can listen to it. This is ridiculous.

Then, in another interview, she added,

> ...we have always been for brotherhood, ...[but] if you say 'Black' don't you automatically think of 'White?' It's a separatist thing.
> (Frank Hains, "On Stage," Jackson, Mississippi *Daily News* [November 15, 1974] D-6).

Another approach to the predicament of Still and other serious Afro-American composers is found in the letters of Donald Dorr. Mr. Dorr observes,

> ...All most people know of "Black" musicians is your typical poor unlettered blues strummer who, born in 1926 or thereabouts, is an

"original" blues strummer, unspoiled by civilization or grammar. These kind are dredged up every year here in an annual "Blues Festival"...One is supposed to get teary-eyed and reverent... Anything in the blues line dating to the 30's will pass for pure holy writ, the whole generation of Handy and Still and their achievements being bypassed for, say, Pete Seeger. Or Lomax... . But how many Blacks, grateful, I suppose, for recognition at last, go along with the charade: after all, isn't Whitey sitting out there on the grass clapping his hands and nodding his head and paying his money for ol' Uncle Bob from the swamps to have a good time in the big city? And Uncle Bob so colorful and primitive and all?

(Letter to Judith Anne Still [March 3, 1984]).

Of course, William Grant Still did not "go along with the charade," and thus on numerous occasions he made an effort to set the record straight. He had always cherished his origins, he said, had fought for civil rights, had tried to express the American Negro in his music,...but he was not a Black composer. He was an American composer who happened to be a Negro. "We're all Americans, regardless of color. We either make it together or we don't make it at all" (Richmond, Virginia *News-Leader* [March 20, 1971]).

Still's viewpoint was rarely given credence unless his music was assessed apart from the "Black" tradition. A critic who was appalled by the lack of support for a concert of works by Black composers, noted that some of Still's work had "freshness, charm and originality," and that "there is nothing distinctively 'Negro' about a serious Negro composer. The music could have been composed by men of any color or ethnic background" (T. E. Foreman, "Music leaders fail to attend concert," *The Riverside Press* [Nov. 2, 1966] D-2).

Such observations, however, were few and far between. Despite Still's desire to be known as an American composer who happened to be a Negro, he was continually labeled as the "Dean of Black Composers," to which he responded, "Why, then, isn't Aaron Copland called the 'Dean of White Composers'?" When conductor Fabien Sevitsky played Still's music he was called a "friend to Black composers," not a friend to William Grant Still. Because Leopold Stokowski felt that Still was "one of our greatest American composers" (Baltimore *Afro-American* [April 21, 1945]), he was greeted at the train station upon his arrival in Los Angeles by a Negro jazz band. It was believed that a musician who liked the compositions of one Negro composer would naturally welcome those of any other Negro musical entity. Everyone was horrified when the Maestro covered his ears and rushed back into the train car as the band began to play.

Donald Dorr's succinct summation of the influence of blackness on Negro culture is given when he discusses the "acclimation of William Grant Still as the Dean of Black Composers." He says,

> Certainly during his long career William Grant Still worked successfully in music not because he was Black, but because he was simply a good musician. He was in the musical marketplace and was valued, as anyone else, white, black or yellow, for what he could produce; I doubt that Artie Shaw hired under the quota system. [Still arranged for Shaw, Paul Whiteman, Don Voorhees, Sophie Tucker, W.C. Handy and others in the 20's and 30's.] But now people are hired so often because they are Black (whatever that means) and we tend to transpose our understanding of the past...Our perception of Blacks--often enough 'used' by Blacks themselves--tends to override the exceptions.
>
> (Letter to Judith Anne Still [March 3, 1984]).

Mr. Dorr's reference to the reverse discrimination that has resulted from civil rights activism goes to the jugular of the racial falsehoods in modern thinking. We have passed through a deplorable period in which standards have been lowered so that minority students could be passed in school, or so that minority candidates might be hired in police and fire departments and government agencies. It has even been urged that students be allowed to speak "Black English," the rationale being that the legitimizing of the idiomatic, non-standard speech of the lower class Negroes would contribute to a sense of Negro identity. Yet the hundreds of thousands of educated Negroes who speak standard, nonidiomatic English should be evidence that identity is no more created by the use of superficial idioms among Negroes than it is among Whites. Negroes are capable of speaking and writing in any idiom or language without loss of identity.

By the same token, Negroes are perfectly capable of meeting standards for diplomas, degrees and jobs. To reward those whose lack of effort or talent deserves no reward, is demeaning to all concerned. Such recognition tells society that the Negro can't achieve, and that, as a result, any legitimate achievements by those who display ability mean nothing. As Sociology professor Charles Boss puts it, "We are learning that equality of educational opportunity does not make us equal, but unequal" (Charles Boss, professor at Los Angeles City College, Los Angeles *Herald-Examiner*, Letters to the Editor [May 16, 1976]).

In order to combat these manufactured inequalities in a society gone culturally and ethically astray, it is necessary for Negroes to avoid demanding acceptance on the basis of wrongs done to them rather than on the basis of talent. The hubris of denying excellence in favor of mediocrity must cease, and Negroes at every level of competence must be expected to make the grade on the basis of their own individual merits. In the words of Dr. Benjamin Alexander, it is the "experts" and the "Boards of Trustees, and not the disadvantaged students, who want these damn doctored math, doctored English, doctored science...and also the meaningless doctored diplomas for the low income group" ("His Truth Is Not Marching on," 11).

Expectation is, after all, a significant aspect of accomplishment. Research studies have shown that students will gain in IQ and self-esteem if they are treated as if they are capable, and adults are more likely to succeed if they are expected to do so (John Kord Lagemann, "Self-Fulfilling Prophecy--A Key to Success," *Reader's Digest* 102 [February 1969] 80-83). If Colored people are presented in the universities and on television as being foul-mouthed, White-hating shoplifters, they will tend to become just that. If they are shown to be respectable citizens living in a high-rise, they will aspire toward that lifestyle.

The proof of this principle of self-fulfillment is being demonstrated by several modern-day educators. The midwestern school superintendent, Gene Mulcahy, is dealing with the low test scores of his Afro-American students by encouraging better study habits among them, and by urging their teachers to expect more of them. Mulcahy is convinced that "low level expectations squelch Black students" (Hattie Clark, "Rousting skeletons in school cloakrooms," *The Christian Science Monitor* 79 [April 24, 1987] 1, 32). Marva Collins, the head of Westside Prep School in Chicago, is teaching unteachable youngsters out of the ghetto by telling them that they are going to be corporate executives, and that she expects them to excel (Bob Herguth, "Marva Collins' Credo," *Friendly Exchange* [Fall 1984] 19-21).

Of course Negroes cannot be expected to find fulfillment if they are stifled by labels and stereotypical notions about the Black experience. An emphasis ought to be placed upon individual virtue and dignity, for virtue and dignity are two qualities which are more important to more Colored people than the academicians and media commentators care to acknowledge. In a volume called *1,000 Successful Blacks* (Charles L. Sanders, ed., The Ebony Success Library I [Nashville, Tennessee: Johnson Publishing Company, Inc., 1973]), the remarkable stories of distinguished Negroes are told. For example, Richard Linyard, executive vice-president and member of the Board of Directors of Seaway National Bank in Chicago, began his career as a janitor. From janitor he moved through the ranks of elevator operator, savings bookkeeper, teller, general bookkeeper, assistant manager of the savings department, assistant cashier, and vice-president of the Chicago branch of the American Institute of Banking (204).

Linyard's case is inspiring, yet it is not necessary to look only among wealthy Negroes to find the anti-"Black" attitude. Madison H. Carter, a retiree from a job at the Alcoholics' Treatment Center in Albuquerque, New Mexico, is known for championing the works of little-known ethnic composers. He writes,

> I cannot see any favorable advancement for the ethnic group since it [the word "Black"] is the "in" thing to say. ...I'm sure that a lot of citizens of African ancestry see the mistake made but go along with the crowd rather than point out the huge blunder that was made in the sixties and seventies by listening to Stokely Carmichael, H. Rap Brown and others. What should be promoted is [that] they are citizens of the United States or United States of America. AMERICANS!

Let's get down to the very important goals in life--first class American citizenship, becoming better educated, seeking knowledge, getting into the technical fields, learning the history of the African American in the Western Hemisphere, and letting the rest of America know we care about the U.S. ...
> (*Albuquerque Tribune* [June 1, 1973]; and, in a letter to Judith Anne Still [October 15, 1984]).

Another person worth mentioning in this regard is Mr. Garron Gordon, a light-skinned Negro whose background blends several ethnic strains and nationalities, especially the Irish. Mr. Gordon is self-educated, having been forced into the work force by the Depression right after completing the third grade. He has labored in many occupations, and in his later years has been employed as both a barber and a security guard. In the 1970's Mr. Gordon and his wife were two of eight Colored people living in a Leisure World community of 250,000 in Laguna Hills, California, and they were so much-loved by their neighbors that, when Mrs. Gordon died, her funeral was one of the largest in the history of the McCormick Mortuary. In speaking of his feelings about the Black experience, Mr. Gordon declares,

> I don't care for the word black. If someone asks me if he should call me Black, I tell them, "just call me Gordon." I act as an individual. I demand respect and I get it, not by taking a militant stand for civil rights, but by being a gentleman and respecting the dignity of others.

Obviously there is a vast area of respectability and individual integrity in Negro life which the term Black seems to obscure. And, Mr. Gordon's Irish ancestry brings up another issue: the espousal of "blackness" also masks the deep damask nuances of color and heritage which contribute to the personhood of every Afro-American.

My great-grandfather was a Scotch overseer who sired two sons by a Negro slave. One of these sons, in turn, married an Indian, and from that union sprang my grandfather. On my grandmother's side, the mixture was just as varied, for it was replete with Negro, Indian, Irish and Spanish forebears. In addition, my father married a Jewish lady with Russian progenitors, so that I was born with "white skin." However, my youngest daughter is dark enough to be classified visually as a light-skinned Colored person, but certainly it would be wrong to call her Black and to ignore, thereby, her luxuriant ancestry. (Artie Shaw, the 40's bandleader and family friend, captured the richness of the blend when he called us, "white chocolate.")

A Negro friend of mine, Ruperta Waters, who is a prize-winning philatelist and horticulturalist from Baltimore, springs from an ancestral line which boasts of a Mohawk Indian, a Dutch woman, and a Spanish Jew who was a member of the House of Commons in England. Mrs. Waters' mother grew up in Bermuda and had friends of so many differing ethnic backgrounds that she learned to speak Yiddish, Dutch, French, Spanish, Portuguese and English.

Dominique-René de Lerma, an author, academician, and historian of the first order, says that the term "Black" is a special problem to him. He explains,

> When Roque Cordero was added to our Columbia recordings and identified as Black, he was upset. Not that he had anything against his African forebears, but he had equal respect for his Indian and Spanish heritage, and a combination of all of these made him Panamanian. ...[This] shows racism in American thinking, which has been accepted by the Afro-American (who also ignores other heritages).
>
> And when we try to define Black music, we come to grips with the question of skin color or culture. If the latter wins out we might have to add Villa-Lobos to the list (the irony being that his first wife was Black, he wasn't, and that any children from this union would have been Black, while the father was not! How can a child have a heritage not common with the parent?).
>
> (Letter to Judith Anne Still [January 31, 1985]).

Assuredly the ethnic treasures in the Villa-Lobos family are lost when it is labeled "Black." And not only is much that is valuable lost in the push for "blackness," but also much that contributes to the understanding of the race problem becomes hidden from view. The term Black is deceptive and simplistic because it suggests that prejudice is simply a Black vs. White issue. In actuality, prejudice is as large a problem within minority groups as it is without.

In pre-Civil War days, the slave-owner taught his slaves to scorn the poor White, while the poor White had contempt for the slave (Shirley Graham, "Spirituals to Symphonies," *Etude* LIV [November 1936) 691-692, 723, 736). Mulattos in Mississippi in the nineteenth century were genuinely disliked by Blacks, just as Blacks were shunned by the Whites. Some light-skinned Colored people owned slaves themselves.

In New Orleans the problem has traditionally had multiple facets in a complex caste system. To the racial animosities among Blacks, Mulattos and Whites are added those between the White Creoles and the Colored Creoles, Creoles being the descendants of the French people who colonized Louisiana. Furthermore, difficulties once existed among the Mulattos and the Quadroons, the fair-skinned free persons of Color who came from Cuba, Guadeloupe and other islands during the Napoleonic wars. While each racial group has stubbornly refused to associate outwardly with at least one other racial bloc, inter-mixing of bloodlines has gone on covertly, allowing many Colored persons to cross the color line.

In the days of segregation, it was very possible for one person designated as White and another identified as Colored to be members of the same family. If both of these persons happened to work in the same place, the one who claimed to be White would receive two or three times as much pay for the same work as the one who looked Afro-American. The one who passed for White would be allowed to ride in front of the streetcar, but the other would be relegated to the rear (Wonk, "The Creoles of Color," 51). The racial absurdities in New Orleans may no longer be as legal or as obvious as they once were, yet they are indicative of the tendency of light-skinned people everywhere to feel superior to those who are dark-skinned. As George S. Schuyler puts it,

> Among Negroes the preference is for pale or light skins and straight hair. This intra-racial color bias is more prevalent among West Indians and Latin Americans than among Negroes in this country, and it is declining here more rapidly than it is down there perhaps because the Blacks here have more education and

economic power.
("Are Negroes More Prejudiced than Whites?," *Negro Digest* X [November 1951] 42).

Unfortunately, Schuyler sees only a portion of the problem. Not only do light-skinned Negroes look down upon dark-skinned Negroes, but also the people of one oppressed minority look down on individuals of another oppressed minority. In his diary on January 14, 1953, William Grant Still lamented,

> Strange it is indeed that people who belong to a race despised since ancient days look on us colored Americans with contempt! Centuries of experience have taught them nothing. Verna's aunt insulted her today. She, a Jewish woman, looks down on her niece who married a Colored man.

Still's lament reaches backward like Lot seeking his wife, calling up memories of Biblical days and of the Holocaust in Europe. It is in fact a lament for the peoples of the world, since the problem of prejudice is a global dilemma. After all, two-thirds of all the people in the world are Colored, not White: they are yellow, red, brown or black, and there are reputed to be sixteen different races among them. Yet, in spite of this diversity, prejudice abounds everywhere.

According to an Associated Press Survey published on July 11, 1963, unreasonable bias exists whether or not it is forbidden by statute. The Arabs in North Africa and the Blacks in equatorial Africa discriminate against Whites and Asians. Australians do not allow Colored races to emigrate there. In India over one-fifth of the population is branded by the census as "untouchable," and there are 41 castes and 3,000 local subcastes. In Ceylon the Hindus and Roman Catholics are prevented by the Buddhists from getting civil jobs. In Pakistan the constitution states that no non-Muslims may serve in the presidency, and Hindus cannot work in the government in any capacity. Indonesia discriminates against the Chinese, while Russia restricts the freedom of Jews and Christians. In Kenya, European and Asian civil servants have been, without exception, replaced by Negroes. Moslems in the Sudan habitually oppress non-Moslem elements. In Ireland, the poor Whites from the south go north to find jobs, and even though they are racially akin to the northern Irish, they become embroiled in religious hatreds which result in the loss of lives.

It is evident that the problem of bigotry transcends the current estimates of it and renders the concept of Black vs. White inoperative. The time has come to set aside the term "Black," and to revive interest in the progress of total, world-wide racial understanding. It is our obligation to re-examine the prevailing view that "Black is beautiful," no matter how compelling and politically relevant that view may seem on the surface.

Undoubtedly the re-examination will offend some people. But those who are offended by a refusal to pay homage to a suspicious choice of words are those who deserve to be offended. If we suffer from the tyranny of a too-frequently-offended political sector, we do so because we have forgotten how language can serve the desires of the greedy and devisive elements in society. The men who create media commercials, as well as the agents of the Kremlin and of Nazi organizations, have often demonstrated that words can mold the minds and attitudes of masses of people. Albert Jay Nock, philosopher and political theorist, has observed,

> Lord, how the world is given to worshipping words! Eschew the coarse word slavery, and you can get glad acceptance for a condition of actual slavery.

> It is a commonplace that the persistence of an institution is due solely to the state of mind that prevails toward it, the set of terms in which men habitually think about it. So long, and only so long, as those terms are favourable, the institution lives and maintains its power; and when for any reason men generally cease thinking in those terms, it weakens and becomes inert.
> (Robert M. Thornton, Ed., *Cogitations from Albert Jay Nock* [Irvington-on-Hudson, New York: The Nockian Society, 1970] 26, 76).

People are more likely to be activated by language than they are to make active use of it.

Surely the public mind was adversely activated in the 50's and 60s when the word "Black" came into prominence as a tool for social comment. The term, carrying as it does the image of protest, does not reflect Negro life as it actually is. Many Negroes are poor, but there are also many who are doctors, bankers, mayors, judges, scholars, scientists, investment brokers, executives, publishers and artists. Some are embittered and aggressive, while a significant number of others are conservative and patriotic. The many are hardly represented by a title which refers to the few.

In fact, the few have attracted so much attention in modern society that observers of current events are sometimes surprised when Negro talent reaches the front pages of the newspapers. When Negro Henry Lewis became conductor of the New Jersey Symphony in 1968, the media evidenced amazement that a Colored man was given such an appointment. Whereupon James G. Rogers wrote in the Los Angeles *Times*,

> Good intentions notwithstanding, we will not overcome prejudice to any significant degree until we abandon this attitude of fatuous toleration toward the accomplishments of others. Much as it may hurt our collective ego, we have got to learn to take for granted that anybody--be he Negro, American Indian, or Australian Bushman--can fall flat on his face, do great things, or simply live an average life.

("Letter to the Editor," Los Angeles Times [May 1, 1968]).

To put it another way, the Negro must achieve natural acceptance and assessment according to his private weaknesses or strengths, but he cannot find this acceptance if racial gulfs are widened by semantic manipulation. The title "Black" must be set aside.

The question arises, however, if we are not to call dark-skinned peoples "Black," what are we to call them? J. A. Rogers campaigns for the word "Negro" by saying,

> Of course there is only one race--the human race. But of all the names used by the stronger group in America to set the dark-skinned citizens apart, Negro is the least objectionable. Not only is it very ancient, but it has a record in America of four centuries of fortitude, endurance and survival power, rare in the annals of mankind.
>
> (*100 Amazing Facts*, 40).

Even so, "Negro" loses integrity when we recall that this word in the romance languages also means "Black." The terms Afro-American and African-American, endorsed by Madison Carter and by Dr. Alexander ("Are We Black?" 47), are more amiable names because they establish a linkage with the dominant group. Colored, on the other hand, is the most accurate descriptive adjective, since most Negroes have skin that has color but not blackness. In the world of art, color clarifies and enhances paintings, just as racial color gives substance to the human condition. Color is so richly varied in creation that the human eye can differentiate 40,000 separate colors, and 36 skin colors. Significantly, when a group of Afro-Americans was asked to make a choice between Negro, Black, Afro-American and Colored, the word Colored was selected by the majority of those polled (Rogers, 40).

A Georgia White man who has some Cherokee blood, says this about the use of the word "Colored" in the South:

> The term "Colored people" or "Colored folks" is applied by White Southerners to those Black INDIVIDUALS who, by their individual conduct and action, are equal to anyone. By the same token, "redneck" is a Southern White whose INDIVIDUAL actions and conduct mark him (or her) as not being equal to anyone. Black people here also use the term "Colored people" and "redneck" and understand what they mean. By the way, in the South a "nigger" is a Black "redneck."
>
> (Name withheld, Letter to Judith Anne Still [January 12, 1985]).

The fact that the word "Colored" acquired a poor reputation in the South--where bathrooms and Jim Crow cars were identified "for Colored only"--is of little consequence. We have already seen that some words can be used as avenues to understanding as much as to misapprehension. If a word is precise and descriptive, it is possible to turn its negative connotations into positive ones through enlightened use. The derisive name, "Yankee Doodle," which was applied to the rebellious colonists in the Revolutionary War, became a jovial and triumphant name when the rebels took it unto themselves. In the same way, titles such as Anglo-Saxon,

Christian, Scotch and Irish were borne up aggressively like battle-standards to remove from them their overtones of scorn and intimidation.

Of course, the word "Black," too, inculcates overtones of scorn and intimidation. But many who use the term today do so, not to elevate the race, but to set the race apart from the nucleus of life and to make it appear that there is some sort of "blackness" that White people can't understand, and some sort of "whiteness" that black people can't fathom. The preeminent awareness will come out of this lexical misappropriation when we realize that every race has much that has never been appreciated, and everything that can and should be understood.

Perhaps the best way to foster an appreciation for the Afro-American people is to call them, not Afro-American or Colored, but "the golden people." This suggestion was made by Dr. Alexander, when he observed that "Americans of African descent...are truly in color more golden than black," and that "golden" is a positive word because it "generally connotes something that is precious, dear, expensive, rich, valuable, good, meritorious, heavenly, exquisite, etc." ("Are We Black?," 47).

Another positive term, which expresses the potential of the race and encourages its ascendancy, is the word, "colorful." "Colorful" reveals the relationship between Colored people and the rest of the human, earthly and cosmic environment, and it holds within it overtones of the richness of creation. Both "colorful" and "golden" might well be adopted by those who wish to work toward brotherhood and human enlightenment.

Whatever name is selected, it is to be hoped that it will be one which expresses the idea of the human family, and the connection between the human family and the natural environment. In nature, there is no prejudice: the leaves on an apple tree differ from those of a peach tree, but the difference renders neither of them inferior. Further, the wise gardener who can deal honestly with the peach tree is not incapable of dealing with the apple tree.

In the human garden, the sage cultivator handles the lush and proliferate vegetation of civilization with the same equanimity. He realizes that there is a fertile harvest in the differences among men and women, and that these differences are more than merely racial distinctions. Each person in each racial community is totally unique, partaking of many parochial, national and universal wholes, yet standing apart from these wholes. Human experience is universal, but human beings are particular. Ultimately, the Negro must decide whether to continue insisting that he is black, or whether to admit that he is magnificently human. Then, if he allows that he is human, he will also be forced to agree that, among men, Black is not always black, nor is White so very white.

# AN EDUCATIONAL APPROACH TO NEGRO INDIVIDUALISM[1]

The need to modernize the English curriculum has nowhere presented more problems than in the development of units dealing with Black literature. Teachers, necessarily committed to principles of literary excellence, have frequent difficulty justifying the study of works with doubtful aesthetic value, such as those by Eldridge Cleaver, James Baldwin, Stokely Carmichael, Martin Luther King, Jr., and Malcolm X. Further, the use of this type of anti-racist literature forces instructors to take a limited approach to the Negro problem, that is, a viewpoint which presumes that all Negroes have been confined within the ethos of the ghetto, and, consequently, that they all nurture feelings of hatred and shame when confronted by the requirements of White culture. In the words of a Chicago educator, this approach tends to minimize the complexities of the Negro for the student (Nancy L. Arnez, "Racial Understanding Through Literature," *English Journal* 58 [Jan. 1969] 56). Ultimately, teachers must exercise care in adopting such a limited viewpoint, and in compromising literary values, in order to champion what seems to be an anti-racist cause. They can as little afford to minimize the complexities of the Negro as they can to minimize the need for standards of literary quality.

Yet, the question will be asked, do not educators, much more than politicians, have a responsibility to understand that the resorts of Negro leaders to militancy and violence reflect widespread deprivation of the Black people? Perhaps, if the Negro militant leadership does indeed represent the Negro population. There are, however, numerous sources which indicate that this may not be the case. J. A. Parker, Negro news commentator in Philadelphia and President of the Foundation for Theological

---

[1] This article was the first nonfiction work by Judith Anne Still to be published. It appeared in the *English Journal* (59 [January 1970] 34-39, copyright, National Council of Teachers of English). It is reprinted here with permission.

Education, suggests that militant leaders are primarily "recognized by the White liberal communications media, overlooking perhaps the most powerful and important Black leaders in America." Continuing along these lines, Parker says,

> If we properly used the standard adopted by the communications media [representation of the people], Dr. Joseph H. Jackson of Chicago, Illinois, president of the largest Negro organization in the world, the National Baptist Convention, which boasts a membership totaling 6.5 million, should be undisputedly the most quoted Black in the nation. Also important is the fact that Dr. Jackson is salaried by his congregation as opposed to the vast majority of the Black leaders who derive the bulk of their support from "Whitey."
> (J. A. Parker, "Reflections of a Black Conservative," *The New Guard* 9 [May 1969] 5).

Along with J. A. Parker and Dr. Jackson, there are other Negro men of consequence, notably George S. Schuyler, author of *Black and Conservative* [Arlington House, 1966], and Dr. Max Yergan, Co-Chairman of the American-African Affairs Association, who do not feel hated and shamed by the mere existence of racial bigotry. There are enough of these men, in fact, to indicate that most Negroes do not promote animosity and violence as the only ways to make themselves felt in a predominantly White world. Rather, they think of themselves as law-abiding and worthwhile individuals, demanding only that their accomplishments, and those of other respected Negroes, be treated with a discernment unsullied by attempts to minimize their complexities.

The desire of most Negroes to be judged as individuals, and to be judged by the same academic and cultural standards applied to Whites, can be amply demonstrated. Doretha Lee, first Negro teacher in a predominantly White district of Orange County, California, rejects stereotyped labels such as Black or Afro-American. Though her mother was a domestic and her father a laborer, Mrs. Lee recalls that, "We were taught that we were individuals and that we could accomplish what we wanted to as individuals." J. A. Parker, in the article already quoted, echoes her attitude, saying, "The pitfall of the civil rights movement was

## An Educational Approach to Negro Individualism

that it attempted to move along or elevate the entire race, even those who did not want to be disturbed." It is thus, he adds, that the movement is "suspect in the black community," for Blacks wish to be "received and respected on the basis of their competence, intellect, and ability to gainfully perform and produce, rather than as subordinates." In other words, what human being wants to be received with the same indiscriminate warmth used to welcome all other members of his group, regardless of their worth?

Of course, the attempt to find eminence apart from a group is an aspect of a need too universal to be confined to members of minority races. Kenneth Keniston, instructor of psychiatry at Yale, has recently identified characteristics of the "hippie" and New Left Movements which probably stem from this larger need. Keniston asserts that these movements are "spontaneous creations of the young" in "strong reaction to the Organized System...of middle-class life" (Kenneth Keniston, *American Scholar* 37 [Spring 1968] 227-245). Indeed, he might say that whatever is spontaneous, honest, and healthy in these movements is not only a reaction to the "Organized System," but also a reaction to any system that tends to discount individuality and self-assertion.

Significantly, the human need for personal recognition renders ineffective any programs which approach students with the attitude that they are inescapably disadvantaged, and that whatever they learn, no matter how little it may be, is to the good. As Harvard psychological studies have demonstrated, there is much truth in Goethe's advice to "Treat people as if they were what they ought to be and you help them to become what they are capable of being." That is, whenever a man is led to educate himself beyond the norm, to get involved in new experiential efforts, to establish new frontiers, to clothe, feed, and house himself more substantially than his peers, he is led to do it to clarify his own self-concept, and to establish an individual image, rather than to enhance pre-existent social patterns.

All of this means that teachers cannot hope to destroy social prejudices through literature which advances the doctrine of environmental determinism. A reading of the *Autobiography of Malcolm X* will, at most, inspire a sense of pity for Negroes who have reason to hate some White people. It will not, however, eliminate the irrational dislike and fear that can only be counteracted by learning to admire each Negro as a separate entity. What is needed is the presentation of biographies or autobiographies of Negro men and women with irreproachable stature, whose individual accomplishments, not environmental difficulties, inspire respect for themselves, rather than for Negroes in general. It is impossible to respect Malcolm X for reacting only with feelings of hatred when his White English teacher discouraged him from becoming a lawyer. But it is also impossible not to admire such Negroes as Anita Glasco, a rising young female lawyer, who was likewise told by a White teacher that her ambition to be a legal expert was ridiculous. Taking the criticism as an individual matter, not as a rejection by the entire White race, Miss Glasco had enough self-respect and faith in her own competence to acquire, eventually, a law degree through Harvard Law School.

It is enlightening to note here that the most artistic works by Negro authors have been written, not in a spirit of disillusionment, but with the same apprehension of competence that prompted Miss Glasco to reach her goal. For this reason, teachers might well adopt an approach to Negro literature which is concerned with books such as Frank Yerby's *The Foxes of Harrow* [Dial Press, 1946], and Arna Bontemps' *Black Thunder* [Macmillan, 1936], rather than with books by Claude Brown or Stokely Carmichael. Biographies or autobiographies more acceptable than *Malcolm X*, include Arna Bontemps' *The Story of George Washington Carver* [Harper, 1954], and *Frederick Douglass: Slave-Fighter, Freeman* [Knopf, 1959], Frederick Douglass' *The Mind and Heart of Frederick Douglass: Excerpts from Speeches of the Great Orator* [Crowell, 1964], Blanche E. Ferguson's *Countee Cullen and the Negro Renaissance* [Dodd, Mead, 1966], Shirley Graham's *Jean Baptiste Pointe de Sable, Founder of Chicago* [Julian Messner, 1953], James Weldon Johnson's *Along This Way* [Viking, 1933], George S. Schuyler's *Black and Conservative* [Arlington House, 1966], Booker T. Washington's *Up From Slavery* [Dell, 1933], and Howard Taubman's biography of Marian Anderson, *My Lord, What a*

*Morning* [Viking, 1966]. Certainly among these works there is much that will inspire the teacher with a broader view of Negroes and their integrity and potential.

However, if instructors still feel called upon, as Nancy Arnez says, in the interest of "sociological and anthropological insights" (Arnez, 57), to present something of the disillusionment of the Negro, they should enhance their presentations with writings that have literary as well as social value. Knowing that Negroes have a fervent desire, just as Whites have, to be respectfully and fairly judged, educators may hardly agree that literary judgments of Negro works need not be made (Arnez, 56). English teachers have habitually selected pieces of English literature for the classroom according to their creative and inspirational worth. It is by such selectivity that Shakespeare, Dickens, Wordsworth, Coleridge, Keats and others have become worthy of our study, and have projected an aura of dignity and authority that recommends them to the student. This same dignity must not be denied to Negro literature by the teaching of Eldridge Cleaver rather than Countee Cullen. Negroes deserve the recognition afforded by selectivity of what their inspired efforts and artistry can produce, in spite of environmental deprivation. Instead of presenting the later poems of disillusionment by Langston Hughes, poems which are far inferior to Hughes' earlier, more optimistic works, instructors might consider reading Paul Laurence Dunbar's superb lyrics of disappointment. For example, Dunbar's "Ships That Pass in the Night," and "The Right to Die," convey a sense of dejection while still preserving the voice of the indomitable, humane spirit:

### SHIPS THAT PASS IN THE NIGHT

Out in the sky the great dark clouds are massing;
    I look far out into the pregnant night,
Where I can hear a solemn booming gun
    And catch the gleaming of a random light,
That tells me that the ship I seek is passing, passing.

My tearful eyes my soul's deep hurt are glassing;
    For I would hail and check that ship of ships.
I stretch my hands, imploring, cry aloud,
    My voice falls dead a foot from mine own lips,

And but its ghost doth reach that vessel, passing, passing.

O Earth, O Sky, O Ocean, both surpassing,
   O heart of mine, O soul that dreads the dark!
Is there no hope for me? Is there no way
   That I may sight and check that speeding bark
Which out of sight and sound is passing, passing?

### THE RIGHT TO DIE

I have no fancy for that ancient cant
That makes us masters of our destinies,
And not our lives, to hold or give them up
As will directs; I cannot, will not think
That men, the subtle worms, who plot and plan
And scheme and calculate with such shrewd wit,
Are such great blund'ring fools as not to know
When they have lived enough.
                       Men court not death
When there are sweets still left in life to taste.
Nor will a brave man choose to live when he,
Full deeply drunk of life, has reached the dregs
And knows that now but bitterness remains.
He is the coward who, outfaced in this,
Fears the false goblins of another life.
I honor him who being much harassed
Drinks of sweet courage until drunk of it,--
Then seizing Death, reluctant, by the hand,
Leaps with him, fearless, to eternal peace!

                 (*The Complete Poems of Paul Laurence Dunbar*)
                   [New York: Dodd, Mead & Company, Inc.,
                         1934]. Reprinted by permission.)

    Certainly, in the area of Negro poetry, there is much that has been written with the sense of beauty and integrity uppermost. Among worthwhile pieces are Claude McKay's "If We Must Die," Countee Cullen's "From the Dark Tower," William Stanley Braithwaite's "Oh, I Have Asked," Arna Bontemps' "My Heart Has Known Its Winter," Langston Hughes' "Dream Variations," Jean Toomer's "Song of the Son," and Paul Laurence Dunbar's

"Sympathy." The teacher has only to search for works like these to discover vast, untapped resources for the study of Negro literature.

To appreciate these resources, however, it has already been noted that current erroneous notions about Negroes and their attitudes must be discarded. The English instructor, like the teacher of history or social studies, should not be pressured into stereotyped channels of thought by political, rather than intellectual, forces. Aside from the misconceptions previously discussed concerning Negro leadership and the basic desires of Negroes, some of the most unfortunate stereotyped notions, advanced by militants and other political extremists, are the following:

1. *That White people share a "collective guilt" for the incidence of bigotry in society, and, concomitantly, that the Negro resorts to violence in protest of that bigotry.*

   Yet, educators and objectivists know that, in social affairs, as in jurisprudence, guilt is an individual phenomenon and cannot be held in common among peoples of a particular race. Too many White people are not guilty of bigotry, and too many Negroes have little reason to feel that all Whites look down upon them. In addition, too much of the violence, supposedly justified by White racist attitudes, has been directed against the lives and businesses of law-abiding Negroes to ascribe its cause to "collective guilt." Finally, the emphasis upon White racism as the motivating force behind today's Negroes is a kick in the teeth to successful Negroes, and to Negroes who do not condone the easy way out through militant turmoil.

2. *That all Negroes wish to be symbolically separated from the White race through use of the term "Black."*

   But, many Negroes still feel that terms such as Negro or Afro-American are more appropriately applied to themselves than "Black." Dr. William Grant Still, recognized in the music world as the "Dean of Negro composers," has said, "This is no more an all Black world than an all White one. Negroes who have a sense of self-worth do not wish to be lost in a multitude through the wide currency of a separatist label. Indeed, 'Black' is a label that denies to Negroes the salvation of universal human understanding."

That Negroes are not all separatists becomes doubly clear from a mention of the efforts of Ferguson Rhemm. Rhemm, teacher of social studies in the Los Angeles ghetto area, member of the N.E.A. Urban Task Force, and Human Relations Chairman of the Association of Classroom Teachers of Los Angeles, has consistently advocated the use of dialogues between Negro and White students to resolve racial misunderstanding. And, though militants demand that such dialogues be used to communicate separatist ideologies, Rhemm insists that the topics of conversation be confined to common human problems, as, for example, "The Generation Gap," in order to mitigate racial hatred.

3. *That there is no hope for the Negro student with a White man's curriculum, because he has been deprived of his rightful place in society by "collective guilt" and by his separatist inclinations. And that, because there is no hope, Negro students must boycott, strike, and riot to succeed* (Miriam Ylvisaker, "Our Guilt," English Journal 58 [February 1969] 193).

On the contrary, there is much evidence to support the belief that victims of prejudice need not riot to succeed, for their victimization alone helps them to gain, not lose, the emotional stability and motivation necessary to cope with curricular challenges. This, in fact, is the conclusion to which Robert Coles comes, in his study of Negro children who faced extreme antagonism in school desegregation test cases (Robert Coles, Children of Crisis: A Study of Courage and Fear [Boston, Atlantic-Little Brown, 1961]. This study was the 1967 winner of the Phi Beta Kappa, Ralph Waldo Emerson Book Award). The fact that Coles' Negro students grew in maturity when isolated by situations of conflict, suggests the operation, again, of the concept of human individuality. By virtue of this concept, it is safe to assume that human beings in general, including Negroes, are likely to become emotionally stronger when they are faced with personal challenges to their self-esteem. However, in situations where there are no personal challenges, but where they are made to feel alienated as a group, a degeneration of their mature attitudes can occur. It is thus that educators working with the culturally disadvantaged must guard against the attitude that they are dealing with students who have been deprived of dignity; rather, they must continually remind themselves of what these students can do with what they have. Undue patronization from well-meaning Whites can only aggravate racial problems.

Aside from this fact that Negroes *can* succeed if they are personally challenged, is the more significant fact that they *have* succeeded, and with what has been dubbed a White man's curriculum. Miss Florence Sprenger, retired English teacher from Manual Arts High School, a school in the Los Angeles ghetto area called Watts, is currently attempting to compress the list of successful Negro graduates of that school in order to fit the names conveniently into a book. The number, she says, is so great that it puts to shame the number of dissidents from Manual Arts who were actually involved in the riots centering around that school in the fall of 1967. Among these notable graduates are Judge Bernard Jefferson, Assembly-woman Yvonne Braithwaite, Deputy Superintendent of Schools James Taylor, actress Mittie Lawrence, actor Paul Winfield, artist Marion Epting, and lawyer Anita Glasco.

Of course, no one is trying to ignore the unfortunate truth that many Negroes do not succeed because they are culturally disadvantaged. Even so, a deficiency in verbal skills does not necessarily indicate spiritual or moral deficiencies great enough to justify resorts to violence and irresponsibility. In fact, perhaps the only thing which saved Watts from a second major riot begun on the Manual Arts Campus was the battalion of mothers who came to the school, voluntarily, to calm the dissidents. And, more often than not, these mothers sent youngsters quietly back to their classes merely by threatening to tell their parents what they were doing.

4. *That Negroes demand special, unreasonable concessions to make up for their inability to cope with the White curriculum. These demands call for a proliferation of courses on Black culture and for representation of the "typical" method of Black speech, that with little verb conjugation, in school texts.*

The idea that there is a "typical" method of speaking among Negroes is as absurd as the idea that the lush residences of the Baldwin Hills in Los Angeles, where Negro families abound, are part of the Los Angeles ghetto simply because Negroes live there. And, Ferguson Rhemm tells us that even Negroes in the ghettos admire those among them who can use standard English skillfully, and insist that their children's Negro teachers avoid ungrammatical speech, although they themselves may not. As for courses on Black culture, it is not everywhere apparent that such courses are more to the taste of deprived students than courses in the traditional curriculum. Indeed, elective courses on Black history were set up at the all-Negro Crenshaw High School in Los Angeles, in response to demands of militants, but surprisingly few of the students elected to take them.

The teacher who finds himself taking an approach to the Negro problem which involves any of the foregoing militant distortions is ignoring his professional commitment to political impartiality. The teacher who, after a close investigation of the lives of many successful Negroes, still feels that a reading of *The Autobiography of Malcolm X* will give his students a "closer inside feeling of what is going on in our Negro culture" (Arnez, 56), is ignoring his commitment to respect the individual worth of Negroes. This teacher must realize that it is only through recognition of the competent individuals of a group, that the recognition of the group itself will come, as an unalterable outgrowth. No educator can, in good faith, deny such recognition to a race from which so many cultural giants have grown.

# FOR THE MAN WHO FAILS[1]

The world is a snob, and the man who wins
   Is the chap for its money's worth:
And the lust for success causes half of the sins
   That are cursing this brave old earth.

• • •

The man who is strong to fight his fight,
   And whose will no front can daunt,
If the truth be truth and the right be right,
   Is the man that the ages want.
Tho' he fail and die in grim defeat,
   Yet he has not fled the strife,
And the house of Earth will seem more sweet
   For the perfume of his life.

     Paul Laurence Dunbar, "For the Man Who Fails"
     in *The Life and Works of Paul Laurence Dunbar*,
Lida Keck Wiggins, Ed. (Dodd, Mead & Co., NY, 1905) 223.

When falsehood is seen as history,
Slavery is accepted as freedom.

                        Unattributed

If William Grant Still had been white-skinned, he would stand today, in the public consciousness, shoulder-to-shoulder with Bach, Beethoven, Mozart, Puccini and Verdi. The fact that he does not so stand is the result of the cruelest and most unremitting social bias: cruel because it is unacknowledged by the majority of

---

[1] This article is a commentary on the book *William Grant Still: A Study in Contradictions* by Catherine Parsons Smith (University of California Press, Berkeley, CA, 2000).

our intelligent and powerful public figures, and unremitting because color prejudice may well be as pervasive in the new millennium as it was in the days of slavery.

How has bigotry against people of color survived so strongly after the end of segregation and apartheid? Primarily through the efforts of writers, publishers, scholars and film producers. The supposed inferiority of the descendants of the African peoples has been codified in our textbooks, in the mass media, and in our thinking. Myths of the deprived, uncivilized, angry, desperate Black man are part of our culture. O.J. Simpson and Louis Farrakhan receive constant and hungry media attention: William Grant Still, George Schuyler and J.A. Parker do not.[2]

Our nation knows what Hitler did not know: that a group of people can be destroyed simply by being discounted, demeaned and/or ignored. Negative attitudes toward people of color have developed over the last 350 years or more, having begun with the African slave trade, and having been strengthened by falsehood, as, for example, when the Whites in South Africa began to teach their children that the thousand-year-old civilization of Great Zimbabwe was built by white Europeans (Henry Louis Gates, Jr., "Wonders of the African World," B8107 [PBS Home Video, 1999]).

When African civilizations as old as 250,000 years were found, archeologists continued to ignore their importance, and went on pretending that the history of civilization began with the Iron Age people of northwestern Europe and Britain (Larry Zimmerman, *The Archeology of Ethnicity* [Sian Jones, Routledge,

---

[2] William Grant Still was the "Dean of Afro-American Composers," the first man of Color to write a symphony played by a major American orchestra, the first to conduct a major symphony orchestra, and the first to have an opera produced by a major American company, among many other firsts in a similar vein.

J.A. Parker is a radio host, media commentator, political essayist, and President of the Lincoln Institute in Washington D.C., a conservative, patriotic organization.

George Schuyler was the Editor-in-Chief of the Afro-American newspaper, *The Pittsburgh Courier*, and the author of *Black and Conservative* (Arlington House, NY, 1966).

1997]). According to Dr. Kay Pace, Africa was actually the source of Western music, but scholars have always "excluded" any mention of Africa in discussing music history (Kay Pace, "Foreword" to 'Africa' by William Grant Still [The Master-Player Library, Flagstaff, AZ, 2001] i).

Some archeologists persist in telling us that the ancient Egyptian pyramids were tombs, and that the tomb-builders had no special scientific knowledge that motivated their construction. Graham Hancock's research, explained in the Learning Channel series, "Quest for the Lost Civilization" (Acorn Media Publishing, Bethesda, MD, 1998), is not widely-praised, probably because it concludes that the Egyptians had dominion over geometry and astronomy as far back as 10,500 B.C., and that the pyramids were not tombs, rather they had a scientific purpose akin to that of "flight simulators." In erecting their immense structures to exactly replicate the layout of the universe, their mathematical calculations, like those of the Maya, were more accurate than ours.

The mulatto writer, Bert Underwood, lists famous people who were part African, or who "mixed" with Africans, including Moses, who married an Ethiopian; Samuel Johnson, who had a Negro son; Napoleon, who loved the mulatto, Josephine; and John Audubon and Alexander Hamilton who were both racially mixed. Underwood concludes, "The politics of America will have you forget that we mixed-race people exist with our history (American history) untaught. It is the vital missing link that makes racism so easy to promote (Underwood, *A Study in Racism: USA* [Chester House Publishers, NY, 1996] 74-75).

Had it not been for the discovery of DNA, historians would still declare that Thomas Jefferson was too high-minded to sleep with his slaves. And this attitude has prevailed, in spite of the testimony of antebellum Blacks that miscegenation was the rule of behavior among the most respected slave owners. Indeed, the nurse who helped my father to deliver me when I was born, Bessie Lawson Blackman, was a direct descendant of the father of Martha Custis, George Washington's wife. According to Mrs. Blackman, White people in the South told her that it was impossible for her family to have been related to Martha Washington, because "there's no such things as 'aristocrats of color.'" (For an extended discussion of the repudiation of racial mixing, see Dalt Wonk, "The Creoles of Color," *New Orleans Magazine* X [May 1976] 55.)

These denials that miscegenation has taken place have been complimented by attempts to show that people of color cannot really fit into any aristocracy owing to their innate primitiveness and degradation. William Grant Still resigned from his position as music director for the film, "Stormy Weather" (Twentieth-Century Fox), when he realized that the producers of the film were trying to present Negroes as deprived, unlettered, oversexed and generally inferior persons. Some forty-two years later, in 1984, the problem of stereotyping still existed, as evidenced by the observation of a newspaper critic that the dance in Still's opera, *Minette Fontaine*, was not "orgiastic enough" (David Foil "Dobish's Career is Soaring" *Louisiana Morning Advocate* [October 26, 1984]).

Some six years later, a review of Still's *Afro-American Symphony* in *The New York Times* stated that the composer had "poor control over form and development" (K. Robert Schwarz, "Composers Who Had to Triumph Over Prejudice" [April 15, 1990] 29). Schwarz found it impossible to admit that a Colored composer knew what he was doing, and so he had to belittle him in some way; the truth is that the symphony is constructed with the utmost attention to form and development (Judith Anne Still, Ed., *William Grant Still and the Fusion of Cultures in American Music*, [The Master-Player Library, Flagstaff, AZ, 1972]).

Even today, the campaign to degrade continues apace: for example, opera companies across the country constantly push *Porgy and Bess* forward, with its "I Got Plenty of Nuttin'," instead of Still's magnificent grand opera *Troubled Island*, characterized by its show-piece setting of the Langston Hughes poem, "I Dream a World." The most disheartening aspect of codified racism is that the public does not see the stereotypes in "Stormy Weather" and *Porgy* as being dangerous, and as implements for intellectual genocide. Stereotypical attitudes are so widespread that they are accepted by people of all colors. It is only when the stereotypes lead to physical distress, as in police profiling, that the victims become concerned.

It should be mentioned that profiling is merely an obvious manifestation of the less obvious ways that people of Color are demeaned, discounted, relegated to lesser status and ignored in our culture. Even academicians who are not really biased, and who outwardly seek to be egalitarian, will perpetuate bigotry in spite of themselves, putting on paper what they believe the public expects to hear, rather than what actually is. A case in point is the book, *William Grant Still: A Study in Contradictions*, which is liberally seasoned with stereotypes and disparaging remarks.

Catherine Smith's articles in *A Study in Contradictions* purport to be thoroughly documented and faithful investigations of the motives and personalities of composer William Grant Still and of his wife, journalist Verna Arvey. The evidence presented, however, does not lead inevitably to the conclusions that Smith draws about the couple. When one observer might see two genuine, talented and altruistic people struggling to survive in a hostile environment, Smith sees desperation, deficiency, disillusion, lack of adaptability to "politically correct" ideas, manipulativeness and obsession. How Smith finds these negative qualities in the bulk of the material she assembles is something of a mystery.

Smith's first chapter on Still seems innocuous enough. She spends considerable time dwelling on the "racial doubleness" of the composer (p. 203), a "doubleness" first referred to by Carol Oja ("'New Music' and the 'New Negro': The Background of William Grant Still's 'Afro-American Symphony'," *Black Music Research Journal* 12, no. 2 [Fall 1992], 145-169). While the formulation of a duality helps to reduce the subject of race to its lowest terms, the concept of duality will one day be rejected by musicologists when they come to understand Still's peculiar spiritual occupations, his non-racial eclecticism, and his repudiation of racial polarization. Lance Bowling, president of Cambria Master Recordings and producer of many William Grant Still compact discs, puts it this way:

> In reading the diaries of William Grant Still, I was struck by the directedness of the man. Disraeli said that the secret of success was constancy of purpose, and Still certainly had that. He used

numerology to develop a life-plan for himself—a lifetime game plan—and he followed that plan in a methodical, inexorable manner. I don't see anything contradictory in his method of attack; he did everything that he wanted to do, producing an enormous amount of fine music, and he did it in spite of unbelievable adversity.

Furthermore, Still, like the entertainer and dancer, John Bubbles, and like George Washington Carver, Mary McLeod Bethune, and other African-Americans of the time, used mysticism as a means of survival; they coped through prophecy, astrology, numerology, visions, and by drawing upon ideas from within. Anyone who does not look into the spiritual strategies of people of color cannot understand their racial attitudes.

> (Lance Bowling, private notes made while preparing the Still diaries for publication, July 5, 2001).

In other words, Still was not a duality, he was a plurality: a man aware of all of the aspects of this life and of the next, and a man capable of expressing these aspects musically. He was faithful to his ideals, purposeful, and never confused about the direction that he would take to accomplish what he wanted to accomplish. (For more information on Afro-American mysticism, see, Joyce Elaine Noll, *Company of Prophets* [Llewellyn Publications, St. Paul, MN 55164-0383, 1991]; also, Judith Anne Still, "Seven Traceries: The Seven Faces of God" [The Master-Player Library, AZ, 1999] v-xi).

Smith affords little attention to Still's spiritual inclinations, while she fails to recognize his firm control over his own musical development. She even misinterprets the composer's many good qualities, including his refreshingly childlike sense of humor. While giving the impression that she is detached and equable in her treatment of the man, she takes frequent stabs at him, and at his wife, revealing an antagonism and a bias. A prime example is in her remark about Still's quip, "He can't dance anymore," on the last page of the score of *The Black Man Dances*. The composer's little funny notes to conductors and musicians in his works are numerous, guileless, non-specific and *never* self-serving. Yet Smith suggests that "He can't dance anymore" refers to the non-release of the piece by Paul Whiteman, even though expert examination of the score shows that the composer penciled in this bit of wit at the same time that he finished the score, not later. Moreover, there was no animosity between Still and Whiteman over the music; Still was paid for the piece, and he was satisfied. Why does Smith turn Still's harmless humor into a disparaging jibe?

Similarly, Smith calls Still's insertion of "The music goes round and round" in the funeral procession for "Lost Horizons," a "desperate" joke. How is it desperate? Still's writings do not indicate any desperation over leaving the studio; he had many irons in the fire at the time, and he was confident that the Creator, who had always sustained him, would send other opportunities of value. He knew what the studio executives thought of him as a man of color, and he was dealing with their disdain in the way that Abe Lincoln would have dealt with it: with humor.

Unfortunately, Smith does not accept Still's humor, his gentleness, his Godliness, or his resilience, nor does she properly attend to his accomplishments. In fact, she manages to downgrade some of his greatest achievements. She lessens the importance of the 1936 Hollywood Bowl concert by noting that Still's part of the program (when he became the first person of Color to conduct a major orchestra in the United States) was less than half of the evening's fare. Further, she does not quote any of the joyful reports from the Afro-American community, reports which clearly saw the event as a monumental blow against segregation.

It has to be said, here, that part of Smith's low opinion of the Los Angeles Philharmonic concert in 1936 comes from her low opinion of West Coast culture in general. She calls Still's move to Los Angeles an "expatriation," indicating that it was a self-imposed exile, a going "against the grain," a move away "from the center." Smith believes that the East Coast was, and is, the arbiter of culture and the arts in the Western Hemisphere, and that New York's Harlem was, in Still's day, the only proper place for Afro-American music, art and literature to flower. It may be her lack of appreciation for the West Coast that leads her to debunk Still's desire to live in Los Angeles in 1934.

But, for Still, the move west was not an exile, but a bid for freedom from a kind of slavery--a move away from the jealousies, social stagnation and cliquishness that gripped New York then, and that some say are still to be endured in the East today. In California, Still found a vibrant cultural oasis where prejudices were less invasive, and where exciting things were happening in the arts. As for the Harlem Renaissance, Still knew that creative people of Color did not have to live together in a certain restricted area in order to do remarkable things in their lives; there were individual flowerings among people of color all across the country, as there had been down through the centuries. The composer took his personal Renaissance with him, went with the grain of his own making, and remained at the center of things. His musical innovations, brought forth in that center, have been copied by other composers so much that we have forgotten where they originated.

Still's decision not to become head of the Music Department at Howard University, in Washington, D.C., is also deprecated by Catherine Smith, and she obliquely intimates that this decision amounted to a rejection of the Harlem Renaissance and of civil rights issues. She does not quote any of the relevant letters from Still which outline his perception of the invitation to go to Howard, letters which allude to a scheme on the part of Olin Downes, the critic who most disliked Still, to hamper Still's productivity by steering him into an administrative position. In addition, Smith does not quote letters which warned Still about the dangers of going to Howard, including that from Alain Locke which said that "Washington is appallingly sterile," and that he (Locke) yearned to get away from there as often as possible (date of the letter not given).

Smith obviously does not take Still's fear of a plot hatched by Olin Downes seriously, no doubt because she presents the concerns of Still and of his wife over conspiracies against them as unjustifiable paranoias. The composer and his wife felt that left-leaning media moguls, critics and composers had engaged in a whispering campaign against them, and that these ill-disposed people had prevented them from receiving performances of their operas, recordings and commissions. The campaign had begun when Still tried to obtain a performance of his opera, *Troubled Island*, and it took its most visible form when the critics collectively panned the first performance of the opera in 1949.

After 1949, Still's career took a downhill slide, during which there were no more major performances of his operas, and no significant recordings. Smith does not document Still's reversal of fortune after 1949; instead, she asserts that Still and Arvey reinforced each other's anxieties and lost perspective. She claims that they isolated themselves through their own delusions, and that their self-destruction was hastened when they failed to embrace the Black Power movement in the sixties. Smith criticizes Still for not being able to "negotiate social change" in the Civil Rights Era.

In order to reach her conclusions, it is necessary for Smith to ignore many documents in the Still-Arvey Archives which deal with links between Black militants and the Communist Party, and the letters from Afro-American right-wingers such as George Schuyler, who stated that the militants were destroying much of the trust that he and the Stills had endeavored to build up over the years. Smith implies that the Stills were alone in their political conservatism, when in fact they were not alone: composers such as Deems Taylor and Arthur Lange agreed with them, as did other prominent persons.

One of the most prominent persons to disclose and to reject the anarchic activities of the Communists in the United States was the Black author, Richard Wright. Wright had joined the Red movement in the thirties, until he discovered that "the very freedom they [he and other Blacks] sought was rejected within the party itself" (*The Washington Times*, February 27, 1985, 2C). When Wright began to oppose the racial attitudes of the Party, he found that even those Reds "who agreed with me would not support me." Wright and many Afro-Americans like him suffered subsequent unacknowledged persecutions for repudiating the radicals.

The persecution of the Stills by the Reds was no less adamant than the opposition incurred by Richard Wright. To suggest that the Stills were imagining their persecution is to suggest that there was no persecution. If Catherine Smith is correct in assuming that the composer and his wife were self-destructively and wrongly paranoid, where is her corroborative data to indicate that Still's music was given the respect that it deserved after 1949? Where is her proof that Still's music was widely-recorded, played and heard by the public after 1949? Where are the documents which show that the left-leaning people in the arts gave Still a chance to seek public adulation, and that the Black militants were capable of, or interested in, empowering Still had he sought their help? Where is there any data that does not show that the Stills were blackballed in a pervasive and absolute manner?

And, what if the Stills were all too correct in their political perspective? What if the leftists and Black militants had in their ranks destructive and misguided elements who were bent on crushing anyone who did not share their opinions? What if Still and Arvey were not isolating themselves, as Smith implies, but were isolated by their adversaries? What if this "extreme paranoia" that Smith deplores was actually a plea for justice and vindication, and what if Catherine Smith has compounded the injustice by minimizing their plight, and by ignoring research in the Still-Arvey papers that would set matters aright?

It is probable that an investigation of newly-opened CIA and FBI files will shed light on the Stills' problem, as will the 160+ political scrapbooks prepared by Verna Arvey to uncover the truth of their situation. In that event, a certain compassion may develop for a couple whose harsh treatment in the media prevented worldwide enjoyment of a rich musical legacy. Given this possible development, Catherine Smith may just as well have blamed Dreyfus for his fate, and castigated him for being broken in body and mind at the end of his life.

Another area of concern that is critical to the study of William Grant Still is also completely bypassed by Smith: that of tacitly applied racism. The fact that Still was a man of color aggravated his career crises, and/or created his crises. The left-wingers who failed to win him to the Communist cause may have used racism against him, or the racists may have turned to revolutionary elements to oppose him: either way, the result was the decimation of two timeless and beautiful careers.

Catherine Smith perhaps has not studied the stories of other great persons of color in history. If she had, she would have noticed a particular pattern: extraordinary accomplishments in spite of huge obstacles, and then swift and unjust attempts by ill-disposed White people to humiliate them, to imprison them, or to rob them of a livelihood.

If we look at only one area of activity, say, for example, the military arena, we see this pattern of retaliation for success quite clearly (Bill Armstrong, "The Buffalo Soldiers," Goldhil Video GH052 [Bill Armstrong Productions, Thousand Oaks, CA, 1996]). Henry Ossier Flipper, the first African-American to graduate from West Point in 1877, endured four years of ostracism during which his fellow cadets would not speak to him. After his graduation, he was assigned to Ft. Davis, Texas, where it was claimed that he went riding with a white lady, and that he stole money from the regiment. After the accusation of theft was made, he was not confined to quarters as a white officer would have been in a similar situation: he was locked up, court-martialed and given a dishonorable discharge. He spent the rest of his days trying to prove his innocence.

John Hanks Alexander, the second African-American man to graduate from West Point, died mysteriously after his graduation from what was said to be "heart disease." Colonel Charles Young, the third man of Color to get through the rigors of West Point (in 1889), was denied a commission because he was accused of being unfit. He rode a horse all the way from Wilberforce to the Capitol to prove that he was fit, but he was turned down again. Had he received his commission, he would have been the first Afro-American to do so in the United States; when he failed to become the first officer of Color, he suffered lifelong disappointment.

Henry V. Plummer, the first Black chaplain in the regular army, appointed in 1884, became a role model for the soldiers at Ft. Riley, Kansas, until he was inexplicably court-martialed and dismissed for fraternizing with enlisted men. Sergeant Brent Woods, who received the Medal of Honor in 1879 for saving civilians and cavalrymen from a massacre in Gavilan Canyon, New Mexico, was demoted to Private *after* he was recognized for bravery. The legendary Buffalo Soldiers were instrumental in winning the battle of San Juan Hill for Teddy Roosevelt, yet, in Roosevelt's speeches after the battle, he falsely accused the Black troopers of cowardice, claiming that he forced them up the hill at gun point.

Tales such as these abound in every area of endeavor where

Afro-Americans have striven for excellence, and William Grant Still was no exception in this horrendous pattern of victimization. Those who write about Still must have the ability and inclination to understand the sufferings of people afflicted by prejudice; those who pretend to be able to recognize paranoia, should also be able to recognize the insidious activities of racists in action.

Catherine Smith does not recognize bigotry as being proactive in Still's life; she simply feels—and unjustly so—that race confined the composer's thinking and development, and caused him to be confused about his identity. Because she does not understand the toxicity of group hatred, she diminishes both Still's pain and his achievement. What is more, she is even more hurtful in her handling of Still's love for Verna Arvey.

Smith takes a negative view of Arvey from the outset. She observes that Verna Arvey would have been a "minor figure" in the cultural arts, had it not been for her association with William Grant Still. She ignores the fact that Arvey was quite prominent in the world of California music in the thirties; because her articles were published in all of the major music magazines, Arvey had artistic influence and widespread connections (Verna Arvey, *Choreographic Music* [E.P. Dutton, NY, 1941]). Smith's notion that New York is the only place to go for cultural direction, causes her to discard Arvey's contention that the greats in music and the arts came out West in increasing numbers, wanting to be a part of a viable, progressive cultural community. Because she was born and raised in Los Angeles, Arvey felt herself to be in an ideal place to pursue her interests in the arts. Smith does not agree.

Smith's evidence that Arvey had no stature in the arts is actually lack of evidence: she does not adequately discuss the prominent people who were known to Arvey, nor does she mention Arvey's brilliant mind, or her true passion for, and knowledge of, music and the dance. As Lance Bowling observed,

> Mrs. Still was a wonderful collaborator for her husband. She had an uncanny ability to synthesize vast amounts of data, years before computers came along. She was not impulsive, or pushy; instead she was reserved, capable, and she had a great reverence and love for her husband. I have an interview from 1975 on radio station KFAC

which shows her kindness and graciousness during Mr. Still's declining years (Steve Markham, "Interview with Mr. and Mrs. William Grant Still, radio KFAC, Los Angeles, CA, "Crossroads of Music," 1974; a tape of this interview is available from Cambria Master Recordings, P.O. Box 374, Lomita, CA, 90717).

Another person who knew the Stills well, Marjorie Lange,[3] told me, upon my mother's death, "Verna and Billy were genuinely kind, loving and enjoyable people, and they were both so talented. I miss them very much." Dr. Annette Kaufman, noted pianist and widow of the distinguished violinist, Louis Kaufman, echoed Marjorie Lange's opinion, calling the Stills, "dear, wonderful people, and true artists" (Message to Judith Anne Still, December 5, 1987).

It is strange that Catherine Smith does not include any such praises of Arvey in her book, even though she met with Marjorie Lange and Annette Kaufman when she came to Los Angeles. Instead, Smith moves the focus of her interest in Arvey to what she supposes to be a love triangle between Still, Arvey and Bruce Forsythe. Forsythe was a writer and musician who worked for a short time as librettist for Still, and who was also a member of Arvey's social group. He probably introduced Still to Arvey when Still visited Los Angeles with Paul Whiteman. Forsythe and a male friend often attended cultural events with Arvey and others, and Arvey and others occasionally came to Forsythe's home. Because Arvey played for the dance and worked as correspondent for many periodicals, her numerous friends joined in lively intellectual discussions and worked on artistic projects together, and Forsythe was often included in their get-togethers.

Smith hints at a romantic relationship between Forsythe and Arvey, probably because Forsythe claimed in one letter that he loved her, but it is not clear from that letter that the love to which he refers is either romantic or sexual. Moreover, Forsythe may have been involved in one or more gay relationships when Arvey

---

[3] Marjorie Lange was a film actress and runner-up to Miss America in 1926. She married the film orchestrator and conductor, Arthur Lange, and she became a psychic medium, involved with automatic writing.

knew him. Smith seems to say that Verna Arvey broke off with Forsythe because Still came into the picture, but such was not the case. Problems with Forsythe arose when he began to lose his eyesight; the fear of blindness caused him to drink heavily, and, eventually, he became an alcoholic. It was Forsythe's substance abuse that led Arvey and her friends to break with him, well before William Grant Still moved to Los Angeles. A letter from Verna Arvey to Forsythe indicates that she wanted the three of them (Still, Arvey, Forsythe) to continue being friends even after 1934 when Still arrived in L.A., but clearly they did not remain friends; by 1934, Forsythe was an embarrassment.

Smith's persistent claim that Verna Arvey felt guilty over Forsythe is an intimation that she felt responsible for his self-destruction, but there is absolutely no evidence of any guilt, written or otherwise. She did not cause his drunkenness—his bad behavior when drunk brought about his downfall; Still did not take her away from his friend because she and Forsythe were never romantically involved.

Ironically, Catherine Smith presents the very document that discounts her conclusions about Still and Arvey. She quotes a letter to Forsythe from March of 1934, before Still arrived on the West Coast to stay, in which Arvey states that she wishes to break off her friendship with Forsythe (*A Study in Contradictions*, 108). Arvey herself gives the reason, when she says that Forsythe has proven himself to be a liar and a drunkard, and that he was not popular among his friends anymore owing to his anti-sociability.

The declaration of Forsythe's son that there was a love triangle between the three was certainly hearsay, echoing the father's fantasies, for the son was not born until the forties. The declaration might also have been in support of the son's interviewer, Catherine Smith, who no doubt expressed her belief in the idea through her questions. If the idea of the love triangle came exclusively from Forsythe to the son, it is well to remember Arvey's statement that Forsythe "lied about her."

Smith's romantic fiction involving Still, Arvey and Forsythe may have been designed to sensationalize *A Study in Contradictions*, and to enliven it with allegations of scandal. But Smith adds professional importance to the supposed scandal by declaring that Forsythe was a major influence on Still by virtue of his work as a librettist. Smith observes that, when Forsythe was no longer Still's librettist, Still began to collaborate with Arvey, and then Still's work changed in some way. The subtle implication here may be that Forsythe was Afro-American and could help Still to recognize his "blackness," where Arvey could not.

However, the composer's sketches in the Still-Arvey Collection (University of Arkansas Libraries, Fayetteville, AR, Special Collections) do not support any notion that Still was led by either Forsythe or Arvey. The composer's own notes, preserved in ninety-nine sketchbooks, reveal his singularity of purpose in composing, and his unwavering development of themes and subject matter that he set down during the 1920s. The composer's adamantine sense of purpose and identity led him to be the influencer, not the influenced, in all of his collaborations. Although the titles of certain works may have been altered after Arvey came into the picture, major changes of philosophy and content were not forthcoming as a result of her work.

Careful reading of all of the letters, diaries and manuscripts in the Still-Arvey papers will ultimately reveal that Bruce Forsythe was an insignificant figure in the Still-Arvey saga. Meanwhile, the Forsythe fiction is not the only distortion of the facts that operates against Still and Arvey in Smith's *Study*. Smith also proposes that Arvey's personality changed after she married Still, and that she became "defensive," "narrow," "angry" and bent on isolating her husband from society.

Smith documents Arvey's supposed change of personality via a letter from Harry Hay, in which Hay says that Arvey's friends, Teru and Waldeen, had bemoaned the loss of the old Arvey "sparkle" and "winsomeness," and that Lester Horton called her "tiresome" and "pushy." No other affidavits other than this one are brought forward to prove that Arvey changed for the worse after her marriage, and reports which give an opposite view of the composer's wife are not mentioned. If, indeed, they did believe that she lost her winsomeness, let it be said that very few people who marry remain the same frolicsome, pie-eyed youngsters that they were in their twenties. Verna Arvey was twenty-nine when she married, and two months later she became pregnant with her first child. Show me the woman who has a baby at thirty and remains "winsome," and she will be an anomaly.

The large volume of evidence, to which Smith had access, indicates that Harry Hay barely knew either Arvey or Still, and that, apart from Hay, the Stills were a popular and respected couple whose home was rarely without friendly visitors. Only the worst kind of pseudo-scholarship would deem Hay's comment to be definitive, particularly when questions can be raised about the purity of Hay's motives. Did he have an axe to grind with Arvey in passing on hearsay as truth? For reasons that will not be discussed here, it is not a certainty that Arvey's three friends spoke ill of her; but, had they done so, were their motives, or Hay's, unblemished by racial prejudice? And what of the motives of Catherine Smith? In a letter to the University of California Press, I myself said,

> I am always amazed when our so-called intellectuals will pick up on a bit of degrading gossip from someone who is not in a position to know, and will turn it into a scholarly theory on paper. Then all other scholars read the paper, and react to that bit of gossip, discussing and developing it into various scenarios, until the reality is lost. In scholarship, theories are more exciting than truth; in the world of great men and women where my parents lived, truth is more lasting than scholarship. (I am reminded that a small mind once criticized Mozart's behavior when he was under the influence, and some offensive playwright turned the anecdote into a play. So now Mozart is, for millions of people, a ridiculous figure. Let's hope that this doesn't happen to William Grant Still.)
> 
> (Judith Anne Still, November 11, 1999).

If Verna Arvey changed after her marriage, it was through growth and through a more serious dedication to what she saw, after her marriage, as her work in the world. Suddenly she was in a meaningful relationship where she could work concertedly with her husband toward a lofty goal; she would no longer have the time or inclination to attend the usual opera parties and museum outings. While she no longer saw the friends of her youth frequently, she and William Grant Still developed new friendships in great numbers. Many of these friends, who were often people of stature, are listed in Arvey's book, *In One Lifetime* (University of Arkansas Press, Fayetteville, AR, 72701, 1984). Far from being isolated, they were in the center of a group of intelligent, creative, personable people who supported and loved them, and the letters that testify to this social and intellectual interaction are available to the public in the Still-Arvey Collection. Testimonies of her closest friends indicate that she never lost her brilliant mind, her wit, or her kind heart.

Meanwhile, in all of this, neither Lester Horton nor Harry Hay, nor Catherine Smith, have mentioned the most important sobering influence in the Still-Arvey marriage: the horrible persecutions visited upon the couple by bigoted people. Smith seems to think that Arvey wanted to enhance herself by marrying Still, and that, having had a choice between two artistic Black men, she chose the one most likely to compensate her for having failed as a concert pianist. Ignoring the fact that Arvey did not really aspire to pianistic stardom—she was primarily a writer who welcomed chances to concertize—Smith implies that the couple had to have opportunistic reasons to get married—other than love, because interracial couples cannot possibly love each other, can they? The truth is that Arvey and Still were painfully aware that their marriage was fraught with danger and sacrifice, and that Arvey was not seizing an opportunity in the eyes of the world—she was giving herself to martyrdom.

Arvey's book, *In One Lifetime*, outlines some of the difficulties that she took on with Still, including being forced to live in a ghetto area, being called a tramp, being refused service and accommodations in hotels and restaurants, and being threatened and prejudged. The most fearful experience for Arvey was the murder of the Short family. Mr. Short was Black and his wife was White, and they and their two children moved into a hostile all-White neighborhood, whereupon the neighbors burned their house with them in it. Verna Arvey's attempts to get the Attorney-General to investigate the case were vain, and perhaps, in Lester Horton's or Catherine Smith's opinion, she was too "pushy." Could she have remained "winsome" after such a horror? Could she have failed to worry over the safety of her own family?

Sadly, Smith wholly accepts Harry Hay's commentary on Arvey, and she asserts that Arvey was so "pushy" that she pushed her husband into an enforced isolation from society. Obviously Smith does not consider racial hatred to be an isolating influence, nor does she believe the couple's huge numbers of friends to be a part of "society:" undoubtedly she means that Arvey kept Still from "negotiating" a place with his people, i.e., the advocates of Black power. In other words, the only legitimate way to be a person of Color is to be a "politically correct" person of Color. The Afro-American friends of the Stills were largely conservative, upper middle-class, and non-stereotypical; they were cultured and intelligent, and they did not spend a lot of time wondering wherein their "blackness" consisted. There is no data which suggests that Arvey forced Still into these friendships, or kept the composer from seeking concourse with the Black militants, had he wished for such associations.

Oddly enough, Smith works against her own theories by positing, on the one hand, that Arvey was so controlling that she was able to isolate her husband, and, on the other, that she was so "weak" that she gave up her personality to Still, submerging her identity in her husband's all-inclusive persona. It is difficult to see how a wife can be both controlling and subordinate, and stay in her marriage without internal conflict for almost forty years, but Smith would have us agree that this is the case. (Perhaps the contradictions in *A Study in Contradictions* belong more to the author than to the subject matter.)

From the perspective of some feminists, it is an injustice for a gifted woman to collaborate with a gifted man without suing for the limelight. And yet, Verna Arvey did not want or need the limelight. She said, and Catherine Smith validates this statement, "I don't want to be a famous artist, I want to do my work and do it well." Even so, she did not submerge herself in her marriage, nor did she give up her identity and her accomplishments in order to promote her husband. In a time when it was absolutely expected that a woman give up her maiden name, she was always just, "Verna Arvey." Her excellent book, *Choreographic Music*, published in 1941, was not written to benefit William Grant Still.

In the remarkable world of symbiotic nature, Arvey retained

her own power while she and her chosen mate advanced and enhanced each other. During her life with the composer she did all that she would have done had she remained single, and she did it without diminishing herself or damaging the career of her husband. They were a team, Verna and Billy, two people who were—in spite of differences in skin color, which were only a problem to others, not to themselves—genuinely in love with each other and faithful to the cause; the cause, not of political correctness, but of intercultural understanding.

Had Catherine Smith dealt with the Still-Arvey papers fairly and completely, her book would reveal a couple not worldly or manipulative, but a warm and friendly pair who loved people and who were comfortable with their commitment to each other. During their 39+ years of marriage, they worked hard to get their compositions and precepts out to the public, but as racial stereotypes gripped the populace in unacknowledged ways, they became less and less successful. They complained about political hurdles and the vituperation of their enemies, but they did not give up their labors, their hopes for future vindication, and their pleasure in family life. They did worry about their inability to get commissions and performances and media attention, but this worry was small when compared to the amount of work that they completed, and the time spent with hobbies, friends and family.

Verna Arvey packed boxes of used clothes and mailed them to the Native American orphans on a reservation. She and Still traveled regularly to Camarillo, California, to visit Arvey's friend Teru, who was in an asylum. They wrote to and visited Henry Cowell, who was wrongfully imprisoned. They gave their old '36 Ford to a newly-married interracial couple in order to help them to get established, even though they had wanted to sell the car for a much-needed sum of money. They collected items to donate to the St. Vincent DePaul Society, and made little gifts for friends, such as a favorite casserole, baked by Arvey, or a set of wooden bookends fashioned by Still. Arvey wrote letters to the editors of the *Times* and *Examiner* to protest fluoridation, vivisection and the murder of the Short family. Arvey went daily to take care of her elderly mother, Bessie Arvey. Both Still and Arvey made sure that their two children had toys to play with, even when they had no money to buy them. They made dolls and doll furniture and train sets themselves.

In their "off-hours," Still and Arvey were not the obsessive, nervous individuals that they appear to be in *A Study in Contradictions.* Verna Arvey read biographies and historical fiction, tried out new recipes, and studied the prophecies of seers like Edgar Cayce. Still immersed himself in philosophical texts, gardened, and solved the most complex crossword puzzles available, in addition to anacrostics and acrostics. Sometimes the couple took their children on picnics to Fern Dell, Marina Del Rey, and Exposition Park. The composer was happiest when he was driving to the beach or to the country with his family. The good things that Still and Arvey provided in their home—the most valuable of which was pure, unselfish love—are not mentioned in Catherine Smith's *Study.*

In the end, it must be suspected that Catherine Smith's research in the Still-Arvey papers is spotty and presumptive. She describes the couple as "anti-social," "anxious," "distrustful," "suspicious," "nervous," "bitter," "paranoid" and "deficient in coping skills." Arvey is "weak," "narrow," "nervous," "angry" and "subservient." Not only are these descriptions totally baseless, but also, they leave the reader wondering what are the Stills' good qualities? Smith fails to find their praiseworthy attributes interesting, and, in fact, her extreme negativity appears almost to be an unqualified dislike. One hesitates to infer that such unsubstantiated repugnance stems from a form of racism.

At any rate, Smith's disapproval of the couple is apparent even in small matters, as, for example, when she quotes Arvey's assessment of Gershwin. Arvey wrote that Gershwin used Negro idioms superficially, while Still expressed these idioms from an internal standpoint, with the sure handling that came with ownership. Smith (p. 165) calls this criticism of Gershwin "snobbish" and "invoking distinctions of class." Disregarding the distinctions of class that direct Smith's own opinions, those who object to Gershwin's blatant appropriation of Negro idioms and his acceptance of fame on their account, will see Arvey's assessment as being rather restrained and quite polite. It is, for the majority of Americans of Color, the absolute truth.

Perhaps the truth for Afro-Americans is not the same as the truth for people of other colors. In Catherine Smith's world, it certainly is not the same. In her world, the enormous achievement of a man of Color is "inability to cope;" the love of a Black man and a White woman is "subordination;" the interaction of an interracial couple with like-minded conservatives of all colors is "isolation;" a sincere faith and a singleness of purpose is "contradiction." With these designations, Catherine Smith joins forces with Teddy Roosevelt, who, by saying what his constituents expected to hear, nearly destroyed a noble heritage. More such politicians among scholars we do not need. Those who have won must now give way to those who have failed to win. And, though William Grant Still and Verna Arvey certainly failed to convince Catherine Smith of their worth, they will one day achieve justice, "if the truth be truth, and the right be right."

# RESTORING PATHS TO DWELL IN[1]

> Yea, they are the greedy dogs which can never have enough, and they are the shepherds that cannot understand; They all look to their own way, everyone for his gain, from his quarter.
> (Isaiah 56:11)

> And they that shall be of thee shall build the old waste places; thou shalt raise up the foundations of many generations; and thou shalt be called, The repairer of the breach, The restorer of paths to dwell in.
> (Isaiah 58:12)

> Go through, go through the gates; ...lift up a standard for the people.
> (Isaiah 62:10)

When Arthur Honegger was asked to comment on composers and music, he said, "The public doesn't want new music; the main thing that it demands of a composer is that he be dead" (*ASCAP Today* 5 [September 1971] 17). With a jaunty verbal wave, Honegger paid his respects to the state of the arts in our time. Ever since the rise of the avant-garde in the 1920's, composers, artists and authors have been eager to do battle with the traditional and the intelligible; and, in their lust for combat, they have rushed onto the battlefield without their audiences behind them.

The relinquishing of contemporary music and art in favor of the work of the "Masters" is a characteristic of the cultural climate in the twentieth century. Everyone knows that the avant-garde has become the rear-guard, but no one seems to know what to do about it, or, indeed, whether anything should be done about it. The artistically well-informed suggest that, if they wait long enough, the public will someday learn to accept that which it does not like in spite of itself. The public wonders secretly whether ugliness can really be beautiful. Time brandishes his scythe and everyone looks away from the horizon. The huddled masses attend fewer and fewer presentations of modern music and art, gravitating instead toward Bach, Beethoven and Brahms, toward

---

[1] This essay is hitherto unpublished.

musical theater, toward the television mini-series, and toward private libraries of tapes, discs and prints. Outward interest in the elevated arts of the day declines amid sighs of apathy and stoic disregard.

Every now and then, in the Pompeian sleep, a call is heard to waken and to rise up. One musician of some stature has made a concerted effort to rally opposition to the decay of the arts: the composer, William Grant Still. Still spent fifty years of his life delivering lectures, writing articles, speaking out in radio and newspaper interviews, crying out in a wilderness not of his own making that audiences should finally and emphatically free themselves from the bonds of the formless, the "harsh and uninteresting," in art and music ("The Composer's Creed," *Music of the West* 17 [October 1961] 13-15) .Said Still,

> ...it is high time for those who truly love music to realize that their help is needed, for today, music stands at a crossroads. Its very survival as a continuing art-form depends on the direction all of us who play a part in the world of music wish to take. We, in short, are faced with the need to make a *great* decision. [We must decide]...what is the good music of today? ...What *is* music and what *isn't* music?
>
> (*Music of the West*, 13).

Still's answer to the "new music" of the ultra-moderns was to try to mobilize a "new audience," not a concert-going public that simply stayed away from modern music, but one that, through its active participation in the arts, would review the ranks of contemporary composers to find compositions that it could enjoy. He wanted vocal devotees who would, in publicized expressions of opinion, demand from their composers and artists works that were dignified and harmonious. He wanted a militant, not an apathetic, public, one that would demonstrate loudly against the purchase of abstract art by the government-owned museums, that would refuse to applaud the "harsher, atonal idioms" (Beverly Wolter, "Composer Conducts N. O. Symphony...," Baton Rouge, Louisiana, *State Times* [March 5, 1955]), and one that was not afraid to decry the "idiotic" stunts of John Cage.

It was only in the defeat of ultra-modernism, claimed Still, that the way could be cleared for world betterment by means of undefaced creativity. He intoned the virtues in the ancient foundations of excellence, spiritual inspiration and craftsmanship. He prodded and exhorted his fellow composers to take heed of those virtues, even though most of them paid little attention to his directives. As the editors of the *Etude* observed in 1950, Still was "almost alone among contemporary composers" in his "courage to reject the experimental cacophonous style which is generally called 'modern music'" (*Etude* 68 [March 1950] 17).

The lack of homage that was given to the voice of harmony had a most pernicious affect upon the refinement of American culture. In fact, the result of the advance of the modernists was as catastrophic as if the trap door had been sealed on the Trojan horse, preventing the Mycenaeans from invading the mainland that was to become Greece. What if the Spartan point of view, not the Athenian, had been allowed to gain control of the reins of civilization; what if the unfeeling, militaristic mind had razed to ashes the philosophical and the aesthetically engaging? Human history might then have lost the modern genesis of drama, poetry, diplomacy and philosophy, wherein Plato, Aristotle, Aeschylus and their followers set the pace for the march of future generations.

Perhaps such a loss has occurred in the last 100 years; certainly William Grant Still thought that the damage suffered has been grievous. According to the composer, what has taken place in music, art and literature, particularly in the United States, is that a constructive movement toward the erection of an inspired, agreeable and well-balanced culture was aborted when the ungodly plunderers, the kidnappers of the fair damsel, made away with the penultimate treasure of civilization--artistic grandeur. Without that treasure, music was engulfed in discord, sculpture crumbled into tasteless heaps of refuse, and literature was impregnated with obscenities and despair.

It was a debacle unparalleled since the fall of the Greco-Romans, and it could not be counterbalanced without courageous tactics. According to Still, the only way to reclaim enchantment in the arts would be to develop a coherent philosophy of artistic creation and appreciation, and to reaffirm the need for value and structure in subjective effort. Inasmuch as such a philosophy of "reconstruction" has never been fully detailed, even by Still, the progress away from the ultra-modern might well begin with an overview of the arts in this century, and with a consolidation of Still's comments upon that view.

Naturally, no observance of present-day culture can begin without mention of the prominence of motion pictures and television. Perhaps the chief reason for public indifference to the absence of radiance and polish in the arts is the presence of the modern counterpart for the Roman circuses, the mass media. Artie Shaw once complained that television was responsible for causing the loss of taste and culture in the United States (Conversation with Judith Anne Still [September 10, 1986]), and he has not been the only one to express that belief. While the media cannot bear the entire blame for cultural degeneracy, it is true that, like hypnotic predators, they feed upon the carcass of personal inventiveness.

In the days before mass media supremacy, serious music and ornamental pursuits were an integral part of life in the average American home. Children learned to play the piano and/or instruments of various sorts, young ladies were commonly taught to paint china and to write poems or novels, families sang together in their parlors and weekends found whole communities attending concerts and plays in parks or theaters.

With the advent of the motion picture and of television--when entertainment became geared to appeal to the eyes and less and less to the ears and to the mind--music ceased to be a central domestic concern. People stopped reading, writing and painting in order to amuse themselves, having welcomed the dominance of the television monitor over their evenings and weekends.

The extent to which the media pervade American life cannot be underestimated. Robert MacNeil has calculated that, for every ten years that a person is alive, he is exposed to 10,000 hours of television, the same number of hours that it would take to get a degree in nuclear physics, to speak several languages fluently, or to earn two bachelor's degrees ("Is Television Shortening Our Attention Span?," *National Forum* 68 [Fall 1987] 21-23). Furthermore, asserts MacNeil, because movie and television producers want to interest the greatest number of people, and because they assume that most people want action, rather than information, they provide fare that shortens attention spans and diminishes the ability to think. Children brought up in front of a screen do not appreciate the rhythms and rich vocabulary of English prose, nor can they deal with complex ideas or stories. The result of the deprivation of the youth is that one-third of America's young enter adulthood as functional illiterates, and that one-million new illiterates and semi-literates are added to this group every year (MacNeil, 22).

Not only does television promote illiteracy, but it also perpetuates mediocrity. Norman Corwin, former producer for CBS, observes that, in our age, the "insipidity" and "shallow fare" of the mass media are taken for significant achievements ("The 365-Day Fantasy," *National Forum* [Fall 1987] 5-6, and *Trivializing America: The Triumph of Mediocrity* [Lyle Stuart, 1986]). The New Coke is presented as having an importance equal to societal and political dignitaries; merit is confused with commercial success. Convicts appear on talk shows and their lives are scrutinized in made-for-TV movies; daytime viewers watch soap operas instead of government hearings. Values are so brutalized that, when diplomats visit this country, they are taken to Disneyland, Magic Mountain and Sea World instead of to places of historical significance.

Because no media distinction is made between "benefactor and malefactor...paragon and parasite" (Corwin, *National Forum*, 6), no such distinction is expected or valued by television viewers. Tending to be partisans of the example that is set for them, human beings allow their language and behavior to degenerate to the level of the movies that are shown to them. They are schooled by habit not to look for subtlety, wisdom and grace on the screen; instead they are habituated to car chases, street fights, four-letter words, explicit sex, and rock music--in general, to variety without content.

As media audiences submit to their environment, directors of programming like George Jellinek of WQXR radio, New York, deplore the growing allegiance to rock-oriented music, and the consequent deterioration of advertising support for concert music stations ("Broadcasting and the Contemporary Composer," *ASCAP Today* 5 [Sept. 1971] 18). When producers are asked to upgrade their offerings, they shrug innocently and insist that they proffer exactly what is demanded of them. The question remains, however, whether the consumer sees in the media what he has always desired, or whether he desires what he has been trained by custom to expect.

In truth, the inculcation of mindlessness in the modern television watcher is exacerbated by the wane of discipline in the upbringing of the youth. More and more children are growing up without parental supervision; twenty percent of American children live below the poverty level and receive little attention from their parents, while the same number are "latchkey" children or offspring from broken homes (C. Emily Feistritzer, *Cheating Our Children: Why We Need School Reform* [National Center for Education Information, Washington D.C., 1985]).

When one-third of the nation's young people are not being neglected at home, they are in classrooms where the environment for deep-thinking and consummate culture is poor. Education, drained of quality by the need to teach everyone, regardless of teachability or motivation, puts less and less emphasis on the arts. Students who watch too much television do inferior work in school, and taxpayers, outraged by the ostensible waste of state funds for curriculums that do not produce results, encourage school administrators to increase drill in grammar, spelling and arithmetic. The "frills" of education--art and music--are cut away, and their critical usefulness in providing mental control, emotional stability and life enhancement is forgotten. Only the marching bands are afforded adequate funding, buoyed up as they are by the American passion for athletics, for bread and circuses.

Indeed, the public neglect of the arts in education is the focus of the recent report of the National Endowment for the Arts, which is appropriately titled, "Toward Civilization" [Washington, D.C. 20506: May 1988]. According to this government assessment, statistics reveal that most Americans believe training in the arts to be unimportant, while between 50 and 80% of Americans have had no education at all in music and art.

Without a complete education, children never gain the ability to think philosophically. By the time young adults enter college, if they do, they are well-practiced in the unquestioning acceptance of persuasion, even as they are seasoned in an educational system that is ruled by the least common denominator. They are ready for the plunderers of intellectual wealth--the academic "abolitionists," as Jacques Barzun calls them ("Romanticism Today," *Encounter* 17 [September 1961] 26-32)--to indoctrinate them in the precepts of abstract art, of existentialist drama, and of atonal or twelve-tone music.

The academic establishment gives cogent arguments for having hoisted the flag of "universal purposelessness" (Barzun, 28) in high art. Rendered skeptical by the "advancements of science, technology and machine idolatry" (Joseph Eger, "Ives and Beatles!" *The Music Journal* [September 1968] 46), "and exasperated by two world wars and twenty abortive revolutions" (Barzun, 27), the thinking man became suddenly and painfully aware of the dark side of human nature. The world conflicts revealed to him the horror of mechanized cruelty, and, in the millions of dead and disfigured war victims, he witnessed the ultimate pointlessness and thoughtlessness of human activity.

Into this world of putrifying ideas and ideals marched Freud, who looked to the genitals for knowledge of motivation, and Schopenhauer, who turned pessimism into philosophic determinism. The economic determinists were verified by the relativists, and by Margaret Mead and Ruth Benedict, who reveled in the amorality of diverse societal systems. The lost-generationists were encouraged by the deconstructionists, the offspring of Jacques Derrida, who magnified the chasm between our perception of things (words) and the things themselves. The deconstructionists concluded that, since reality only exists for us through our definition of it, and since definitions can be arbitrary and based on individual interpretation, then reality itself is arbitrary and not governed by absolutes. It was this repudiation of absolute principles of truth and beauty which supported the growth in painting of impressionism, surrealism and abstractionism, and in literature of naturalism, existentialism and expressionism.

Scholars in America were excited over the innovations in expression, having long-hoped for liberation from European-based traditions and techniques. Paul Fromm, one of those who promoted the Festival of Contemporary American Music at Tanglewood in 1967, announced that contemporary music was "musical liberation from the constraints of the past" (*Tanglewood Festival Report* [Chicago, Illinois: Fromm Music Foundation, 1967] 14). Unfortunately for the arts, however, repudiation and rejection cannot themselves engender innovative manifestations; they must be assisted by talent and imagination. If a creative man escapes from tradition, he develops new art forms; but if an uninspired man does so, he merely destroys old ones. The leaders of the abolitionist movement had neither the inspiration nor the talent to produce an uplifting American idiom in the arts.

Onto the American stage came numerous grave spectacles of human futility. Even the most widely-acclaimed playwrights were weighed down by a sodden sort of literary despair. While Willy Loman killed himself over obsolescence, the seven weak figures in Sam Shepard's *Buried Child* demonstrated that they would not, could not, grow or change, enrich or impress, inside or outside of the drama. And Shepard, in receiving his Pulitzer Prize for *Buried Child*, was labeled "one of the greatest writers in the history of American drama" (Jack Richardson, "Sam Shepard's *Buried Child*," *South Coast Repertory Theater Newsletter* [Spring 1986] 4).

Among painters, abstractionists like Kandinsky, and their champion, Clement Greenberg, were the most bombastic proponents of art as visual anguish. Because art was a reflection of our age, they said, it could not transcend that which it mirrored. Greenberg even developed a system of thought to prove that paintings had to be abstract in order to constitute a "significant human enterprise" (Hilton Kramer, "The Idea of Tradition in American Art Criticism," *The American Scholar* 56 [Summer 1987] 319-327). Art, explained Greenberg, had lost its function after the Enlightenment. Having ceased to be a necessary adjunct to communication, education, decoration and architecture, it could now go no further than its "area of competence," that is, it was suddenly confined within the hitherto unrecognized barriers of the two-dimensional canvas. This restriction to its boundaries was the apparent result of art's newly-acquired purpose, which was the criticism of man and civilization. Anyone who denounced the limitations of human endeavor had, perforce, to abide within his own personal limits.

The argument was contrived and pompous, in addition to being deleterious to the exploration of artistic possibilities. It was something near to deciding that, since breeding exotic flowers has no real function in society, breeders ought not to be allowed to cross one breed with another, but should be morally confined to enjoyment of the varieties of plants that exist already. Where once civilization had been predicated upon the compulsion to scale the heights of the probable, now it was consumed by self-conscious references to its receding potential.

The mental gymnastics of Greenberg, which were negative and artificial (and tended subjugate and abuse the art-lover), were echoed in the mathematical theories and esoteric precepts of the serialists and twelve-tonists in music. The latter set up systems that were so complex that they seemed to forbid the common man to seek access to them. As Still put it, the composers of the "new music" developed long explanations for what was essentially a lack of form and grace in their compositions. In their prolixity they looked down upon their audiences from a perceptual and artistically superior vantage point, as if to write consonant music would be a fault because the public might understand it ("Our American Musical Resources," *Showcase* Music Clubs Magazine [Fall 1961] 8).

The supercilious banter of the musical theorists became one of the trappings of their formidable armor. George Perle, in *Serial Composition and Atonality* [University of California Press, 1962], warned his readers that the music of Schoenberg-through-Webern-to-Babbitt could not be understood at all if the techniques for writing it were not understood. Whereupon he launched into a study of those techniques which proved them closer to nuclear or statistical theory than to aesthetic prescription. What Perle was really saying, and has said on other occasions, is that composers of serial, twelve-tone and atonal music do not write to communicate with or to please the public; as Roger Sessions put it, the composer of today writes "what's in him," not what people want to hear ("The New Sound of Music: No Longer Do-Re-Mi,"

Flint, Michigan, *Journal* [*Tanglewood Report*] 14).

It has not seemed to matter to composers like Sessions that people have not cared to hear what's in them, nor have they cared to understand it. At the Contemporary Music Festival in Tanglewood [August 1967]--a festival brought forward to make the public curious about contemporary music--only a few hundred people attended, while thousands went instead to the Tanglewood Theater-Concert Hall to listen to Bach and Mozart. A reporter from the *Worcester Daily Telegram* who heard the work of the modernists said that the composers and performers were "fiercely serious," attempting to disguise their "hollowness" with "mysterious" titles like "Plahn," "Pien" and "Junctures." Program notes were rarified and righteous, containing "such brow-wrinkling phrases as 'complementary modes in opposite regrstal movement,' 'Differing attitudes toward the basic compositional material,' and 'expanding and contracting intervallic cells.'" In spite of the profundity, however, the journalist concluded that it amounted to "'plink, plank, plunk' for varying numbers of instruments, in the course of which explosive sound clusters punctuated the fracas," and "piano strings were plucked while other instruments made isolated, eerie sounds and noises" ("Music: Contemporary Fete at Tanglewood," *Tanglewood Report* [August 17, 1967] 17).

Significantly, the adverse reaction of this reporter was not an isolated fulmination: everywhere the modernists have been shunned by their hearers. When the Oakland Symphony Orchestra went bankrupt, the experts posited that it may have expanded its services too rapidly, or it may not have attracted big-name soloists, or it may have been hurt by the rise of rock-and-roll (Michael Walsh, "Let's Do the Time Warp Again," *Time* [January 11, 1988] 68-70). No one would confess that the real reason for the fall of Oakland was that the "innovative programming" of works by Várèse, Penderecki and Lutoslawski had left Northern California music-lovers cold. As Erich Leinsdorf admitted, conductors cannot play contemporary music because the public is not receptive to it ("In the Berkshires, A Musical Feast," *Kansas City Star* [August 27, 1967]). The same is true of radio audiences, who express displeasure over Bartok, "Le Sacre" and any dissonant and discordant music that they hear on the air (Jellinek, 18).

Recalling the large number of people in the NEA Report who think that arts instruction is worthless, one wonders whether this belief is not based upon public reaction to contemporary music and art. Interestingly enough, the same educators who deplored the general lack of concern for the arts in America (NEA Report) also suggested that students should study Katherine Hepburn, Jackson Pollock and Aaron Copland along with Shakespeare, Cervantes and Bach. The implication is, of course, that the first three figures deserve equal status with the last three. It does not occur to the NEA that Americans may deem arts instruction to be worthless simply because their mentors often try to deify the artistically trivial, and to worship the culturally insignificant.

Thus, the exaltation of the unimportant continues. The pretensions of the avant-garde override their susceptibility to bombardment: the protests of the people are ignored by the fervent conquerors of delicacy and charm in art and music. When Albert Goldberg attacked the modernists (*Times* Calendar Section [April 16, 1961; June 16, 1963]), he sang the anthem of "Nobility, Beauty and Expressiveness" in music, and lamented the demise of ability, wherein it was "possible to be hailed as a great composer in the 20th-century without even having a sense of pitch." Readers of his column sent hordes of letters to his defense, most of which said, in effect, "Down with the twelve-tones!" But Lawrence Morton, proponent of modernism, refusing to believe that the inundation of mail was the result of the clear mind and informed will of the populace, accused Goldberg of "demagoguery" (*Times* Calendar [July 21, 1963]), and of brainwashing people into rejecting anything that was different from the norm. While Morton lambasted the critics for their "tyranny," Paul Fromm blamed the exclusion of the "new music" upon the ignorance of audiences. The fault, he avowed, lay with people who are uninformed and uneducated, and who make the "environment" "unhealthy" for musicians and composers. "Great art," he said flatly, "does not appeal to everybody." What he might have wanted to say was that art ought not to have to appeal to anybody (Panel Session, Annual Conference of the Music Critics Association [August 11, 1967]).

Other contemporary musicians and composers have surpassed Fromm by intimating that the public has an obligation to listen to their music regardless of its artistic appeal. They are sure that it will gain credence if listeners will bear up long enough. Composer Robert Starer, grumbling because a man walked out of the concert hall after hearing the first "loud," "harsh chord" in one of his compositions, writes of the need for audiences to learn to listen ("The Case of Mr. X, or, The Man Who Walked Out of the Concert Hall," *Musical America* 107 [Nov. 1987] 18-21). His discourse includes the alarming statement that "any horror movie has more dissonance in it" than his music (Starer, 18); that this comparison should be deemed a recommendation is indicative of the level to which taste has plummeted in this country.

Starer goes on to indulge in an almost tongue-in-cheek summary of people's attitudes toward contemporary music, a description that may be closer to the essence of truth than he wants to admit. Says Starer, the modern concert-goer despises music that "gesticulates wildly" without "discernible melody or rhythm." For him, the mathematical formulae that are used to compose the music produce only "meaningless sounds," as in the work of Sessions, Elliott Carter and Wuorinen. Crumb and Druckman present sound effects, or silly theatrical gimmicks "To cover up their emptiness," while John Cage wants "to prove that noise is music." Minimal music is "for minimal minds," a "cushion of sound" so that people can think of other things. Audiences want intelligent thoughts that have sequence, musical variation and development, modulation, and "harmonic and contrapuntal treatment of themes." They want "music of some complexity and depth which gains upon repeated hearing" (Starer, 21).

Starer seems to agree that this coherence is what audiences desire from composers, and yet he does not promise that his contemporaries will give it to them. He assumes, after all is said, that Mr. X will eventually pay homage to his "loud, ...harsh chord," just as he did to Stravinsky's "Rite of Spring." With continued exposure to the muck and clang, attitudes will change, and fledgling awareness will burgeon, if not to actual enjoyment, at least to apprehension and understanding of the invisible meanings in non-traditional outpourings. As Norman Pelligrini of WFMT Chicago radio put it, "Today's clangor is tomorrow's consonance" ("Broadcasting and the Contemporary Composer," *ASCAP Today* 5 [Sept. 1971] 19). If radio stations will continue to insinuate Lukas Foss in between Beethoven and Barber, the public will learn to idolize one along with the other.

The arguments of Pelligrini and Starer are formidable. The purveyors of the abstract are fond of recalling the hue and cry over Van Gogh, Gauguin, Matisse and Picasso, who were once anathema to the critics and the people, and whose works now hang in hallowed halls everywhere. In fact, it is an unchallenged fact that all of our anointed geniuses were, each in his time, the victims of disapproval: how shall the literary persecution of Wagner by Eduard Hanslick and Stravinsky be ignored? By extension, therefore, the productions of the most radical abstractionists will one day be revered. So say the liberators of the arts.

The presumption is that all of the bodies have been safely buried, and that the current estimate of the conflict will achieve historical codification. Just as Ramses II thought that he could hold history at bay by erasing Tutankhamen's name from the Temple of Luxor, so the abstractionists and atonalists glory in their victory over the universal artistic standard. It does not occur to them that perhaps two-hundred years from now even Matisse, Picasso and Stravinsky may be disallowed, while Michelangelo, Rembrandt and Sibelius will retain their vitality and authority.

The centuries have a way of breaking and turning the sod in endless fields of human war and endeavor, so that tenacious weeds will fertilize the more vital and lovely species. At one time the English embraced Jacobean drama to the exclusion of Shakespeare, confident that the stage would always be held captive by that grandiose form of entertainment. Yet, two-hundred years later, Shakespeare had resumed his throne, and the Jacobeans occasionally merited a paragraph or two in theatrical textbooks. Galileo was tortured into ignominious demise by the far-seeing scholars of his time, while today their cause brings shame to their memory.

Of course, the predominant shame of mankind is that the

earthbound multitudes can never see beyond the tallest of their number. The public avoids concerts of contemporary music, but secretly it wonders whether the composer of obtuse, noisome music is not in a realm of cognition high above the ordinary art-lover, privy to some hidden secret that hovers in the dingy clatter. It allows itself to be accused of weakness and of a timidity in meeting the real world head-on. It retaliates, not only by avoiding anything composed after 1920, but also by embracing the Masters. It knows that it cannot be condemned for naiveté if it patronizes Brahms, Bach and Schubert; if it stays close to Chopin and Liszt, no incident will be provoked wherein it must take a firm stand on the avant-garde. The emperor is permitted to keep his new clothes; few are brave enough to say that bad art is bad art.

It is in the avoidance of confrontation that the intellectual and cultural dictatorship gains strength. Even the vocabulary and definitions with which music and art are discussed are determined by mental strangulation and the obliteration of options. Just as Clement Greenberg imprisoned artists within two dimensions instead of three, so, too, the music critics speak of all compositions as if they are bound by two opposing factions only--the clash of the "Titans": the minimalists vs. the serialists (Andrew Stiller, "Who Owns American Music?" *Opus* 3 [December 1986] 18-19, 60). Stiller defines all of American music in terms of the modernist idiom, declaring that "quintessentially" American composers distrust system, structure and form, ignore the practical and the traditional, and embody "gadgeteering" and "indeterminacy" (Stiller, 18).

The same presumptions that constrain Stiller were operative in World War II. By limiting the choices for action and by altering the definitions of human worth, the Third Reich justified the pursuit of all that was antithetical to basic human needs, morals and pleasures. The primary difference between American culture and Nazi Germany is that the latter was comparatively short-lived, while the former has been under the fire of ultra-modern snobbery for more than half-a-century. After this long barrage, the pull away from narrow aesthetic notions will involve a difficult psychological process.

This arduous process of psychological reevaluation was

alluded to by Robert McClintock, composer and director of the Summer Chamber Orchestra in Sacramento, when he reported on several performances of the works of William Grant Still. According to McClintock,

> The members of my orchestra responded rather tepidly to *Summerland* upon first exposure. By the end of June some wanted to play it in their quartet. The same was basically true of *Danzas*, except the acceptance was quicker due to its rhythmic interest. But in both cases I saw in these musicians a similar reaction that meets my music. Essentially, modern musicians don't really care for contemporary music; yet when they "see" music they can recognize--major chords, etc., then they automatically assume it to be outdated, old-fashioned, and of little artistic worth.
> 
> Then they stop looking at it and start hearing it. With a little more exposure they begin to feel it (something they don't do much with so-called contemporary music). And then they discover that this music with major chords, etc., is much more difficult to execute than first "sight" would have them think; appreciation as a musician and a lover of fine music quickly develops.
> 
> (Letter to Judith Anne Still [September 4, 1986]).

What McClintock's musicians came to discover was that the composition of melody is difficult, as is the infusing of form in inanimate matter. Only those with real genius can originate that which is simple and beautiful--the no-talents can only produce dissonance and claim that it has merit. If all creatures could conceive perfect forms and endearing harmonies, then the earth would be peopled by Gods. But the earth is virtually godless. It has lost sight of the fact that great art is a rare event in the annals of man, scarce in it propagation, yet fecund in its influence; it accomplishes more than it intends with more effort than is immediately evident.

As William Grant Still wrote, there is much that is "new" in the tonal realm that has not been done before. The genuine creator "can give a fresh approach to accepted procedures," and "old traditions," and only those progenitors will survive who never completely repudiate the old "to bring forth the new." Indeed, that which is new is not necessarily better than that which is old (*Music of the West*, 14, 15). In other words, "I don't understand why a piece that was judged wonderful yesterday cannot still be wonderful today. It's like eating ice cream. Just because you ate it yesterday, doesn't mean it still won't taste good today" (Robert Finn, "Still Opus Premieres Tonight at Oberlin," Cleveland, Ohio, *Plain Dealer* [November 9, 1970]). Still's wife, Verna Arvey, expanded upon her husband's denial of newness for the sake of newness, suggesting that,

> He never believed harmonic resources had been exhausted. Schoenberg and others went far afield in seeking new sounds with their dissonance and twelve-tone scales, but he didn't think it was necessary. He would spend hours on one harmony, picking it apart and trying various things, but always staying within tonality--and always coming up with something interesting.
> (Tony Thomas, "William Grant Still," *Canadian Stereo Guide* 4 [Fall 1975] 69-71).

Certainly the same abundant resources for invention also exist in the visual arts, for subtle changes of feeling can be effected with the smallest inflection or alteration of treatment. A painter can transform the entire personality of a landscape wherein a building is steeped in half-darkness, by putting a lamp in the window of that building.

Still continually spoke of the indispensability of subtlety and character in art and music, waging his private campaign against the Fromms and the Mortons who, he said, were themselves demagogues, replacing the riches of cultural heritage with "calculated noise" and dark, disjointed sounds. He called them the "ruthless dictators" who want us to give our "allegiance to false gods;" that is, subscribers to "the false idea that it is sophisticated to take all the beauty and pleasure out of an art," and "that melodic music is reactionary" ("Modern Composers Have Lost Their Audiences: Why?" *Australian Musical News* 47 [July 2, 1956], and, Speech to the Southern California Music Teacher's Association, Williamsburg Inn [June 13, 1967]).

When not writing or lecturing, Still and his wife collected newspaper articles to chronicle the ludicrous results of avant-gardism. In one news item in their files, Schoenberg admitted that he had no idea what he was trying to do in a particular piece of his music because he had lost the mathematical diagram that he had prepared for composing it. Another bit of news copy told how a Matisse painting was turned upside-down in the New York Museum of Art, and for forty-seven years no one noticed it, not even Matisse' own son. A third clipping concerned a composer who thought that someone else's work was his and who rushed forward to take a bow. Still another was a review of a first performance of a composition by Roy Harris for two choruses, in which the reviewer announced that this was one of Harris' best works, even though the two choruses had been eight measures apart throughout.

Still could chuckle over these antics of the modernists because he perceived that they were not a smokescreen for some hidden sapience or ability. The claim that the "innovators" may know something that the masses do not was discounted by Still's own life-experience: he was not ignorant of the internal precepts of the serialists and twelve-tonists; in fact, he studied with the Grandfather of the atonal idiom, Edgard Varèse. He credited Varèse with opening up certain new vistas for him, and in his exploration of the ultra-modern theories, he was able to invent a few of his own abstract tonal effects (Letter to Burt Korall [June 14, 1968]; Boris Nelson, "The World of Music," *The* Toledo, Ohio, *Blade* [November 22, 1970]). His early compositions in the "new" idiom were "performed auspiciously in New York" between 1925 and 1929 ("The History and Future of Black American Music," *Music Department Bulletin* 2 [Lincoln University, Pennsylvania: August 4, 1969]).

In many musical areas Still was, indeed, one of the world's most intrepid venturers into virgin territory. He was the first to use non-traditional instruments such as African drums and banjos in orchestral compositions. He was the first to elevate the blues to an unadulterated symphonic level (his efforts in that realm preceded and surpassed Gershwin), and he was the first to use voices as integral aspects of an American ballet. Furthermore, his ballet, *Sahdji*, was the first ballet to depict a serious African subject, and his opera, *Troubled Island*, was the first major American production with a Negro subject.

Yet, through all of his "firsts" in music, he drifted farther and farther away from the atonal and the mathematical. A thorough knowledge of the techniques of Ives and Cowell led him to the discovery that individual styles and idioms lose their identity when subjected to the avant-garde treatment (*Music Department Bulletin*). As Barbara Tischler has pointed out, the modern idiom makes nationalism "irrelevant" (*An American Music: The Search for an American Musical Identity* [Oxford University Press, 1987]). Radical music, conveying neither the individuality of the artist nor the shape and texture of the culture, raises "cultural barriers" and obliterates folk and racial idioms (Frank Gagnard, "On the Square Music Notes," *The* New Orleans, Louisiana, *Times-Picayune* [April 16, 1968]).

Ultimately Still decided that arithmetic could not step beyond the mind into the heart in order to communicate feelings (*The* Miami, Florida, *Herald* [October 29, 1961] 19E). He agreed with his friend, Meredith Willson, who said that, if modernism describes emotions at all, they are hostile ones, such as "Indigestion" and "Cyclone" (Speech to the Southern California Music Teachers' Association, [1967]). Versatility, taken for its own sake, has no power to elevate or to please, and the avant-garde has no strength to generate ingratiating effects unless it is "contrasted with other idioms" (John B. Barker, "Composer praises individuality...," *The* Elyria, Ohio, *Chronicle-Telegram* [November 10, 1970]). Dissonance, Still concluded, had to be used just like other musical elements, "with discrimination, with good taste, in a personal idiom," not as an end in itself, but when it is appropriate to express a particular mood or subject (*The Blade*).

Still's *Dark Horsemen*, for example, in the piano suite *Three Visions*, encompasses difficult dissonances which are necessary to the apocalyptic picture being drawn. However, concentrated dissonance is absent from the second part of the suite, *Summerland*, when a realm of heavenly abundance and peace is represented. No glimpse of heaven or of hell could be recognizable if the entire suite were dissonant, for the result of applying modernist modes would be a "dull sameness" (*Australian Musical News*).

In Still's view, the composer should abjure this sameness, as well as the sense of duty to confine himself to the methods of every other composer (Speech for the Music Teachers' Association). He should not "arbitrarily discard" that which is tonal and consonant, nor should he be forced "to limit himself to any single style or method," especially to the "overly contrapuntal, dissonant, formless" (Speech for the Music Teachers' Association; and, *Showcase*, 7).

Still spoke from the lofty platform of personal mission, for the textbook editors had tried to force him to write like "every other composer." In 1967, when he composed a short piece for a schoolroom anthology, the evaluation committee told him to delete the broken chords in it because they were a "nineteenth-century device." He refused, with the comment, "The fact that broken chords had been used a century ago didn't mean that they had to be discarded today, particularly when there was an artistic reason for their inclusion" (Verna Arvey, *In One Lifetime* [Arkansas: University of Arkansas Press, 1984] 175).

Still looked down the endless ranks of the highly-educated, self-possessed guardians of the contemporary mode, he listened to the "long statements" of the abolitionists which vindicated their methods, and he repeated his accusation that "mediocrity" was "trying to distinguish itself by the use of big words" (*In One Lifetime*, 176). "Simply declaring that a succession of notes is a melody does not make it a melody, nor a few odd beats a recognizable rhythm" (*Australian Musical News*). There will always be, he promised, "a difference between music and sound." "If they [the avant-gardists] could write music, they would" *In One Lifetime*, 176).

As the avant-gardists disregarded his conjuration to begin writing music, Still then incited the public to stand by its own intuitive grasp of what was pleasing and what was not--to raise a tumultuous cry for works that conformed to its apprehensions. "Just as the spark of freedom burns in the hearts of people all over the world, whether they be free men or oppressed, so does the inner love of beauty, and so does the public appreciation of all that is worthy in the arts" (*Australian Musical News*). The Fromms and Mortons could spew flames and storms everlastingly; the public is the final judge of what will live.

And, since the public must judge, the public must learn to defend its judgments. Still deplored the vast panorama of wasted words, wasted talent, lack of orientation, distrust of personal likes and dislikes, and artistic hypocrisy in the United States. He called for immediate changes to be made in attitudes and objectives.

He was aware, however, that changes were already coming--that the germ of revolution had already begun to fulminate. By refusing to attend concerts where contemporary music was programmed, audiences had already forced a return to traditional music. In other ways, too, people were revealing a slow march away from the waste of talent and time in the twentieth century, in the direction of that which is solid yet subtle in their lives and surroundings. Two small indications of the return to perceivable form and firmness in art and music have been the sharp upswing in the use of carved stone in architecture, and the return to the popularity of ballroom dancing. The *Smithsonian* magazine has recorded the fact that, today, builders are using eight times as much marble and twenty times as much granite, while limestone quarries are laboring around the clock to fill a growing demand for material that can be exquisitely sculpted (19 [October 1988] 88). Significantly, most of this stone is not being used to make abstract forms: it is the source of aspiring columns and shapely façades. In addition, the number of ballroom dancers in the United States has doubled in the last five years (*Smithsonian* 19 [March 1989] 84), surpassing the number of people who are interested in the contemporary, "formless" kinds of dancing.

Even so, more is required than for the populace to bring splendid architectural shapes back into its structures, or to return grace and elegance to dancing. Still wanted the citizenry to improve the embellishments and entertainments in every aspect of its private and community life. His desire for uplift in music and in art was a pressing issue for him, as he beheld with dismay the manner in which the media have been destroying literature as a prolific ingredient of existence. Still knew that, in future years, as people read less and less, they will be forced to depend more and more on music, painting and sculpture for enrichment. Furthermore, they cannot always look to the past--to the Masters--for that enrichment, for a virile civilization cannot progress

# Restoring Paths to Dwell In

without continuing to create and to objectify its special identity.

The composer's strategy for preserving and enhancing the identity of American culture was three-pronged, and involved seven basic operations. The tenets of his plan for action were:

I.  *Composers and artists should*:
    1. Return form and structure to their creations.
    2. Effect a fusion in their work between the popular and the serious.

II. *Communities and national organizations should*:
    3. Bring higher forms of art and music into the schools.
    4. Sponsor and promote "concert picnics" for the people.
    5. Sponsor reading orchestras for composers which would involve the public.

III. *Audiences should*:
    6. Rely on their own instincts to determine what is emotionally satisfying.
    7. Become more aggressive (in and out of concert halls and galleries) in expressing approval or disapproval of what is offered to them.

Still's thoughts on each of the aspects of this master-plan gave substance and impulsion to his philosophy of coherence, and to his hopes for a counter-attack in the war against cultural deconstruction. A consideration of each of these seven thrusts and foci will merge all of his perceptions into a coherent muster for vigor and freedom in the arts.

## Composers and artists should return form and structure to the arts:

The first principle of cultural liberation is so central to it that it alone might suffice if all other imperatives are neglected. This precept is erected upon the notion that art is not art if it does not upgrade attitudes and feelings, and that it cannot improve the mental environment unless it has discernible coherence.

Among the reiterated verities that appear in the volumes of the philosophers is the notion that art must "give joy" (Robert M. Thornton, ed., *Cogitations from Albert Jay Nock* [Irvington-on-Hudson, New York: The Nockian Society, 1985] 55). From Hesiod to Nock, thinkers have said that great art, poetry and music are meant to deliver a "release from sorrows and a truce from cares," and to elevate and sustain "the human spirit through the communication of joy, of felicity" (Nock, 56).

Often it is added that this joy has something to do with the apprehension of beauty and structure in art, and that beauty should be a given quantity. Andrés Segovia, master of the guitar, insisted that life without musical expression that is both beautiful and well-made is merely subsistence. Said Segovia, there is an insanity to life that has not had in it music that is "the most beautiful, the most noble, the best that she has to offer" (John Farrell, "A Conversation With Andrés Segovia," University of Southern California *Trojan Family* 19 [December 1986] 20).

It must be confessed, of course, that the concepts of joy and of beauty are abstract and not subject to proof, thus their elusiveness and dependence upon subjective taste lead frequently to the conclusion that they do not really exist. The philosophy of the good, the true and the beautiful, the fortress of artistic excellence, had to fall to this argument before formlessness could be raised on the dais of power and regard. The mind-bullying mentors announced to the credulous world that anything could be beautiful if it were deemed so. Opinion, they contended, was the arbiter of all things, yet opinion was an unknown factor, as indefinite and as various as individual fingerprints or voice-prints.

The world was told that the purpose of art was not to uplift, but to express our innermost thoughts and to mirror our outermost absurdities. Only through self-disembowelment could we be led to see the meaning of life, for the self can be no more nor less ugly and turbulent than its encircling environment is bruised and arbitrary. That orange and blue splash on the art gallery wall makes us *feel* something, doesn't it? And what we *feel* makes us human, makes what we are seeing a work of art. Anything that reveals human complexity is a component of the culture, and lends meaning to existence.

Yet the art-lover looks at the orange and blue smear, or hears cyclonic experiments with sound, and he senses that he could make splashes and crashes exactly like those if he so chose. He wonders if art can be something that anyone might do. Further, he notes that he also *feels* something when he witnesses a car accident on the freeway. Is there deep meaning in the automobile collision just because he feels something in viewing it? Does the meaning make him human even though he does not stop to aid the bleeding victims? Is the anguished metal and tortured rubble a work of art?

The abstractionists would have us think so--would have us believe that a conglomeration of twisted metal can be art. But they have forgotten their own definition of art--that it is an expression of self or of life, no matter how repugnant. And, by their own definition, nothing that is completely turbulent and displeasing can be an artistic expression, for there is nothing in the universe that is totally devoid of form, purpose or harmony--that has nothing with which another entity can identify. As Still pointed out, reaction to anarchy and chaos in world affairs does not have to be anarchy and chaos in the arts, for the modern world "isn't necessarily ugly" (*Australian Musical News*).

Indeed, cosmic theory and biology dictate that art shall have structure and beauty, and that there is a universal and forceful standard of loveliness in the world. There are things that have been called art in this century that will never be art, regardless of the variousness of opinion. Although it is often said that one man's meat is another man's poison, oleander leaves will always kill us if we eat them.

The spiritualists have claimed, and Still agreed with them, that art is the visible manifestation of the fixed laws of the universe. Everything in the cosmos is structured, has form, and operates with everything else inexorably, pleasurably and eternally, in the same way that the planets move on course according to calculable laws. These laws are paramount in the mathematical axioms set down by Pythagoras, the axioms which denote the unity, order and structure of all life; they are also the laws referred to by Ruskin, in his statement that the laws of nature (or, Life) are the power which forces the several parts of a plant to help each other. And, they are the laws discussed by Dr. Richard Steinpach in his writings about Truth:

Truth is basically simple. It is just in simplicity, which is the result of the uniformity of the whole, that true greatness lies. We do know today...that the immense variety of plants, animals and human beings has its foundation in the same four genetic building-stones, that the cells in plant, animal and man are built up in the same way, that every cell, in whatever organ it may be located, always contains the master-plan of the whole; we know that arms, legs, wings and fins have issued from the same fundamental design; we know that the same forces are at work within an atom as between solar systems.

Ecology, the science of natural co-operation, indeed reveals to us how one thing gears into the other, completing and furthering one another. In this interplay of the great household of Creation, everything fulfills the role assigned to it. How then could we assume that just man is without function in this system?
(*How is it That We Live After Death* [Stiftung Gralsbotschaft, Germany, 1979] 41, 43).

Steinpach's discourse is seconded by Ernest Schuettler, who asserts that Truth, or the absolute, universal standard of correctness, is nothing more than the "Laws of Nature," by which all things operate. "A bird singing his song of Thanksgiving into the early morning sun, ...a rose opening its dew-bedecked petals to admit the light of day, ...and bacteria thriving in the absence of light," all of these things manifest the laws of nature. "Only man refuses to recognize these principles as absolute and thinks they are subject to compromise;" man "beclouds" the principles "with so many words that even the highest authorities rarely agree on any interpretation as the correct one" ("Truth," *A New Approach* 2 [January 1979] 6-8).

In spite of the obfuscations of men, however, the principles remain, ready to be objectified in art and music; and, because art is a glimpse of the eternal beauty and structure of life, it, too, must have form and some kinship with the natural world. As the religious philosophers insist, "Beauty is the law made manifest" (Eduard Bauer, "On the Nature of Art," *A New Approach* 2 [Jan. 1979] 16). Furthermore, the artist has an obligation to align himself with "the law" when he sets out to paint, sculpt, draw or compose, for man

...is meant to form the bridge by which, uplifting and ennobling, the beauty and harmony of that higher world flows down into the earthly. True art, which outlives the ages, is an example of the fulfillment of this task.

(Steinpach, 48).

The obligation of the artist to reflect eternal principles in his work is so strong that even the non-spiritualist thinkers have spoken of it. Edmund A. Opitz, a Christian clergyman, has said,

The human person is emphatically *not* the mere accidental end result of the chance interaction of physical and chemical forces, however much it might please certain of our contemporaries to believe this. ...To the contrary, every man and woman is a work of divine art; through our beings flow the primordial creative forces of the universe. Coordinate with those forces and we become creators too, some of us in small and others in large measure.

("The Liberating Arts," *The Freeman* 38 [December 1988] 479).

Creativity, then, requires a recognition of the relationship between visual or aural comeliness and the purposeful order of the cosmos. It is also tied in with the realization that art and music must accomplish something, inasmuch as everything in the cosmos has function and purpose as well as order. If art does not have purpose, it is not creative, nor is it art.

The close relationship that should exist between that which is beautiful and that which is functional renders the two almost inseparable, so much so that many of the evidences of universal laws border on artistic sublimity. The migrating Canada geese fly in a spit-and-polish V-formation in order to make the best use of air currents that they both generate and employ. Any other formation would lack the comeliness of the "V," and would stifle their progress and their chances for survival. A suspension bridge inculcates superb form and efficacy of design, taking into account the laws of physics, that is, the stress it can bear from its own weight, from the weight it must bear, and from the force of the wind. (As Still observed privately, if the atonal composers built bridges in the same way that they composed music, all of their constructs would collapse prior to completion.)

The discordant composers and painters think that they can alter concepts of beauty by ignoring them. Yet beauty in art is like time, which operates according to fixed principles. We can set the hands of a clock askew, but we cannot thereby change the time. As Edward Bauer contended, no amount of pontification will turn obtrusive forms into art. Nothing can be called art that brings "no tidings of eternal beauty" (Bauer, 16).

In addition, we can do harm to ourselves by not conforming to standards of natural beauty. Even as our concepts of universal magnificence are indigenous to the cosmos, therefore subject to its unchanging laws, so our personal need for affirmation of those concepts is governed by our unalterable biological make-up. For example, it has been discovered that the intellect does not determine our response to music; rather, certain circuits in the brain bring about reactions to musical stimuli (Andrew Stiller, "The Biology of Music," *Opus* 3 [August 1987] 12-15). Human beings have a basic bodily impetus toward music that is rhythmic, just as they have a need to learn to talk; both music and talk are forms of necessary communication, and normal humans cannot be prevented either from talking or from making music.

As Stiller explains, music aids humans to survive by assisting in their emotional communication and cooperation. "Musical patterns are not abstract and mathematical in their rationale," they are dictated by physical realities (Stiller, 15). It is the body that requires melodies to be "made mostly of major seconds," to "employ dynamic accents, and notes of varying lengths," and to make "extensive use of variation and repetition" (Stiller, 13).

Because our need for non-abstract music is a biological dictum, it stands to reason that discordant music is detrimental to our health. Still, who became physically ill when he listened to discordant compositions, believed absolutely that we need "good" music in order to be healthy, positive human beings. He insisted that, "There is a natural feeling for good music" (Stanley Williford, "William Grant Still: Time to Discover a Musical Giant," Los Angeles *Sentinel* [February 8, 1973] A10), and that "bad" music is a destructive force that can "do harm" (*Music of the West*, 14). Since the body operates by natural rhythms, disjointed and incoherent cadences can cause the body's patterns of function to be disrupted, in the same way that a singer who is off-key in a chorus can cause others to sing off-key.

In this regard, what we see and hear around us influences our physical and emotional balance. A person crossing a raging river on horseback, or on a suspension bridge, may become dizzy if he looks down at the churning, swirling water below. Unless he glances up and away, he may lose his balance. Nothing physical has caused his instability--it is simply the result of the mental response to what he observes that affects him in a physical way.

Noise, lack of tonality, jarring notes and shocking art forms cause stress, and stress leads to mental and physical imbalance. Studies have shown that stress causes the brain to send forth chemicals which contribute to heart disease and perhaps to other maladies. The supply of calcium to the brain, the chief ingredient which allows brain impulses to be transmitted, can be curtailed by excessive exposure to that which is visually or audibly unsettling.

Moreover, just as we can damage our physical well-being by listening to noisy and incoherent music, so we can slow our spiritual and intellectual progress as a civilized people by ignoring the fixed laws of cosmic activity. Dr. Jacob Bronowski, in his BBC film series, "The Ascent of Man," noted that civilization did not emerge on the earth until man became aware of the order in matter and "the grain" in wood and stone, that is, until he learned to cut building materials with, rather than against, the grain. As all things in the cosmos have a "grain," or a pattern of existence, and as all of the patterns relate to each other, it follows that there are forms and relationships which exist unseen in nature and are available to us for the enrichment of our own feelings and relationships; the genuine composer and the true artist intuit these relationships, reflect and express them outwardly, and use them to communicate with their audiences.

It must be observed here that the concept of communication is pivotal where the arts are concerned. Maya Angelou, in one of her National Public Television presentations, defined the difference between noise and sound in terms of communication. Birds, she said, sing to communicate with other birds, and they cannot convey messages if they use random, unstructured noises. In the same vein, Still remarked, "Music can step in where words fail to communicate" (*Showcase*, 6), especially in cultures where no written texts are present. A clipping in one of Verna Arvey's scrapbooks discusses the Bantu tribes in Africa, and observes that Bantu music must be understood in order to understand Bantu history, culture and values; it is in the peculiar stresses and rhythms of the African chants and songs that the best expression of tribal culture exists ("Bantu Can be Better Understood by Appreciating His Music," *Australian Music and Dance* [January 1962]).

In the same way that the Bantu communicate their values through their music, and cannot do so without musical structure and form, so the artistic language of the world's consummate composers and painters must have coherence and proportion. As Still declared, a composer must have an "innate rhythmic sense," and his music must have "natural sequence" and "symmetry;" without it, the hearer will be unable to retain a coherent impression "of what he has heard, he will not remember it or desire to hear it again" ("The Structure of Music," *Etude* 68 [March 1950] 17).

The composer who disregards the laws of form replaces recurring themes and melodies with "bizarre sounds." He explores "new harmonic effects because that is so much easier than constructing a well-proportioned composition." His "occasional consonant intervals are weak because of bad handling;" his "vaulted counterpoint is incorrect, disjointed and muddled" (*Etude*, 61). His hearers are not brought to a state of deep thought, nor is their humanity enriched by the music that they hear.

If the composer is to enrich humanity, he must realize that uplifting thoughts, musical themes and profound ideas have their own designs and personalities, and they are part of the cosmic material that surrounds us. (Perhaps, as Plato suggested, ideas are the *only* reality.) Like solar energy that can be tapped for domestic and industrial use, artistic energy is ever-present for those who reach out to pluck it from the Edenic life-source. This creative energy cannot be tapped, however, through mathematical computation, it must be intuited "spiritually" and then allowed to impose its own outline upon that which is painted or composed. As Still explained it,

> There is no set rule for composing. One is inspired by many things one sees or hears. Thoughts are realities. Inspirations or ideas belong to the cosmos; they are universal in their availability to all who can reach out and take them. Some composers can reach higher than others, and for that reason too much credit should not be taken by the individual. Thoughts are realities. God is a reality. As we evolve, God evolves. Life is but a system of governments, each working toward perfection. The process of getting ideas and themes is spiritual, after which the human mind must take over with its inventive and technical ability to put the musical idea on paper, and in the proper form. However, the composer should let his theme or musical material dictate its own development.
> (J. Douglas Cook, "Visits to the Homes of Famous Composers #3," *Opera and Concert* [November 1946] 9).

Still consistently repeated that the process of turning universal harmonies into art forms is subliminal, not objective, and that the use of the scientific mind--"mathematical formulae" and "specially devised scales"--is of no practical value in producing that which has grandeur and longevity. The subjective mind brings forth the melody, extending a motif into a phrase. "The motif dictates its own development, its own treatment, and even its own form." As in architecture, "form follows function" (*Etude*, 61). Later, the scientific approach can be used to help select combinations of instruments that can be used to approximate the abstract tone color of the motive, but not until the spiritual process is completed. As Still summed up his thoughts about the creative mind, he said, "No amount of technique can make up for this God-given sense of life. Somewhere in his nature, the real composer must have a spiritual quality which enables him to come close to God" (*The Blade*).

It is almost as if artistic creation is a matter of following a universal map which reveals the many routes to spiritual perfection. No one insists that any particular course is followed-- the individual may develop his strategy according to the map, or in any other manner that he chooses. Those who use the map to its best advantage will arrive at their destination without pointless wandering or despair. Those who do not may be hopelessly lost.

It was to prevent his fellow human beings from becoming lost that Still spoke against that which is fragmentary and not well-defined or unified in the arts. And it was through his philosophy of form that he hoped to lead composers, painters and writers to spiritual redemption in modern culture.

## **Composers and artists should effect a fusion in their work between the serious and the popular**:

Once the contemporary composer acknowledges the necessity for a framework in each of his compositions, he must then proceed to infuse that structure with human interest, or, "to write for the people" (*Stadium Concerts Review*, 41). Still praised audiences for their discernment, intelligence and honesty, and warned that composers must never feel themselves to be superior to their audiences. The imperiousness of the expressionistic overlords must give way to an exalted public; the hospitable reaction of the hearer and viewer is the only thing that should matter if the purpose of the arts is to be realized.

Furthermore, the youth must be included in this exalted and emancipated public. To release the young people from their willing servitude to degenerative popular music, and to offset the affects of media promulgation of popular culture, Still suggested that composers begin to take elements from the popular idiom and to raise them to a higher level of treatment and manifestation. By giving attention to the music of the common man, the modern composer will enlist the interest of the ranks of adolescents in spite of the predominance of television and rock music. After all, Still insisted, the popular composer values rhythm and melody, he makes use of appealing folk sources, and "he has never underestimated the value of pleasing his audiences" (*Showcase*, 7). It is this attention to melody and to the rich musical heritage of the people that has made American popular music the only truly American music (*Showcase*, 7).

Still first recognized the "unique rhythmic possibilities and other distinctive characteristics" in blues and jazz when he built his first symphony around an original blues theme (Rex Stewart, "An Interview of William Grant Still" [April 4, 1966]). Later, in the 1940's, he suggested that the love of young Americans for swing was prophetic, and meant that "The people of tomorrow are going to want these things in their serious music" ("Co-Art Forum # 4," *Hazard's Pavilion* 1 [Fall 1986] 22). Much to the dismay of his fellow serious composers, Still asserted that symphony concerts and operas would be far better-attended if the concert halls presented music that contained elements of the things that were heard in dance bands, in rhythmic jazz, and in the virile folk idioms. Observing that Beethoven's "Minuet in G" was once a commercially successful popular song, Still maintained that composers ought not to overlook the rich musical resources of the people, for folk music was nothing more than music that had outlived the fame of its originators.

Not only would serious music obtain both universality and appeal if it explored and blended the folk musics of the many racial groups in the United States (*Showcase*, 7), but also it would acquire an attractiveness that would open a path to invasion of the mass media. Had Still lived into the 1980's, he would probably have encouraged the manufacture of videos that would fuse serious music with popular visual effects. While the eyes of the youth were engaged, they could be intellectually habituated to the esoteric in musical products.

## Communities and national organizations should bring higher forms of art into the schools:

Not only should the interest of the youth be captured by the employment of their own musical resources, but also the attention of the young people must be everywhere directed to the best that art and music have to offer. It is important that the process of redirection take place in the schools, since the media and popular culture hold the field in the child's world when he is not in class, and since it is clear that the majority of parents are not providing the moral and cultural enrichment that is needed.

The importance of good music to education is not emphasized enough by educators and school boards. It has already been pointed out that the higher types of tonal music activate and boost the rhythms by which the mind and the body operate. Sociological experiments have also indicated that high art fosters cultural values, optimism, creative impulses, and clean, well-balanced attitudes. Studies of the human brain have shown that, whenever a person learns new things or expands his horizons artistically, the connections in the wiring of the brain are improved, and the brain itself matures and develops. All of these improvements contribute to intellectual success, even in disadvantaged environments: when Walter Turnbull, leader of the Boys' Choir of Harlem, introduces disadvantaged youths to beautiful music, he transforms their lives; in an area where one-in-ten boys do not graduate from high school, 98% of Turnbull's boys go on to college (*Reader's Digest* 67 [May 1988] 65).

In Chicago, similar successes are occurring among the students of Marva Collins. Collins emphasizes cultural literacy in her school, filling her classrooms with good books, good music, knowledge of past and present values, and historical awareness. Above all, she speaks against educational "relevance," which "limits perspectives to the grim scenes children see in their everyday lives" (Mark Evans, "Cultural Illiteracy," *Lincoln Review* 7 [Winter 1987] 24).

Everywhere that educators have forsaken relevance for elegance in youthful experience, the results have been convincing. And, the protestation that children will not understand or enjoy the most elevated art forms has proven to be insubstantial: even opera can be an educational experience. In 1986, the Cleveland Opera introduced fourth and fifth graders to opera, using the children in the production and in the audience for a presentation of *Carmen*. The children loved it, got involved, and "never missed a cue or broke character" (Brian Tombaugh, "From C to Shining C," *The* Lorain, Ohio, *Journal* [November 20, 1986]). In Baton Rouge, in October of 1984, Still's own *Minette Fontaine* was a huge triumph when presented to the children of the school system.

Certainly opera should become a part of the educational curriculum in the schools, as should field trips to other performances of serious orchestral music, and to art galleries and museums. Habits of taste cannot develop without repeated exposure and cultivation. Every school should have a full-time music teacher and music program, and community leaders should appear before local boards to speak for better music, art and literature in the curriculum. If such programs become nationwide, then, as Still commented, the interest of the young people in the sublime arts "would be whetted," and "their appreciation would be made the more intense" (Bob Martin, "An Interview of William Grant Still" [May 1964] 19).

## Communities and national organizations should sponsor and promote "concert picnics" for the people:

Once the appetites of school children are whetted for high culture, there must be fertile oases in the community where they can be indulged. Every town, neighborhood or suburb ought to have its own park and community center where families can gather for live performances and art exhibits on weekends. The gatherings should be informal, and full of creature comforts: the people might well bring picnic lunches to eat on park lawns while they listen to concert music. Later there may be games and social get-togethers.

The interjection of food and fun into the concert-experience is not without precursors. In the Elizabethan period, dramas were staged for sociable crowds, spirits full with eating, drinking and frivolity. Playwrights had to please their audiences, or risk the physical disapproval of the commoners standing in the pit, or of nobles perched on the platform with the actors. Both low-born and well-born folk were attentive to the dramatic display, and could memorize long passages from the plays after only one hearing.

Although the atmosphere in cultural gatherings became less jovial after the time of Shakespeare, the casual aspect remained until the twentieth century. Max Rudolf has pointed out that, prior to 1910, the composer and the performer were more important than the conductor. Ordinary people knew more about music then than they do today, therefore they were more interested in the expertise of the instrumentalists than in the charisma of the conductor. In those days, concerts were "casual affairs" or "festive get-togethers" where the audiences were not separated from the orchestra, where the lights were not dimmed, and where conductors were not grand or aloof ("A Medley of Thoughts on Conductors and Composers," a lecture at Juilliard School, New York [Dec. 18, 1982] 1-2).

As the distance between the audience and the conductor has widened, as the baton-wielding tuxedoed Maestros have courted the adulation of the worshipful public, the personal involvement of that public with concert music has lessened. American concert-goers do not clap or stamp or shout spontaneously during a piece of music, even if they like what they hear; musicians do not smile even if they enjoy what they are playing. Only at appointed moments is everyone permitted by custom to applaud, and they must do so, even if they do not care for what has been presented. The significance in, and the reason for, attending concerts of live music is nearly forgotten.

Perhaps, with a resurgence of frivolity and informality in concert programming, the vitality of live orchestral music will be rediscovered, and the importance of taking delight in live performances will be recognized. Along with this recognition will come the apprehension that sound transcends itself when we can see the mechanics involved in making music: then sound becomes a part of human experience and enters into the realm of physical intelligibility. As Amanda Smith of "Dance Wyoming" explains, "live music has a different penetration. We feel the energy from the musician with live music, so that the music goes to the bone, and then touches the soul" (Telephone conversation with Judith Anne Still [Jan. 12, 1988]). Her description is echoed by the British painter, Walter Roberts, when, in discussing art work, he comments, "...a print is never quite the same as an original, just as, say, a tape recording does not have the same vitality as a live orchestral performance, when magic seems to spin around and make the hair at the back of (at least) my head stand on end!" (Letter to Judith Anne Still [December 28, 1986]).

It is out of this "magic"--this energy that is generated by live musicians--that a powerful attitudinal force is unleashed in audiences. Members of these audiences are exposed to a community of feeling and a spiritual oneness that increases their humanity. As Still expressed it, music "forms a common bond" between us when we share it (*Stadium Concerts Review*, 41). Because we sense, when we are in a group, that all men respond as we do individually, our feelings of brotherly love are fostered, as are our "social and spiritual ideals," and our sense of the operation of spiritual laws in the universe.

The more the public is encouraged to draw together in groups to hear music played, and to witness stirring works of art or inspiring dramatic presentations, the more human and spiritual men and women will become. To that end, therefore, every avenue toward encouragement ought to be taken, even those that inculcate picnics in the park and light-hearted Saturday romps for young and old from all walks of life. As Still concluded, "Music should be for the people" of every class and interest. "Perhaps our sharing of it and other forms of art will hasten the coming of the ideal society wherein every person will devote part of every day to life-sustaining activities, and the other part to cultural pursuits" (*Stadium Concerts Review*, 41).

## **Communities and national organizations should sponsor reading orchestras for composers which would involve the public**:

Certainly the ideal, cultured society is desired by many, but it cannot be established without the development of a culture that is desirable. To make applause genuine, to see that musicians smile when they are performing, there must first be music composed that is enjoyable for both musicians and audiences. In order for modern composers to create music that satisfies audiences, they should be provided with a sort of a laboratory orchestra that will play their compositions and that will allow them to hear whether or not they have succeeded as composers. Still's origination of this orchestral laboratory concept occurred in 1964, when he said in an interview,

> ...I wish that it could be possible for there to be some sort of an orchestra, a sort of laboratory group, that, say, might travel throughout the country. It could be maintained on a yearly basis, and it could go around and give composers a chance to hear their things. They could come here [to Los Angeles], and they could stay here probably two or three weeks...giving concerts and so on, and the composers would have the use of that orchestra just to hear their efforts, and for those who were interested to hear them.
> 
> (Bob Martin, "Interview," 27).

By "those who were interested to hear them," Still meant the public, whose members should be allowed to attend such performances, and to express their feelings about the new compositions, either via applause, or in brief discussion sessions. Through honest displays of approval or disapproval, audiences will be able to encourage inventive ability in composers and to discourage mediocrity.

As a further encouragement to creativity, when composers in the community are found who have talent, the best compositions by native or local composers should be included in the regular concert series of the regional symphony orchestra. Every concert program should include "one American work and one contemporary work by a foreign composer" (*State Times*), both on the local level and where the large, metropolitan orchestras that tour nationally are concerned.

## Audiences should rely on their own instincts to determine what is emotionally satisfying:

It goes without saying that no plan to encourage creativity will prevail unless a new audience mentality is nourished by the public. The individual music-and-art-lover must steel himself with cultural courage, looking only within himself for artistic leadership and judgment. No longer may he assume that newspaper critics, university professors and internationally-recognized artists, authors and composers are the final arbiters of what should and should not be accepted. It is his to take up the challenge put to him by pedantic catch-phrases and erudite nomenclature, and to decide for himself what is good and what is not. Nor should he fear that personal dislike denotes a lack of understanding, for it is the emotional response, not the intellectual, that is the Achilles tendon of artistic power.

## Audiences should become more aggressive (in and out of concert halls and galleries) in expressing approval or disapproval of what is offered to them:

Once the public learns to trust its own emotional responses, it would do well to don the plummed-crest of privilege and to sally into the open. Still exorted audiences to write letters to conductors and to newspaper editors, to directors of art museums and to cultural boards, clearly identifying pieces of music, or dramas, or art works that are aesthetically impoverished. He implored concert-goers to avoid applauding compositions which are unpleasant, even as he warned music-lovers not to presume that all contemporary music is, by nature, inferior. He urged citizens to object loudly and confidently if their state-supported museums spent money on salvage-yard sculpture and chimpanzee-oils. If you don't like grotesque art, he declared, say so; say it loudly, and say it to anyone and everyone who is responsible for placing such monstrosities in places of prominence.

Furthermore, do not be afraid to make-known your opinions in the concert-hall. Audiences, particularly American audiences, are governed by a snobbery in the rules of applause that ought to be overcome. This snobbery was largely inspired by Wagner, who did not want his *Parsifal* and *Ring Cycle* to be interrupted by audience response, and who therefore began the practice of not applauding between musical segments. It was he who was largely responsible for our reluctance to intrude between movements of a symphony, and to clap between sections in a suite. This reluctance, added to the growing distance between conductors and musicians and the members of the public, forces an unnatural bondage of reaction and emotion during musical performances.

Yet Still believed that appreciation for music and art should be spontaneous, exuberant and unashamed. Artificial rules of decorum, ignoring as they do the necessity for genuine praise or blame, should not be allowed to carry culture into the realm of the stilted and the uncomfortable. The liberated audience should be allowed to applaud when and if it pleases, to sit near to the musicians in the bright light of enjoyment and perception, and to shout, stamp, clap or maintain silence as it deems appropriate.

In all of his precepts for cultural liberty, Still placed the pleasure of the ordinary human being uppermost. Even so, this pleasure was the refined gratification achieved after careful exposure to the loftiest human creations, it was not the sensual or violent joy encouraged by those who would profit from man's inhumanity to man. If human life is infused with high art, it will be human life; if it is filled with the noise and rubble of pseudo-art, it will constitute a new Dark Age, without valor or victory, a panorama of hubris and waste.

It was to build in these waste places that Still defined and redefined his thoughts on modern culture, and that he unfolded his scheme for renovation of the American cultural environment. He lamented the spoilation and imprisonment of an inventive people, and hoped that his lectures and writings would raise a counter-siege to the abolitionists, the abstractionists, the avant-gardists and the expressionists. That he failed in his mission was inevitable, for the common man and woman, in whom emotions season deference to the cerebral, have ever been discounted and subjugated.

But it is in the abjectness of this subjugation that an epic future may take shape, for it is in changing attitudes, goaded by hindsight and castigation, that revolutions are engendered. There may yet be for Still, temples of harmony and decorum rising over the charred remains of contemporary despair, and, instead of "new music" and "new art," hosts of "new" audiences clamoring for all that is intelligible and endearing in native cultural resources. If so, the composer, who died unheeded and disappointed, shall have earned the right to wear, in the afterlife, a breastplate of righteousness and a helmet of salvation (Isaiah 59:17).

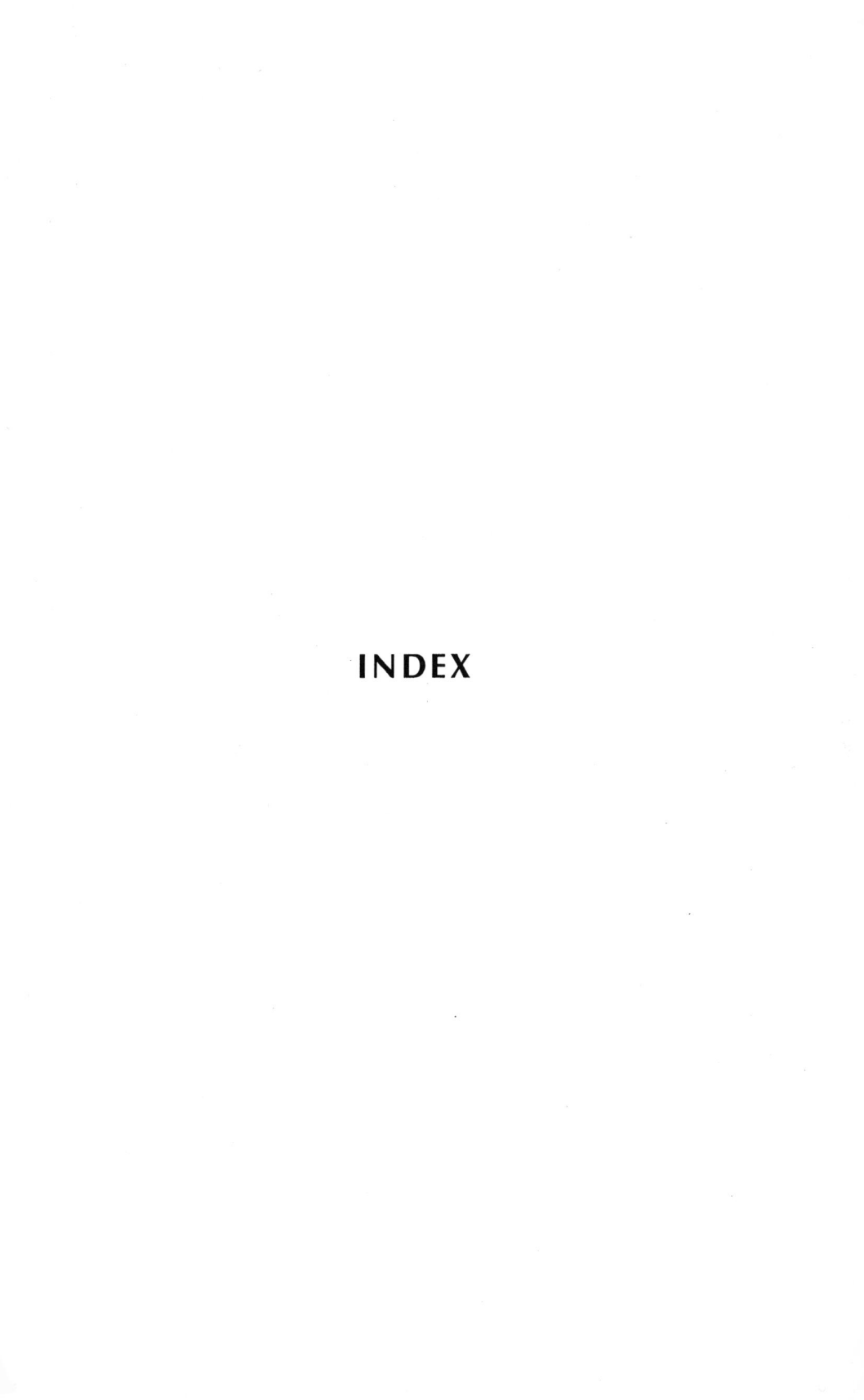

# INDEX

# INDEX

## A

*Achille Lauro*, 170
Achilles, 119, 127, 290
Acorn Media Publishing, 235
Acquired Immune Deficiency Syndrome, 165
Adams, Sherman, 57
Addison Wesley Publishers, 165
Aeolian, 77
Aeolian Foundation, 88
Aeschylus, 257
Africa, 171, 184, 187, 195, 214, 235, 282
*Africa*, 101, 235
African(s), 94, 173, 184, 188, 192, 210, 212, 234, 282
African-American, 211, 217, 238, 243
African music, 78, 79, 271
Afro-American(s), 170, 174, 175, 180, 181, 182, 185, 191, 193, 194, 195, 196, 199, 203, 205, 206, 209, 211, 212-213, 217, 218, 227, 234, 238, 239, 241, 244, 247, 250, 253
*Afro-American*, 119, 208
Afro-American newspapers, 98, 137
*Afro-American Symphony, The*, 14, 68, 76, 93, 94, 100, 115, 116, 155, 156, 159, 236
Ahab, 4
AIDS, see Acquired Immune Deficiency Syndrome
Ainlay, George W., 143, 144, 148, 149
Alabam, see Club Alabam
Alabama, 6, 201
Alabama Agricultural and Mechanical College, 29
Albuquerque (NM), 210
*Albuquerque Tribune*, 211
Alcoholics' Treatment Center, 210
Alexander, Benjamin, Dr., 186, 187, 193, 199, 209, 217, 218
Alexander, John Hanks, 243
Ali, Muhammed, see Clay, Cassius
Allan, 8
Allen, George Wesley, 200-201
Allen, Nimrod B., 117
Allport, Gordon, 165
Allred, Nellie G., 108
*Along This Way*, 224
*Alternative: A Study in Psychology, The*, 151
Altschuler, Ira M. Dr., 148
Amadeus, v
*Amadeus*, 113, 114, 115
America, 68, 87, 94, 101, 117, 202, 235, 261, 265
American(s), 7, 14, 18, 49, 86, 88, 94, 95, 98, 120, 132, 141, 143, 160, 165, 169, 174, 178, 188, 190, 194, 196, 197, 200, 203, 204, 205, 207, 210, 211, 212, 214, 216, 234, 235, 252, 257, 258, 259, 260, 262, 265, 268, 271, 275, 284, 285, 288, 290, 291
American-African Affairs Association, 222
American-Arab Anti-Discrimination Committee, 170
*American Dancer*, 132

*American Harp Journal, The*, 75
American Harp Society, 82
American Institute of Banking, 210
American Legion, 42
*American Mercury*, 36
American Music, v
*American Music*, 205
*American Music: The Search for an American Musical Identity*, 272
*American Scene, The*, 68
*American Scholar, The*, 223, 262
American Society of Composers, Authors and Publishers (ASCAP), 35, 255, 260, 267
*Among School Children*, 65
Amway Corporation, 125
Anacreon, 131
Andersen, Hans Christian, 17, 97
Anderson, Eddie "Rochester," 83
Anderson, Marian, 205, 224
Andrew (turtle), 48
Angelou, Maya, 281
Anglo-Saxon, 192, 197, 217
Anne (turtle), 48
Anti-Defamation League, 170
*Anti-Jacobin, The*, 191
Ants, 53
Apocalypse, 72
Arabs, 214
*Archaic Ritual*, 72
*Archeology of Ethnicity, The*, 234
Argus, Trafford William, 148
Aristotle, 20, 80, 139, 257
Aristotelian, 18
Arizona, State of, 160, 180, 235, 236
Arkansas, State of, 3, 7, 8, 9, 30, 98, 121, 159, 172, 247, 249, 273
*Arkansas Historical Quarterly*, 3, 100
Arlington House Publishers, 222, 224, 234
*Armonía*, 147
Armstrong, Bill, 243
Arnez, Nancy L., 221, 225, 230
Arnold, Matthew, 142
*Art Linkletter's House Party*, 39
Arvey, Bessie, Dr., 26, 32, photo insert, 251
Arvey, Dale, photo insert
Arvey, Edna, photo insert
Arvey, David, 32
Arvey, Verna, dedication page, 11, 16, 19, 21, 25, 26, 32, 34, 78, 79, 81, 97, 101, 105, 107, 108, 116, 117, 131, 132, 134, 172, 175, 177, 188, 191, 195, 214, 237, 242, 244-247, 249-253, 270, 273, 282, photo inserts
ASCAP, see American Society of Composers, Authors and Publishers
*ASCAP Today*, 255, 260, 267
*Ascent of Man, The*, 281
Asians, 214
Associated Negro Press, 93
Associated Press, The, 214
Association of Classroom Teachers, 228
Athenian, 257
Atlanta (GA), 5, 6
Atlanta University, 6
Atlantic-Little Brown, Inc., 228
Atlantic Ocean, 12
Attorney-General of the United States, 249
Audubon, John, 235
Australia(n), 180, 214, 216
*Australian Musical News*, 270, 272, 273, 277

# Index

*Australian Music and Dance*, 282
*Autobiography of Malcolm X, The*, 223, 230
*Autochthonous Symphony, The*, 68
Automatic writing, 62

## B

Babbitt, Milton, 258
Bach, Johann Sebastian, 97, 107 149 185, 206, 233, 255, 264, 265, 268
*Back to Baltimore*, 10
Baldwin Hills (CA), 230
Baldwin, James, 204, 221
Baldwin, Lillian, 142
Baltimore (MD), 119, 147, 208, 212
Bantu Tribe, 282
Baptists, 170
Barber, Samuel, 267
Barbirolli, John, Sir, 174
Barker, John B., 272
Barnett, Claude, 93
Baroque Period, 97, 131
Barrymore, Lionel, 132-133
Bartok, Bela, 264
Barton, Mary Jane, 81
Barzun, Jacques, 261
Bates College, 14, 57, 95
Baton Rouge (LA), 117, 181, 256, 286
Baton Rouge Opera, 117
Bauer, Edward, 278, 280
Baum, L. Frank, 17, 47
Baum, Vicki, 77
*Bayou Legend, A*, 12, 117, 178
BBC, see British Broadcasting Corporation
Bean, Louis John, 147
Beatles, The, 261

Becton, Mrs., 101
Beethoven, Ludwig Van, 105, 107, 110, 113, 116, 117, 140, 185, 233, 255, 267, 285
Belafonte, Harry, 6
Belgium, 98, 120, 200
Bellevue Hospital, 147
Benedict, Ruth, 261
Bennett, Robert Russell, 108, 109
Bennett, Tony, 75
Benny, Jack, 83
Benton, Thomas Hart, 132
Berkeley (CA), 233
Berkley, Tom, 181
Berkshires, The, 264
Berlin, Irving, 65
Berlioz, Hector, 108
Bernstein, Leonard, 67, 140
Bermuda, 212
Bersezio, Carlo, 107
Berta, Music Critic, 107
Bethesda (MD), 235
Bethune, Mary McLeod, 238
Bible, The, 20, 77, 98, 120, 123, 214, 255, 292
Bill Armstrong Productions, 243
Billheimer, Stephen, 8
Bizet, George, 107, 117
*Black Aesthetic, The*, 205
*Black and Conservative*, 222, 224, 234
Blackman, Bessie Lawson, 13, 26, 27, 28, 29, photo insert, 235
*Black Man Dances, The*, 238
Black militants, 241, 250
*Black Music in Our Culture*, 186
*Black Music Research Journal*, 237
Black Nationalists, 194
Black Panthers, The, 194

*Black Perspective in Music, The*, 13
Black Power, 241, 250
Black Silent Majority Committee, The, 194, 198
Black Sparrow Press, 130
Black Swan, The, 91
*Black Thunder*, 224
*Blade, The*, 184, 186, 189, 271, 272, 283
Blake, Eubie, 173
Blues, 69, 93, 94, 95, 160, 172, 182, 207, 271, 284
*Blue Steel*, 101
B'nai B'rith, 170
*Bohême, La*, 107
Bonaparte, Napoleon, 235
Bontemps, Arna, 224, 226
Borodin, Alexander, 106
Boss, Charles, 209
Boston (MA), 11, 31, 184, 228
*Boston Sunday Globe*, 140
Bowling, Lance, 237, 238, 244
Brahms, Johannes, 106, 255, 268
Braithwaite, William Stanley, 226
Braithwaite, Yvonne, 229
*Branch of Velvet, A*, 202
Brant, Leroy V., 57, 58
Bridgman, Juliet, 133
Brimmer, Andrew, 201
Britain, see England
British (people), 288
British Broadcasting Corporation (BBC), 281
Bronowski, Jacob, Dr., 281
Brown, Anne, 205, 206
Brown, Claude, 224
Browne, Thomas, Sir, 119
Brown, H. Rap, 210
Brown, R. Donald, 68, 84-94, 122, 142, 191

Brussels (Belgium), 98, 121
Bubbles, John, 238
Budapest (Hungary), 144
Buddha, 135
Buddhists, 214
Buffalo Soldiers, The, 243
*Buffalo Soldiers, The*, 243
Bull, Evelyn Benham, 124, 126, 137, 146, 147, 149, 150, 151, 152, 153, 154
Burbank (CA), 125
Bureau of Musical Research, 128, 145
*Buried Child*, 262
*Burning of Rome, The*, 10
Byrens, Florence Cooles, 145

## C

Cage, John, 256, 266
California, State of, 11, 16, 32, 34, 51, 57, 58, 66, 76, 81, 94, 101, 119, 123, 125, 128, 140, 145, 146, 147, 153, 155, 159, 174, 175, 179, 182, 192, 196, 199, 200, 203, 233, 240, 243, 244, 245, 251, 264, 270, 272
California Arts Council, 155
California State University, Dominguez Hills, 203
California State University, Fullerton, 13, 68, 83, 84, 122, 191
Callahan, J. D., 75
Camarillo (CA), 251
Cambria Master Recordings, 237, 245
Canada, 67, 279
Canadian, 191
*Canadian Stereo Guide*, 270
Canning, George, 191
Capitol Hill School, 10, 30

# Index

*Carmen*, 107, 286
Carmichael, Stokely, 201, 210, 221, 224
Carr, Francis, 110, 111, 112
Carroll, Earl, 177
Carroll, Eva May, 125
Carter, Elliott, 266
Carter, Madison H., 210, 217
Carver, George Washington, 89, 237
Catalina Island, 58
Catholic(s), 71, 197
Cayce, Edgar, 252
CBS, see Columbia Broadcasting System
Census, Unites States, see United States Census
Center for Media and Public Affairs, The, 196
Central Avenue, 92
Central Intelligence Agency (CIA), 242
Cervantes, Miguel de, 265
Ceylon, 214
Chadwick, George, 88
Chamber of Commerce, San Jose, 57
Chaucer, Geoffrey, 4, 170
Cherokee tribe, 217
Chester House Publishers, 235
Chicago (IL), 152, 210, 221, 222, 262, 267, 286
*Children of Crises*, 228
Chinese (people), 214
Choctaw tribe, 6, 160
Chopin, Frédéric, 65, 66, 106, 133, 147, 268
*Choreographic Music*, 36, 244, 250
Christ, 197
Christian(s), 111, 127, 166, 190, 197, 214, 218, 279

*Christian Science Monitor, The*, 210
Christmas, 38, 155, 156
*Chronicle Telegram, The*, 272
CIA, see Central Intelligence Agency
Cimarron Street, 13, 83
Cincinnati Symphony Orchestra, 88
Civil Rights Act, 179
Civil Rights Era, 241
Civil War, The, 159, 171, 180, 193, 201, 213
Claiborne, Clay, 194, 195
Clark, Hattie, 209
Classical Period, 131
Clay, E. R., 152
Clay, Cassius, 181, 196
Cleaver, Eldridge, 195, 221, 225
Cleveland Opera, The, 286
*Cleveland Plain Dealer*, 270
Cleveland Symphony Orchestra, 88
Club Alabam, 90, 92
*Co-Art Forum*, 285
Coca-Cola, 58, 259
*Cogitations from Albert Jay Nock*, 215, 276
Coleridge, Samuel Taylor, 225
Coleridge-Taylor, Samuel, 182
Coles, Robert, 228
Collins, Marva, 210, 286
*Colored Soldiers, The*, 90
*Color Purple, The*, 159
Columbia Broadcasting System (CBS), 31, 33, 86, 179, 259
Columbia Records, 179, 212
Columbus (OH), 31
*Columbus Magazine*, 201
Columbus Urban League, 117
Communism, 61
Communist Party, 61, 189, 190,

299

194, 199, 241
*Company of Prophets*, 238
*Complete Poems of Paul Laurence Dunbar, The*, 226
*Composers Creed, The*, 256
Conference of College Composition and Communication, 203
Confucianists, 190
*Conjure*, 203
Cooke, James Francis, Dr., 130, 143, 144, 145
Cook, J. Douglas, 178, 179, 184, 188, 283
Coon, Wendell, 21
Cooper, William, 15
Copland, Aaron, 116, 140, 207, 265
Cordero, Rogue, 212
*Coronet*, 70, 144, 148
Corwin, Norman, 259
Cosby, Bill, 196
Cotton Club, The, 90, 92
*Countee Cullen and the Negro Renaissance*, 224
County General Hospital, 147
Coventry (United Kingdom), 132
Cowell, Henry, 272
Craft, Lois Adele, 75-81,
Crenshaw High School, 230
Creole(s), 68, 94, 185, 201, 213
Crile, George W., Dr., 145, 154
Crocker Street Hospital, 32
Crosby, Bing, 86
Cross Street, 11
Crumb, George, 266
Cuba, 213
Cullen, Countee, 87, 204, 225, 226
Custis, Martha (Washington), 235

## D

DaCamera Schallplatten Records, 71
*Daily News*, 206
Daisy (duck), 47
D'Aleria, Marguerite, 33
Damrosch School, 146
Dance Wyoming, 288
*Danzas de Panama*, 269
Dark Age(s), 292
*Darker America*, 68
*Dark Horsemen*, 72, 272
David (King), 77
DaVinci, Leonardo, 132, 133
Dawson, William L., 174
Deep River Hour, 31, 86
Deep River Orchestra, 174
De La Pagerie, Josephine Tascher, 235
De Lerma, Dominique René, 186, 212
Delibes, Leo, 107
Dell Publishing Company, 224
Democrat(ic Party), 196
Denmark, 200
Depression, The, 100, 155, 198, 211
Derrida, Jacques, 261
Desto Records, 71
Detroit (MI), 148
*Detroit Free Press*, 75
Detroit Symphony Orchestra, 202
Dett, Nathaniel, 87, 88
Dial Press, The, 224
Dickens, Charles, 225
Dillard University, 191
Disc Company of America, 128
Disneyland, 259
Disraeli, Benjamin, 237
Dobbs, Mattiwilda, 59
Dodd, Mead & Company, 224,

# Index

226, 233
*Dog Owner's Digest*, 152
Dominguez, Albert, 71
Dominguez Hills (CA), 203
Donald (duck), 47
*Doorways to the Mind*, 97
Dora (duck), 47
Dorr, Donald, 183, 184, 200, 206, 208
Doubleday & Co., 205
Douglass, Frederick, 224
Downes, Olin, 184, 240
Dreams, 71, 72
*Dream Variations*, 226
Dreyfus, Alfred, 242
Dreyfuss, Henry, 59
Druckman, Jacob, 266
Dudley, Uncle, 140
Duke of Milan, 132
Dumas, Alexander, 204
Dunbar, Paul Laurence, 16, 89, 90, 159-160, 204, 225-227, 233
Duschek, Franz Xaver, 110
Dutch (people), 212

**E**

Eachus, Ann, 33
East Germany, 170
East India, 143, 152
Eastman School of Music, 119
Ebony Success Library, The, 210
Eden, Garden of, 106
Edison, Thomas Alva, 123
Educational Press Association, 83
Eger, Joseph, 261
Egypt, 57, 58, 192
Egyptian(s), 125, 143, 192, 235
Eighteenth century, 145
Einstein, Albert, 133
Eisenhower, Dwight, President, 57
Eliot, George, 132
Elizabethan Age, 287
Ellington, Duke, 90, 116
Ellis, Mildred, Miss, 71
El Toro (CA), 199
Elyria (OH), 272
Emperor of Wurtemburg, 109
*Encounter*, 261
England, 200, 212, 234
English (people), 267
English (language), v, 5, 6, 10, 35, 132, 183, 192, 204, 208, 212, 221, 224, 225, 227, 259
*English Journal, The*, 221, 228
Enlightenment, The, 262
*Ennanga*, 75-82
E. P. Dutton Publishing, 36, 244
Epting, Marion, 229
Equal Employment Opportunity Commission (EEOC), 194
*Eroica Symphony*, 107
Ethiopia(n), 192, 235
*Etude, The*, 33, 36, 107, 108, 122, 130, 132, 135, 141, 142, 143, 144, 145, 147, 148, 149, 213, 257, 282, 283
Europe(an), 71, 166, 192, 200, 202, 205, 214, 234, 261
Evans, Mark, 286
Exposition Park, 252

**F**

Fairchild, Halford H., Dr., 192-193
Falkenstein, Waldeen, 247
Fambro, Anne, 5, 6, photo insert
Fambro, Carrie, see Shepperson, Carrie
Far East(ern), 138
Farrakhan, Louis, 234

Farrell, John, 276
Fayetteville (AR), 105, 115, 121, 247, 249
Feather, Leonard, 205
Federal Bureau of Investigation (FBI), 194, 242
Federal Reserve Board, 201
Feinstein, Nathan, 102
Feistritzer, C. Emily, 260
Ferguson, Blanche E., 224
Fern Dell, 123, 252
Ferry Building, 58
Festival of Contemporary American Music, 262, 264
*Festive Overture*, 155
Fetta, Frank, 73, 155
Fields, Richard, 71
Fifield, Reverend, 197
Finn, Robert, 270
Fischer, Eddie, 75
Fisherman's Wharf, 58
*Five on the Black Hand Side*, 196
Flagstaff (AZ), 159, 160, 235, 236
Flagstaff Symphony Orchestra, 159, 160
*Flint Journal*, 264
Flipper, Henry Ossier, 243
Florida, State of, 6, 7
Flying saucers, 62
Foil, David, 181, 236
*Folk Suites from the Western Hemisphere*, 68
Ford (motor car), 19, 26, 34, 56, photo insert, 251
Foreman, T. E., 206
Forsythe, Bruce, 245, 247
Fort Davis (TX), 243
Fort Riley (KS), 243
*Forum*, 3
Foshay Jr. High School, see James A. Foshay Jr. High School
Foss, Lukas, 267
Foundation for Theological Education, 221-222
*Fourth Symphony, The*, see *Autochthonous Symphony*
Fox, Daniel, 170
*Foxes of Harrow, The*, 224
Fox Studios, see Twentieth-Century Fox
France, 130
Franck, César, 107, 117
Franklin, Benjamin, 77, 122, 133, 141
Fraternal Cemetery, 12
*Frederick Douglass: Slave-Fighter*, 224
Freedman, Roma Sachs, 143
*Freeman, The*, 190, 199, 279
French (language, people), 130, 190, 212, 213
Freudian, v
Freud, Sigmund, 261
*Friendly Exchange, The*, 210
Fromm Music Foundation, 262,
Fromm, Paul, 262, 265, 266, 270, 273
*From the Dark Tower*, 226
Frost, Robert, v, 65, 66
Fuller, Hoyt, 205
Fullerton (CA), 13, 68, 83, 84, 122
Fuss, Marilyn, 154
Futuro Press, 192

G

Gabriel, Thomas, 203
Gagnard, Frank, 69, 89, 272
Gainsborough, Thomas, 132
Galilei, Galileo, 19, 267
Galt, Martha, 133

# Index

Gaskill, Merle, 32
Gates, Henry Louis, Jr., 234
Gauguin, Paul, 267
Gavilan Canyon, 243
Gayle, Addison, Jr., 205
Georgia, State of, 5, 6, 173, 217
German (people, language), 8, 13, 166
Germany, 170, 200, 268, 278
Gershwin, George, 65, 88, 102, 173, 252, 271
Gilbert, L. Wolfe, 21
Gilkey, Josie, 11
Gillam, Professor, 4
Glasco, Anita, 224, 229
*Gloomy Sunday*, 144
*G-Minor Symphony* (K550), 65, 66
God, dedication page, 15, 20, 21, 23, 32, 35, 36, 49, 61, 69, 70, 73, 74, 77, 80, 81, 97, 98, 99, 100, 101, 102, 103, 113, 120, 123, 124, 137, 138, 150, 155, 156, 163, 166, 169, 170, 190, 197, 201, 239, 269, 283
Goethe, Johann Wolfgang von, 223
Goldberg, Albert, 265
Goldhil Video, 243
Goldstein, Clifford, 169, 170
Goosens, Eugene, 174
Gordon, Garron, 211
Gospel music, 182
Gould, Charles, 198, 199, 200
Gould, Norma, 177
Graham, Frances, Mrs., 200
Graham, Shirley, 213, 224
Grainger, Percy, 147
*Gralswelt*, 164-165
Grand Prix Records, 71
*Grapho-Therapeutics*, 153
Great Depression, The 100, 155, 157, 198, 211
Great Divide, 87
Greco-Romans, 26
Greece, 131, 252
Greeks, 125, 131, 143
Greenberg, Clement, 262, 263, 268
Greene, Patterson, 117
Gretry, Andre Erneste Modeste, 144-145
Grieg, Edvard, 147
Griffith Observatory, 59
Griffith Park, 16, 122
Guadeloupe, 213
Guggenheim Fellowship, 32
*Guideposts*, 168-169
Gumpert, Gustav V., 145, 149

## H

Haas, Robert Bartlett, 5, 130, 134
Hains, Frank, 206
Hall, Felipe, 71
Hall, Frederick, 191
Halloween, 38
Hals, Frans, 106
Hamilton, Alexander, 235
*Hamlet*, 67
Hancock, Graham, 235
Handy, William Christopher, 11, 21, 31, 86, 172, 173, 179, 207, 208
Hanslick, Eduard, 267
Hanson, Howard, 73, 95, 100, 119, 130, 174, 198
Harlem (NY), 65, 87, 88, 90, 92, 99, 173, 174, 239
Harlem, Boys' Choir of, 286
Harlem Renaissance, 87, 90, 92, 240
Harper and Row Publishers, 224

Harrison, John, 113
Harris, Roy, 140, 271
Harvard Law School, 224
Harvard Medical School, 199
Harvard University, 223
Hathaway, Anne, 67
Hathaway, Homer, 69
Hawaii, State of, 33, 127
Hayakawa, S. I., Dr., 201
Hayes, Roland, 91, 205
Hay, Harry, 247, 248, 249, 250
*Hazard's Pavilion*, 285
Hazlitt, Henry, 199
Heaven, 72
Hebrews, 127
Heifetz, Jascha, 144
Hepburn, Katherine, 265
*Herald, The*, 272
*Herald-Express, The*, 140
*Herald-Examiner, The*, 117
Herguth, Bob, 210
Hesiod, 276
Heylbut, Rose, Miss, 69
*Highway I, U.S.A.*, 117
*Hi Jinx*, 43
Hindemith, Paul, 131
Hinderas, Natalie, 71, 73
Hindu(s), 143, 190, 214
Hines, Jerome, 21
Hines, Mildred, 21
Hinton, William A., M.D., 199
Hitler, Adolf, 234
Hobson-Pilot, Ann, 81
Hofdemel, Franz, 110, 112, 113
Hofdemel, Johann, 112
Hofdemel, Magdalena, 110, 112
*Holiday*, 122
Holland, 106
Holliday, Billie, 179
Holliday, Thomas, 110, 114
Hollywood (CA), 18, 59, 66, 87-88, 128, 153, 177

Hollywood Bowl, 59, 66, 88, 239
Holocaust, The, 197, 214
Holt, Mrs., 39, 40
Homer, 131
Honegger, Arthur, 255
Horne, Lena, 177
Horton, Lester, 247, 249
House of Commons, 212
Howard University, 81, 240
*How is it That We Live After Death*, 278
Hudgins, Mary D., 100
Hughes, Langston, 87, 90, 92, 225, 226, 236
Hyatt, Laura Oliver, 7

**I**

*I Dream a World*, 236
*If We Must Die*, 226
*I Got Rhythm*, 173
Indiana State Prison, 147
India(ns) (East Indians), 143, 152, 190, 213, 214
Indian(s) (Native Americans), 5, 6, 7, 9, 16, 59, 68, 94, 143, 160, 185, 211, 212, 213, 216, 217, 251
Indonesia, 214
*In Memoriam*, 17
*In One Lifetime*, 67, 105, 249, 268
Inquisition, The, 19, 166
Institute for Historical Review, 197
Institute of Musical Art, 88, 146, 287
*Interview with William Grant Still*, 84-94, 142, 191
Iowa, State of, 41
Ireland, 169, 214

# Index

Irish, 211, 215, 218
Iron Age, The, 234
Irvington-on-Hudson (NY), 215, 276
Isaiah, The Prophet, 255, 292
*Isthmian Negro Youth Congress Bulletin*, 142
Italians, 170
Italy, 200
Ives, Charles, 261, 272

## J

Jackson, Calvin, 87
Jackson, Catherine, 132
Jackson, Jesse, 181
Jackson, Joseph H., Dr., 222
Jackson (MS), 206
Jackson (TN), 169
Jacksonville (AR), 8
Jacobean drama, 267
James A. Foshay Jr. High School, 41-43
Japan, 135
Japanese, 13, 40, 135
Jazz, 160, 182, 184, 205, 208, 284
*Jean Baptiste Pointe de Sable*, 224
Jefferson, Bernard, Judge, 229
Jefferson Boulevard, 83
*Jeffersons, The*, 195
Jefferson, Thomas (President), 133, 235
Jellinek, George, 259, 265
Jesus, The Christ, 105
Jew(ish), Jews, 21, 32, 40, 101, 102, 105, 121, 134, 160, 166, 170, 175, 187, 190, 195, 197, 202, 212, 214
Jim Crow, 7, 172, 217
Jinarajadasa, C., 136

Jivaros, 143
J. M. Dent and Sons, Publishers, 110
John Muir Jr. High School, 33
Johns Hopkins Hospital, 147
Johnson, Hall, 116, 173
Johnson, James Weldon, 224
Johnson Publishing Co., 210
Johnson, Samuel, 235
Joint Board on Science and Engineering, 193
Jo-Jo (the dog), 46
Jones, Bill, 200
Joplin, Scott, 90, 172
Josephine, see De La Pagerie
Joseph II (Emperor), 111
Judas, The Disciple, 106
Judson, Arthur, 174
Juilliard School, The, 88, 146, 287
Julian Messner Publishing, 224
*Junctures*, 264
*Jupiter Symphony* (K551), 66

## K

*Kaintuck'*, 34
Kandinsky, Wassily, 262
Kansas City (MO) Philharmonic Orchestra, 75, 76, 77
*Kansas City Star*, 264
*Kansas City Times*, 75
Kastendieck, Miles, 140
Kastner, Alfred, 78
Kastner, Stephanie, 78, 80
Kaufman, Annette, Dr., 21, 59, 245
Kaufman, Louis, Dr., 21, 59, 245
KCET-TV, 130, 135
Kearney, Paul W., 144, 148
Keats, John, 159, 225

Kelly, Karen, 125
Keniston, Kenneth, 223
Kennedy Medallion, 21
Kenney, A. K., 201
Kent State University Press, 186
Kentucky, State of, 147
Kenya, 214
*Keyboard Classics*, 65, 83
KFAC (Radio), 244-245
KHJ-TV, 123, 153
King, Martin Luther, Jr., 195, 221
Klemperer, Otto, 34
Klinghoffer, Leon, 170
Kniest, John, 71
Knopf, Alfred A., Publishing, 224
*Know Your American Music*, 133
Knox, Barbara, Mrs., 187, 190
Korall, Burt, 184, 185, 271
Kosloff, Alexander, 33
Kramer, Hilton, 262
Kremlin, The, 215
Krueger, Karl, 76, 174, 198
Ku Klux Klan, 165, 168, 197
Kupferberg, Herbert, 113

**L**

Labor Conciliation Board, 102
Lagemann, John Kord, 209
La Guardia, Fiorello, Mayor, 4, 14, 198
Laguna Hills (CA), 211
Lahaina (Maui), 127
Lake Placid, 66
*Lancet, The*, 146
Landau, Maestro, 81
Lange, Marjorie and Arthur, 21, 26, 61, 62, photo insert, 125, 241, 245
Lanier, Sidney, 97

Lansburg, Alan, 123, 153
Laski, Michael, 194
Latin (language), 41, 42
Latin America(ns), 33, 213
Laurida Books Publishing, 153
Lawrence, Mittie, 229
Lazarus, 121
Learning Channel, The, 235
*Learning '54*, 39-40
Lee, Doretha, 222
Lee, Peggy, 75
Legend Records, 71
Lehmann, F. J., 129, 134
Leinsdorf, Erich, 264
Leisure World (CA), 211
*Lenox Avenue*, 68
Lert, Richard, 77
Lert, Vicki (Baum), 77
Leviero, Anthony, 133
Lewis, George H., 202-203
Lewis, Henry, 216
Lewis, Robert C., 124
*Liberty*, 169, 170
Liberty Bell, 42
Library of Congress, The, 83
Lichter, Linda S., 196
*Life and Works of Paul Laurence Dunbar, The*, 159
Lincoln, Abraham, President, 239
Lincoln Institute, The, 181, 194, 234
*Lincoln Review, The*, 181, 186, 191, 193, 199, 286
Lincoln University (PA), 123, 173, 271
Lindbergh, Charles, 12
Lind, Jenny, 97
Linkletter, Art, 39
Linyard, Richard, 210
Lionel trains, 51
Liszt, Franz, 268

# Index

Little Hiawatha, 9
Little League, 163
Little Rock (AR), 3, 7, 8, 9, 11, 12, 30, 31, 159, 172
Llewellyn Publications, 238
Locke, Alain, 240
Loman, Willy, 262
Lomax, Alan, 207
Lomita (CA), 245
London (U.K.), 110, 147, 152
London, Jack, 204
*Lorain Journal*, 286
Los Angeles, City of, 11, 13, 21, 32, 35, 50, 66, 81, 82, 83, 84, 88, 90, 91, 98, 117, 119, 123, 130, 133, 135, 137, 140, 147, 153-154, 163, 176, 178, 184-185, 187, 192, 193, 196, 208, 209, 216, 228, 229, 230, 239, 244, 245, 251, 252, 280, 289
Los Angeles Board of Educ., 39
Los Angeles Bureau of Adoptions, 176
Los Angeles City College, 209
Los Angeles Community Orchestra, 78
Los Angeles High School, 33
Los Angeles Philharmonic Orchestra, 34, 66, 78, 88, 239
*Los Angeles Times*, 147, 154, 182, 184-185, 187, 205, 216, 251, 265
Los Feliz School, 39
*Lost Horizons*, 239
Lot, 214
Lotus Club, 8, 159
Louisiana, State of, 181, 201, 213, 236
Lubin, Steven, 114
Lutoslawski, Witold, 264

## M

MacDowell, Edward, 106
MacNeil, Robert, 258
McClintock, Robert, 269
McCormick Mortuary, 211
McDaniel, Hattie, 5
McDonald's, Ronald, Restaurants, 125
McDowell, Leander, 4, 8
McDowell, Melba, 11
McGarry, Nola, 70, 114, 138-139
McGraw Hill Publishers, 113
McKay, Claude, 87, 226
McKay, George Frederick, 120
McNelly, Willis, Dr., 13
Macmillan Press, 224
*Madame Butterfly*, 107
Magic Mountain, 259
Maine, State of, 57
Malcolm X, 195, 204, 221, 224
*Malcolm X*, 224
Malibu (CA), 122
Manual Arts High School, 33, 34, 41, 229
Marina del Rey (CA), 252
Marina-Westchester Symphony, 73, 155, 157
Marina-Westchester Symphony Society, 155
Marina-Westchester Symphony Society Newsletter, 149
Markham, Steve, 245
Martin, Bob (Robert), 287, 289
Marxism, v
Maryland, State of, 147, 235
Mason, Daniel Gregory, 135-136, 141, 142
Masons, The, 111
Master-Player Library, The, 235, 236, 238

Matisse, Henri, 267, 271
Matthew, Gospel of, 105
Matthews, Miriam, 21, 89, 119
Maui (Hawaii), 127
Maya, The, 235
Mayan, 58
Mayflower, The, 132
Mayo, Charles H., Dr., 145
Mayo Clinic, The, 145
Mead, Margaret, 261
Medusa, 66
Melville, Herman, 4
Mendelssohn, Felix, 148
*Merchant of Venice, The*, 10
Merriweather, Evangeline, Mrs., 38
Methodist, 169
Metro-Goldwyn-Mayer (MGM), 87
Metropolitan Opera, 21, 59, 103
Mexican(s), 40, 58, 170, 197
Mexico, 34, 35, 58, 130, 175
Miami (FL), 188, 272
*Miami Herald*, 188, 272
Michelangelo, di Lodovico, 267
Michigan, State of 147
*Micro Magazine*, 73, 98, 120
Middle Ages, The, 166
Middlebrooks, Mrs., 169, 190
Middle East, The, 169
*Midsummer Night's Dream, A*, 10
*Midwinter*, 122
Miller, Mitch, 130
Mill Valley (CA), 123
Milner (GA), 6
Milton, John, 132, 159
Milwaukee (WI), 200
*Mind and Heart of Frederick Douglass, The*, 224
*Minette Fontaine*, 117, 181, 232, 286

Minimalists, 268
Minnesota, State of, 234
*Minuet in G*, 285
Miss America, 21, 61, 245
Mission Viejo (CA), 125, 163
*Mission Viejo Newspost*, 201
Mississippi, State of, 6, 7, 12, 16, 29, 171, 172, 200, 213
Missouri, State of, 75, 76
Miss Washington, 61
*Modern Study of the Harp*, 77
Mohawk tribe, 212
Monterey (CA), 58
Moor, 192
*Morning Advocate, The*, 181, 236
Morton, Lawrence, 265, 270, 273
Moses, 235
Moslem, 189, 214
Moten, Etta (Barnett), 205, 206
Mount San Antonio College, 203
Mount Shasta, 56
Mozart, Constanze, 111, 112, 113
Mozart, Leopold, 109, 110
Mozart, Wolfgang Amadeus, v, 65, 65, 109-115, 133, 185, 233, 248, 264
Mulcahy, Gene, 209, 210
*Mumbo-Jumbo*, 203
Murphy, Carl, 98, 137
Museum of Natural History, The, 16
*Musical America*, 36, 143, 266
*Musical Digest, The*, 133, 136, 145, 149
*Musical Mainstream*, 83
*Music and Dance*, 97, 132
*Music and Dance in California*, 128, 145
Music Clubs Magazine, (see also *Showcase*), 263

# Index

Music Critics' Association, 265
*Music Department Bulletin*, 173, 184, 185, 186, 271, 272
*Music Educators' Journal*, 83
Music Educators' National Conference, 83
*Music Journal, The*, 133, 143, 147, 173, 261
*Music of the West*, 256, 269, 280
*Music on my Beat*, 178
Music Teachers' Association, 140, 141, 270, 272, 273
*Music Therapy in Action*, 147
*Music Therapy: Its Future*, 124, 126, 137, 138, 147, 150, 151, 152, 153
M. W. Gibbs High School, 3, 30, 85
*My Heart Has Known Its Winter*, 226
*My Lord, What a Morning*, 224
Myceneans, The, 257

## N

Nagy, Daniel, 111
Napolean, see Bonaparte
Napoleonic Wars, 213
Nashville (TN), 210
National Baptist Convention, 222
National Broadcasting Corporation (NBC), 73, 86
National Center for Education Information, 260
National City (CA), 35
National Council of Teachers of English (NCTE), 221
National Education Association Urban Task Force, 228
National Endowment for the Arts (NEA), 260, 265
National Federation of Music Clubs, 88
*National Forum, The*, 203, 258, 259
National Foundation for Music Therapy, 146
*National Insider, The*, 200
National Public Television, 281
Native American, see Indians
*Nature of Prejudice, The*, 165
Nazi Party, The, 165, 166, 197, 215, 268
NBC, see National Broadcasting Corporation
*Negro Digest, The*, 214
Negro History Bulletin, 193
Negro History Week, 206
Nelson, Boris, 184, 271
Neo, 56
Neoclassicism, 140
Nevada, State of, 81
New Age, The, 164
*New Approach, A*, 278
New England, 198
New England Conservatory of Music, 31, 88
*New Guard, The*, 222
New Guinea, 13
New Jersey Symphony Orchestra, 216
Newman, Al, 93
New Mexico, State of, 210, 243
*New music*, 255, 256, 263, 265, 292
New Orleans (LA), 36, 57, 69, 89, 117, 172, 201, 213, 236, 272
*New Orleans Magazine*, 201, 236
New Orleans Philharmonic Orchestra, 36
New Orleans Symphony Orchestra, 256
*News-Leader*, 207

Newton, Huey, 195
New York (NY), 4, 11, 14, 18, 19, 31, 36, 57, 59, 67, 71, 77, 85, 86, 87, 90, 92, 97, 98, 113, 128, 147, 155, 159, 173, 178, 192, 199, 215, 226, 229, 233, 234, 235, 239, 244, 259, 276, 287
New York City Center, 115
*New Yorker, The*, 140
New York Museum of Art, 271
*New York Times, The*, 36, 133, 202, 236
New York World's Fair, 59, 88, 117
Nihilist(s), 65, 66, 134
Nimoy, Leonard, 123, 153
Nineteenth century, 213, 273
Ninety-fifth Street Elementary School, 32
Nixon, Richard, President, 133
Nock, Albert Jay, 215, 276
Nockian Society, The, 215, 276
Noll, Joyce Elaine, 238
Normandy (France), 120
*Nozze di Figaro, Le*, 109
Numerology, 70, 134, 154

## O

Oakland (CA), 58
Oakland Symphony Orchestra, 66, 264
Oberlin (OH), 31, 56, 57
Oberlin College, 31, 56, 67, 85, 129, 134, 270
Ober, William M., Dr., 111
Ocean Park, *vi*
Oceanside (CA), 124
Odeh, Alex, 170, 190
*Oh, I Have Asked...*, 226
Ohio, State of, 31, 159, 184, 186

Oja, Carol, 237
Oklahoma City (OK), 187
Oleander, 277
Olmstead (AR), 8
*Omnitron Associates Newsletter*, 123
*One-Hundred Amazing Facts About the Negro*, 192, 216
*One-Thousand Successful Blacks*, 210
*Opera and Concert*, 178, 179, 184, 283
*Opera Journal*, 110, 114
Opitz, Edmund A., 202, 279
*Opus* magazine, 268, 280
*Orange and Lemon*, 8
Orange County (CA), 196, 222
Orient(al), 73
Orion Recordings, 71, 81
*Ovation*, 110, 111, 113, 114
Owensboro (KY), 147
*Oxford English Dictionary*, 192
Oxford University Press, 272
*Oz (Wizard of Oz)*, *vi*, 17, 47
Ozma, 46, 47

## P

Pace, Kay, Dr., 235
Paganini, Niccolò, 108
Paige, Raymond, 33
Pakistan, 214
Palestinian, 170
Palevsky, Joan, 81
Palomar Observatory, 59
Panamanian, 212
Pan-American Union Conference, 130
*Paradise Lost*, 132
Parent-Teacher Association (PTA), 38
Parker-Faye, Bradley, 129

# Index

Parker, J. A. "Jaye," 181, 194, 195, 221-222, 234
*Parsifal*, 291
Pasadena Interracial Women's Club, 195
Patterson, David, 128, 140
Paul (The Apostle), 127
Pelligrini, Norman, 267
Pendericki, Krzysztof, 264
Pennsylvania, State of, 123, 173, 271
Perle, George, 263
Pershing, Warren J., General, 132
Peters, Brock, 196
Phenomenologists, 134
Phi Beta Kappa, 228
*Phi Delta Gamma Journal*, 3, 83
Philadelphia (PA), 194, 202, 221
Philharmonic Orchestra, see Los Angeles Philharmonic
Phillips, Theodore, Mr. and Mrs., 21
Phipps Psychiatric Clinic, 147
*Piano Guild Notes*, 65
Picasso, Pablo, 267
*Pien*, 264
Pilate, Pontius, 105
*Pittsburgh Courier, The*, 166, 174, 234
*Plahn*, 264
*Plain Dealer, The*, 270
Plato, 139, 257, 282
Plummer, Henry V., 243
Pollock, Jackson, 265
Pompeian, 256
*Porgy and Bess*, 102, 236
Portanova, Joseph, 21
Portanova, Mary, 21
Portuguese (language), 212
Powell, Adam Clayton, 196
*Prayer, Praise and Dreams*, 98, 99, 101
Presbyterian, 169
Price, Florence, 87
Priestley, M., 147
Princess of Wurtemburg, The, 109
Psalms, The, 11, 20, 98, 126
Psychic, 62, 70, 125
Public Broadcasting System (PBS), 130, 135, 234
Puccini, Giacomo, 65, 107, 117, 233
Pulitzer Prize, 262
Puritans, The, 198
Pushkin, Alexander, 204
Pythagoras, 124, 277

## Q

*Quest for the Lost Civilization*, 235
Quickie Grill, 187
Quin, Carolyn, Dr., 182

## R

Rachmaninoff, Sergey, 70, 132
*Radiant Pinnacle*, 73
Radio, 31, 49, 85, 146, 256, 264, 267
Railroad(s), 49, 50, 51, 52, 58
*Rain or Shine*, 177
Ralph Waldo Emerson Book Award, 228
Ramses II (The Pharoah), 267
*Rancho Reporter, The*, 199
Raymond Paige Orchestra, The, 33
*Rays*, 164
*Readers' Digest, The*, 209, 286
Reagan Transition Team, The, 194
Reed, Ishmael, 203, 204

*Register, The*, 196
Religion, 60, 69, 73, 97, 98, 104, 120, 137, 138, 164-171, 188, 215
Rembrandt, Harmenszoon van Rijn, 267
Renaissance, The, 124
Reno, Doris, 188
Republican Party, The, 196
Resta, Francis, Colonel, 57
Revolutionary War, The, 217
Rhemm, Ferguson, 228, 230
*Rhythm Boys, The*, 86
Richardson, Jack, 262
Richmond (VA), 207
*Right to Die, The*, 226
Rimsky-Korsakoff, Nicolay, 106
*Ring Cycle, The*, 291
Ringo Street, 11
*Rising Tide*, 14
*Rite of Spring, The*, 266
*Ritmo*, 36
*Riverside Press, The*, 207
Roberts, Allen, 133
Roberts, Walter, 288
Robinson, Bojangles, 178
Robison, Willard, 31
Rochester, Eddie (Anderson), 83
Rochester Philharmonic Orchestra, 73
Rockne, Knute, 132
Rodriguez, José, 128, 145
Rogers, J. A., 192, 199, 200, 216, 217
Rogers, James G., 216
Rollin, Henry R., 147
Roman Age, 192, 257
Roman Catholics, 214
Romantic Period, 131
Rome (GA), 173
Roosevelt, Eleanor, 4, 14, 198
Roosevelt, Franklin Delano, President, 101
Roosevelt, Theodore, President, 243, 253
Roseville (CA), 58
Rosicrucian Fellowship, 16, 57, 124
Rosicrucian Museum, 57
Routledge, City of, 234
Rubiks' Cube, 121, 122
Rudolf, Max, 287
Ruskin, John, 277
Russia(n), 102, 170, 189, 200, 212, 214, 215

S

Sacramento (CA), 58, 269
*Sacre, Le*, 264
*Sacred Word and its Creative Overtones, The*, 124
*Sahdji*, 100, 119, 271
Sainte-Colombe, Paul de, 153
Saint Francis of Assisi, 124
Saint Georges, Chevalier de, 182
Saint John, Gospel of, 123
Saint Jorisdoelen Almshouse, 106
Saint Joseph, 71
*Saint Louis Blues*, 173
Saint Paul (MN), 238
Saint Paul Lutheran Church Missionary Society, 98, 137, 138
Saint Vincent de Paul Society, 251
Salieri, Antonio, 109, 110, 112, 113, 115
Salvi, Professor, 75
Salzburg (Austria), 115
Salzedo, Carlos, 77, 78
San Antonio (TX), 194
Sanders, Charles L., 210
Sand, George, 65, 66

# Index

San Francisco (CA), 56, 58, 198
*San Francisco Examiner*, 198
San Francisco Opera, 117
San Francisco World's Fair, 56
San Jose (CA), 57, 58
San Jose Municipal Chorus, 57
San Juan Hill, 243
Santa Barbara (CA), 81
Santa Barbara Music Club, 81
Santa Monica (CA), 22, 79
Santa Monica Boulevard, 187
Santa Monica Symphony Orchestra, 61
Sargeant, Winthrop, 140
Saul (The King), 77
Scheibe, Johann, 107
*Scherzo, The*, 76, 115
Schoen, Max, Dr., 148
Schoenberg, Arnold, 131, 136, 140, 263, 270
Schopenhauer, Arthur, 261
Schubert, Franz, 105, 268
Schuettler, Ernest, 278
Schuyler, George S., 181, 204, 213, 214, 222, 224, 234, 241
Schuyler, Philippa, 116
Schwartzman, Jack, Dr., 189, 190
Schwarz, K. Robert, 236
Schweisheimer, Waldemar, Dr., 142
Schwerin, Erna, 111
Scotch (people), 211
Scotch-Irish (people), 6, 7, 160, 171, 218
Seattle (WA), 56
Seaway National Bank, 210
Sea World, 254
Seeger, Pete, 207
Segovia, Andrés, 276
Selassie, Haile, 192
*Sentinel, The*, 178, 193, 196, 280

*Serial Composition and Atonality*, 263
Serialists, the, 140, 240
Sessions, Roger, 263, 264, 266
Seventh Avenue School, 38
*Seven Traceries*, 73, 238
Sevitsky, Fabien, 207
Seymour, Harriet Ayer, 146
Shaffer, Peter, 113, 114
Shakespeare, William, *v*, 3, 10, 67, 97, 114, 159, 225, 265, 267, 287
Shaw, Artie, 11, 17, 31, 179, 208, 212, 258
Shep (the dog), 34, 46, 47, photo insert
Shepard, Sam, 262
Shepperson, Carrie Still (Carrie Lena Fambro), 3-12, 26, 29, 67, 105, photo insert
Shepperson, Charles B., 5, 9, 10, 30, 31, 66-67, photo insert
*Ships That Pass in the Night*, 225
Shockley, William B., 197
Short case, Mr. and Mrs. Short, 175, 190, 249, 251
*Showcase*, 263, 273, 282, 284, 285
*Shuffle Along*, 173
Shulkin, Lou, Mr. and Mrs., 187
Shylock, 3, 203
Sian Jones Publishers, 234
Sibelius, Jean, 14, 108, 206, 267
Silverwoods, Inc., 8
Simmons, Calvin, 66
Simpson, O. J., 234
Sipchen, Bob, 187
Sirens, The, 119
Sixth Avenue School, 37, 39
*Slow Through the Dark*, 90
Smith, Amanda, 288
Smith, Catherine Parsons, *vi*,

313

233-253
Smith, Edward J., 133
Smith, G. E. Kidder, 134-135
*Smithsonian* magazine, 274
Society for the Prevention of Cruelty to Animals, 46
Socrates, v
Sokolsky, M., *Los Angeles Times* Critic, 140
Solomon, Isler, 102
*Song of the Son*, 226
Sonneck Society Bulletin, The, 163
Sonoma Valley, The, 126
*Soul on Ice*, 95
*Sounding Board, The*, 149, 155
Sousa, John Philip, 148
South (Deep South), 4, 8, 14, 29, 36, 66, 89, 97, 159, 172, 174, 182, 183, 200, 215, 217, 235
South Africa, 234
*South Coast Repertory Theater Newsletter*, 262
Southern, Eileen, Dr., 13
Southwest Indian Museum, 16, 59
Spain, 200
Spanish (people), 4, 160, 185, 211, 212
Spanish (language), 33, 35, 130
Spartan, 257
Spastics' Home, 147
Spirituals (Negro), 172
Spiritualism, 70, 77, 101, 105, 120, 121, 126, 136, 277
Sprenger, Florence, Miss, 229
*Stadium Concerts Review*, 284, 288, 289
Stalingrad (Russia), 13
Standifer, James A., 205, 206
Standish, Miles, 132
Starer, Robert, 266, 267

*State Times, The*, 256, 290
Steel industry, 102
Steinbeck, John, 204
Steinpach, Richard, Dr., 164, 277, 278, 279
Stephenson, Shirley, 84
Stewart, Rex, 284
*Stiftung Gralsbotschaft*, 164, 278
Still, Duncan Allen, 13, 26, 35, 41, 42, 50, 51, 52, 58, photo inserts
Still, Duncan, Sr., 200
Still, Judith Anne, photo inserts
Stille, Lewis, 200
Stiller, Andrew, 268, 280
Stille, Thompson, 200
Still, Gail, 67
Still, Milton, 200
Still, Verna Arvey, see Verna Arvey
Still, William Grant, Sr., 6, 67, photo insert, 171-172
Stockton, Ann Mason, 78, 80, 81
Stokowski, Leopold, 14, 21, 59, 95, 119, 174, 198, 207-208
*Stormy Weather*, 93, 177, 178, 236
*Story of George Washington Carver, The*, 224
Stravinsky, Igor, 131, 140, 266, 267
Stuart, Lyle, 259
*Study in Contradictions, A*, 233-253
*Study in Racism: USA, A*, 235
Sturzaker, James, 125, 143, 151, 154
Sudan, The, 214
Suessmayr, Franz Xaver, 112
Summer Chamber Orchestra, 269
*Summerland*, 71, 72, 269, 272
*Summertime*, 173

# Index

Supreme Court, The, 199
Surif, Gregorio, 147
Sutter's Fort, 58
*Sympathy*, 227
*Symphony #1*, see *Afro-American Symphony, The*

## T

Tanglewood (MA), 262, 264
*Tanglewood Report*, 262, 264
Tanglewood Theater-Concert Hall, 264
Tarchanoff, Dr., 145
Taubman, Howard, 224
Taylor, Deems, 105, 106
Taylor, James, 229
Taylor, J. D., 146
Television, 39, 45, 46, 49, 72, 117, 123, 153, 184, 194, 195, 196, 202, 209, 256, 258, 259, 260, 281, 284
*Tempest, The*, 97
Temple of Luxor, 267
Tennessee, State of, 169, 172, 182, 210
Tennyson, Alfred Lord, 159
Teru, 247, 251
Texas, State of, 194, 243
*Theosophical Order of Service*, 124, 125, 130, 136, 147, 149, 151
Theosophical Society, The, 124, 138-139
Theosophy, 124, 138-139
Third Reich, The, 268
Thomas, Dylan, 130
Thomas, Tony, 270
Thomas Y. Crowell, Inc., 224
Thornton, Robert M., 215, 276
*Three Visions*, 71, 72, 73, 272
Tijuana (Mexico), 34

*Time*, 138, 264
*Times-Picayune, The*, 69, 89, 272
Tiomkin, Dimitri, 116
Tischler, Barbara, 272
Toledo (OH), 184, 271
*Toledo Blade*, 271, 272, 283
Tombaugh, Brian, 286
Toomer, Jean, 226
*Tosca, La*, 107
*To You, America*, 17
Train(s), 49, 50, 72, 102
Trimborn, Harry, 182
*Trivializing America*, 259
*Trojan Family*, 276
Trojan horse, 257
*Troubled Island*, 14, 18, 36, 67, 72, 102, 115, 178, 236, 240, 271
Troy, City of, 98
Troyer, Charles, 143
Truman, Harry, President, 102, 133
Tucker, Sophie, 31, 208
Turnbull, Walter, 286
Turtle(s), 47, 48
Tuskegee Institute, 201
Tutankhamen (The Pharoah), 192, 267
*TV Guide*, 195
*Twelfth Night*, 67
Twentieth century, 87, 124, 255, 274
Twentieth-Century Fox Studios, 76, 93, 178, 236

## U

Uncle Tom, 18, 186, 204
Underwood, Bert, 201-202, 235
Unidentified flying objects (UFOs), 62

315

Union School, 30
United Nations Educational, Scientific and Cultural Organization (UNESCO), 184
United States, 33, 60, 89, 97, 115, 169, 170, 171, 177, 184, 197, 198, 199, 210, 241, 257, 258, 274, 285
United States Attorney General, 249
United States Census Bureau, 22
United States Committee for UNESCO, 184
United States government, 116
United States Navy, 31, 85, 95
United States Presidents, 133
University of Arkansas, 68, 115, 121, 247
University of Arkansas Press, 67, 105, 191, 249, 273
University of California at Los Angeles, 192, 193
University of California Press, vi, 233, 263
University of Houston, 3
University of Iowa, 145
University of Miami, 117
University of Mississippi, 206
University of Southern California, 276
University of Washington Orchestra, 56
*Up Beat*, 105
*Up From Slavery*, 224
Urban League, 117
*Urn-Burial*, 119

V _____

Van Gogh, Vincent, 267
*Vanities*, 177
Van Vechten, Carl, 87
Várèse, Edgard, 11, 68, 86, 87, 264, 271
Venerable, Grant D., Dr., 123, 126, 127, 129
Verdi, Giuseppe, 233
Vermont, State of, 57
Victoria Avenue, 84
Victorian Age, 131
Victory garden, 15, 45
*Victory Tide*, 101
Vienna (Austria), 109, 110, 112
Vienna Conservatory of Music, 77
Viking Press, 224, 225
Villa-Lobos, Heitor, 212
Vinetz, Rose Cooper, 33
Virginia, State of, 207
Vodery, Will(iam), 87, 174
Voice of America, 18
Voorhees, Don, 31, 85, 100, 156, 208

W _____

Wagner, Richard, 65, 107, 267, 291
Waldeen, see Falkenstein
Walker, Bree, 168, 169
Walsh, Michael, 264
Warthin, Dr., 145
Washington, Booker T., 224
Washington, D.C., 81, 130, 191, 194, 196, 234, 240, 243, 260
Washington, George, President, 133, 235, see also photo insert of Bessie Lawson Blackman
Washington, Martha Custis, 235, see also photo insert of Bessie Lawson Blackman
Washington, Mary Helen, 195
Washington, State of, 61
*Washington Times, The*, 241

Waters, Ethel, 91
Waters, Ruperta, 212
Watts, 194, 229
Wayne County Hospital, 147
Webern, Anton von, 263
Westerman, George, 142
Western Avenue Elementary School, 32
Western Hemisphere, 211, 239
West Indies, The, 195
West Point Military Academy, 57, 243
Westside Jewish Community Center, 81
Westside Prep School, 210
*We Wear the Mask*, 90
WFMT-Radio, 267
*When All is Done*, 90
Whistler, James McNeill, 134
White, Clarence Cameron, 87
Whiteman, Paul, 11, 17, 31, 86, 100, 208, 238-239, 245
Whittier, John Greenleaf, 159
Wiggins, Lida Keck, 233
Wilberforce (OH), 159, 243
Wilberforce University, 10, 31, 85
Wilkinson County (MS), 200
*William Grant Still and the Fusion of Cultures in American Music*, 130, 134, 236
*William Grant Still: A Study in Contradictions*, 233-253
William Grant Still Community Arts Center, 89, 119
William Grant Still Festival, 155, 157
Williamsburg Inn, 140, 270
Williford, Stanley, 178, 280
Willoughby, N. D., 164
Willson, Meredith, 141, 272
Wilson, Woodrow, President, 133
Winfield, Paul, 229
Wisenberg, Charles, 184
*Wizard of Oz*, see *Oz*
Wolter, Beverly, 256
*Wonders of the African World*, 234
Wonk, Dalt, 201, 213, 236
Wood, Barbara, 147
Woods, Brent, Sergeant, 243
Woodville (MS), 6, 7, 29, 171
WOR-Radio, 86
*Worcester Daily Telegram*, 264
Wordsworth, William, 159, 225
World's Fair, New York, 14, 101
World War I, 17, 31, 85, 95, 132, 143, 261
World War II, 45, 71, 87, 116, 138, 144, 145, 193, 261, 268
Worthington, Donna, 147
WQXR Radio, 259
Wright, Ellen, 104
Wright, John, 104
Wright, Richard, 204, 241
Writers' Day Conference, 203
Wuorinen, Charles, 266
WWs, 62

## XYZ

Yale University, 223
*Yankee Doodle*, 217
Yeats, William Butler, 65
Yerby, Frank, 204, 224
Yergan, Max, Dr., 222
Yiddish, 212
Ylvisaker, Miriam, 228
Young Americans for Freedom, 194
Young, Charles, Colonel, 89, 243

Zimbabwe, 234
Zimmerman, Larry, 234
Zone, Fran, 206
Zuckert, Leon, 191
Zuni, Indians, 143

## OTHER BOOKS AUTHORED BY JUDITH ANNE STILL

***In Foundling Fire***
The biographical account of the life-crisis of a Jewish couple during the turmoil of World War II.

***Little David Had No Fear***
A biography for children and young adults of the boyhood years and adult achievements of William Grant Still.

***William Grant Still and the Fusion of Cultures in American Music***
A collection of essays and musicological and historical articles on William Grant Still and his achievements in music.

**For these and other publications, contact:**

THE MASTER-PLAYER LIBRARY
P. O. Box 3044
Flagstaff, AZ 86003-3044

Fax: (928) 526-0321
Catalog Requests: wgsmusic@bigplanet.com
Website: www.williamgrantstill.com

**For audio recordings, sheet music, and additional biographical information on William Grant Still, contact:**

WILLIAM GRANT STILL MUSIC
1109 So. Plaza Way, Suite #109
Flagstaff, AZ 86001-6317

Fax: (928) 526-0321
Catalog Requests: wgsmusic@bigplanet.com
Website: www.williamgrantstill.com